SAGE Publications
London ● Thousand Oaks ● New Delhi

in association with

MEDIA AND CULTURAL REGULATION

Edited by KENNETH THOMPSON

The Open University, Walton Hall, Milton Keynes MK7 6AA

© The Open University 1997

First published in 1997

The opinions expressed are not necessarily those of the Course Team or of The Open University.

SAGE Publications Ltd
6 Bonhill Street
London EC2A 4PU

SAGE Publications Inc.
2455 Teller Road
Thousand Oaks
California 91320

SAGE Publications India Pvt Ltd
32, M-Block Market
Greater Kailash - I
New Delhi 110 048

British Library Cataloguing in Publication data

A catalogue record for this book is available from The British Library.

ISBN 0 7619 5439 2 (cased)

ISBN 0 7619 5440 6 (pbk)

Library of Congress catalog card number 97–065517

Edited, designed and typeset by The Open University.

Printed in the United Kingdom by Bath Press Colourbooks, Glasgow

MEDIA AND CULTURAL REGULATION

edited by Kenneth Thompson

Introduction

Kenneth Thompson

regulation

Regulation is one of the most controversial topics in modern societies at the end of the twentieth century, not just in the cultural sphere, but also in economics and politics. With capitalism established as the unchallenged global economic system, exerting pressures on states to privatize industries and dismantle barriers to free trade and communication, nation-states find themselves facing questions about how they will protect their national autonomy and the rights and interests of their citizens. Economic

de-regulation

de-regulation in the newly-privatized public utilities in Britain gave rise to so much controversy that new forms of regulation had to be developed, with a proliferation of regulatory bodies to protect the interests of customers. In some sectors de-regulation has been resisted. For example, in 1993, the European Union opposed American proposals to de-regulate trade in films and television in the latest round of international negotiations over GATT (General Agreement on Tariffs and Trade). The EU's demand for 'cultural exemption' may have been inspired by Canada, which obtained a similar, if ineffective, exemption in the USA–Canada free-trade pact. The Canadians, the French and some other countries were fearful that treating culture simply as merchandise, subjected to de-regulation that would abolish quotas and fiscal incentives, would weaken their distinctive national cultures. Similarly, nation-states have sought to maintain national regulations not just on the origin of mass media communications, but also on their content, as in the case of British efforts to ban satellite-transmitted pornographic television programmes, on the grounds that they would harm citizens.

However, cultural regulation and de-regulation raise issues broader than matters of free trade and transnational communication. Some commentators have even spoken of the contemporary period as a time of 'culture wars'. The reasons for this are not hard to find. The production and consumption of cultural representations affects the construction of identities – national, ethnic, religious, occupational, familial, sex and gender. Modern societies are increasingly pluralistic and multicultural, composed of groups holding very different cultural meanings, values and tastes. Meanings regulate and organize conduct and practices – they help to set the rules, norms and conventions by which social life is ordered and governed. They are, therefore, what those who wish to govern and regulate the conduct and ideas of others seek to structure and shape. Contestation over the regulation of culture includes struggles over meanings and interpretations, as in debates about what constitutes the national heritage. It is not just coincidence that in some countries the ministry concerned with cultural affairs is called something like the Department of National Heritage (for example, in Britain and Canada). Certain forms of culture are given a privileged status because of what they represent and the social functions they are believed to serve; they are to be preserved and promoted because they are part of the 'national story'. Other cultural forms may be defined as a threat to the nation and its cultural heritage, and they are deemed unworthy of support or even subjected to restrictive regulation.

Regulation of the mass media has become a constant concern of modern governments, even when they are ideologically committed to support policies of de-regulation. It seems as if there are some aspects of culture that are judged to be too important to be left in the hands of an unregulated market. But equally, if it seems that market forces might serve ideologically approved cultural ends, they may be positively encouraged.

Of course, it is not just governments at national and local level that are concerned with cultural regulation. Managers or organizations seek to shape and harness culture to their corporate ends and may find themselves struggling with others' meanings and interpretations (see the discussions of organizational culture in **du Gay**[*] (ed.) 1997, Chapters 5 and 6). Minority groups of various kinds may seek to change the ways in which they are represented in the mass media. Feminists have sought to bring pressure on newspapers to stop the publication of pictures of women's bodies that they judge to be demeaning. Pressure groups such as the National Viewers' and Listeners' Association (founded by Mrs Mary Whitehouse in the 'swinging Britain' of the 1960s) attempt to mobilize public opinion to force broadcasting organizations to regulate their programme content in line with certain moral standards, as well as lobbying regulatory bodies such as the Broadcasting Standards Council and the Independent Television Commission. For their part, mass media institutions claim that self-regulation is best, or appeal to libertarian and commercial ideologies which support the individual citizen's or customer's right to free choice. Other voices are raised in favour of cultural regulation which serves other values – such as education, enlightenment, the duty to inform – and speak of the need for a public sphere which facilitates rational communication and debate. For all these reasons, the regulation of culture in its broadest sense has become an arena of intense argument, debate and contestation.

This book's concern with issues of regulation involves focusing on a 'moment' in what has been called the 'circuit of culture'. It has been suggested that in order to gain a full understanding of any cultural text or artefact, such as the Sony Walkman, it is necessary to analyse the processes of *representation, identity, production, consumption* and *regulation* (**du Gay, Hall et al.**, 1997). A cultural artefact like the Walkman has an impact upon the regulation of social life through the ways in which it is represented, the identities associated with it, and the articulation of its production and consumption. In the case study of the Walkman, the focus on regulation also involves the transgression of boundaries between the public and private spheres, for example in its use, listening privately to music within public spaces, on the street, in the train. So, although this book focuses specifically

---

[*]A reference in bold indicates another book, or a chapter in another book, in the series.

on regulation, the other moments in the 'circuit of culture' are also implicated in processes of regulation, and vice versa. For example, Woodward explained that sexual identities are represented through cultural texts and symbolic systems which are produced and consumed at particular historical moments at which they are subjected to regulatory systems of which they also form part (**Woodward**, 1997). In other words, although we separate the different moments of the cultural circuit for analytical purposes, processes of regulation are implicated in the moments of representation, identity, production and consumption.

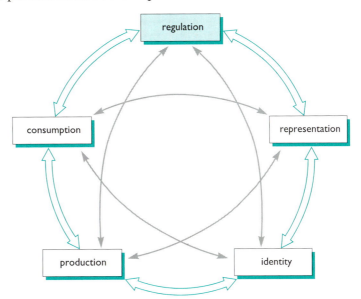

The circuit of culture

Regulation has a number of meanings, depending on the context. It can refer to something as specific as government policies and regulations (and their change or abolition, as in policies of *de-regulation*). At other times it has the more general sense of the reproduction of a particular pattern and order of signifying practices (so that things appear to be 'regular' or 'natural'). The study of forms of regulation inevitably raises questions both of cultural policy (by some regulating authority) and of cultural politics, involving struggles over meanings, values, forms of subjectivity and identity. Regulation does not mechanically reproduce the status quo. It is a dynamic process that is often contested, and while the outcome is likely to be affected by economic pressures and power structures, we will argue that it also depends on the specific circumstances and on the creative actions of individuals and groups. As we will see in Chapter 1, some theories of regulation proceed from the assumption that there will be a close correspondence between the mode of economic production and the forms of consumption in each historical period, and that the maintenance of this regime *requires* a particular mode of cultural or moral regulation. This is not an approach taken by the authors of this book, although economic factors are discussed where it seems appropriate. However, attention *is* given to political or power factors, particularly in the case of the ideological project of the New Right (or neo-liberalism) which played a prominent part in struggles over regulation and de-regulation in the 1980s, and thus provoked a series of controversies in the 1980s and 1990s about heritage, morality, multiculturalism and control of the mass media.

Chapter 1 outlines some of the theories that have been drawn on to analyse the relationship between forms of cultural regulation and economic, political and social forces. The seminal theorist of regulation and of ideology was the Italian Marxist, Antonio Gramsci, and his ideas are given prominence, but there is also consideration of other theorists – Althusser on ideology and Foucault on discourses – who addressed questions of subjectivity and identity. Attention is also given to sociological theories of communication and the public sphere, such as those inspired by Jürgen Habermas.

The usefulness of these theoretical ideas is demonstrated by examining some examples of studies that have been informed by them. The first example is that of the politics of leisure in successive periods from the beginning of the nineteenth century. It considers the extent to which economic developments have determined the direction taken by state regulation in the sphere of leisure in different periods. The second example focuses on the New Right ideology of the 1980s, which promoted economic de-regulation but also some cultural **re-regulation**, and asks to what extent it managed to reconcile the competing pressures of market forces and the desire to preserve a sense of national cultural heritage. The third example is concerned with the **mediazation of society** – the process by which in modern society the transmission of symbolic forms is increasingly mediated by the mass media industries. It asks whether the mass media as presently organized provide the necessary public sphere for the rational communication and debate that are said to be essential in constituting a modern democratic society. An overarching theme linking the examples is that of changes in the forms of regulation. In some respects, there seems to have been a shift towards de-regulation, and in the direction of **self-regulation**. But it is also possible to trace a rather more complex picture, in which there are competing tendencies, involving regulation, de-regulation and re-regulation occurring simultaneously.

re-regulation

mediazation of society

self-regulation

According to some theorists, especially those influenced by the work of Michel Foucault, the key site (or battleground) of social regulation in modern society is that of sexuality. In Chapter 2 Robert Bocock examines some of the controversies that have accompanied changes in the regulation of sexual practices and representations in recent decades. These range from protests about the sexual content of television programmes, especially some 'pornographic' satellite channels, to opposition to the sympathetic portrayal of gay and lesbian relationships and lifestyles. For some people these developments are symptomatic of an increasing moral permissiveness in the post-war period, part of a general process of secularization, in which religious institutions lose their authority and the capacity to exercise moral regulation. However, it can be argued that the heritage of puritan moral discourses is still there to be called upon by moral campaigners, including politicians, as happened in the ideological appeals of the New Right for a return to 'Victorian values' in the 1980s or the political slogans about 'family values' and 'back to basics' in the 1990s. Whether there still exists a 'moral majority' that shares the heritage of puritan moral discourses is open to doubt, but that has not stopped moral campaigners from appealing to it.

Chapter 2 also examines a set of rival discourses, such as those deriving from secular liberal philosophy, which stress individual liberties and are sometimes accused by their opponents of promoting moral libertarianism. These different sets of moral discourses can sometimes lead to interesting and surprising alliances in debates about sexual morality, such as the alliance between some feminists and conservative religious groups campaigning against pornography.

Two important reasons why sexuality seems to be the key site of social regulation in modern society are: firstly, that the family is seen as vital to the reproduction of society and social order; and secondly, that sexuality is central to identity construction. Both of these factors feature in debates about homosexuality and the regulation of gay and lesbian practices and representations. Chapter 2 touches on some of the changes that have occurred in television's representations of gays and lesbians, and discusses whether a shift is occurring in their regulation – from tight regulation to a more permissive regime.

One of the problems faced by governments seeking to regulate representations of sexuality on television is that cultural globalization through new technologies, such as satellite broadcasting, makes it very difficult for one country to maintain a kind of cultural integrity or isolation, free from outside influences. In Chapter 3, John Tomlinson looks at issues of regulation arising from responses to globalization, taking as his focus a critical model of globalization, based on the notion of cultural imperialism. For some critics of globalization as cultural imperialism, the supposed dominance of a worldwide, standardized, 'homogenized' consumer culture, emanating from western (particularly American) capitalism, represents a form of global cultural regulation. This is the sense of regulation, described in Chapter 1, derived from the Marxian idea of the shaping of culture in conformity with the economic-political demands of capitalism. This view is contrasted with that put forward by those who regard these developments as the benign fruit of a de-regulated, international cultural market, with increased freedom of cultural choice and practice. Tomlinson shows how thinking about the politics of global cultural flows in terms of regulation/de-regulation reveals a much more complex situation than either view originally envisaged.

In the end, the balance of Tomlinson's argument comes down against the cultural imperialism thesis as an adequate view of cultural globalization. However, he acknowledges that it has generated debates that raise some important issues: about the specific nature of cultural as distinct from economic power and domination; about the relationship between cultural identity, place, space and time; and about cultural regulation – 'protection' – by the state.

Although the modernizing forces that accompany globalization frequently entail secularization, in the sense that religious institutions lose their once pre-eminent role in shaping culture, it is not necessarily the case that religious symbols and values lose all significance. On the contrary, global population movements and the increasingly 'multicultural' or socially plural character of modern society means that groups may react by striving to construct their collective identities through discourses incorporating religious symbols in order to assert their difference from others. This is the case with many ethnic groups, as discussed by Bhikhu Parekh in Chapter 4. The problem for modern 'liberal' societies is that their tolerance of difference is based on certain western notions of individualism and individual rights, which may not fit in with the demands of ethnic groups to secure equal respect and rights for practices that are offensive to the majority culture. The most famous recent example of this was the support of some British Moslems for an Islamic authority's proclamation of a *fatwah* (in effect, a death sentence) against Salman Rushdie for blasphemy in his novel, *The Satanic Verses*. It was not just the death sentence, but also the notion of a criminal offence of blasphemy that offended the liberal sensibilities of many British people. However, as mentioned in Chapter 2, it was only a decade previously that Mary Whitehouse, of the National Viewers' and Listeners' Association, had brought a successful prosecution for blasphemy against the editor of *Gay News* for publishing a poem about the feelings of a Roman soldier looking at Jesus being crucified. Another source of contention is that the British blasphemy law only applies to Christianity, so denying other groups equal recognition.

Chapter 4 examines the various forms of 'multiculturalism' and the different regulatory strategies that each of them may give rise to, comparing the situations in the USA, Britain and Canada. Each country has experienced the impact of the same global trends, particularly large-scale immigration at times, which has increased the multicultural character of their populations, but their regulatory strategies with regard to multiculturalism exhibit significant differences that are worth considering.

In Chapter 5, Stuart Hall reflects on some of the issues that have been raised about the different moments in the 'cultural circuit', and on the very centrality of culture, and the study of culture, to contemporary society.

References

DU GAY, P. (ed.) (1997) *Production of Culture/Cultures of Production*, London, Sage/The Open University (Book 4 in this series).

DU GAY, P., HALL, S., JANES, L., MACKAY, H. and NEGUS, K. (1997) *Doing Cultural Studies: the story of the Sony Walkman*, London, Sage/The Open University (Book 1 in this series).

WOODWARD, K. (1997) 'Introduction' in Woodward, K. (ed.) *Identity and Difference*, London, Sage/The Open University (Book 3 in this series).

REGULATION, DE-REGULATION AND RE-REGULATION

Kenneth Thompson

Contents

1   Introduction

In the last quarter of the twentieth century it has sometimes seemed as if the dominant economic and political trends could be summed up by the words *globalization* and *de-regulation*. It is certainly the case that the increasing globalization of markets has meant that national economies have been exposed to greater international competition and that there has been an upsurge of neo-liberalism and the promotion of an ideology of 'enterprise culture' (see **du Gay**, ed., 1997). At the same time, globalization in communications and consumer cultures, and increasing international travel and migration, has meant that nation-states have become more socially plural and multicultural. Not surprisingly, these developments have provoked counter-pressures for *regulation* or *re-regulation* to maintain or restore national social order and cultural heritage. In this chapter three cases relevant to the regulation of culture will be discussed in terms of these competing demands for change and order. In the first case we will look at the ways in which these competing pressures have affected the politics of leisure in successive periods from the beginning of the nineteenth century. The second case discusses the tension between these pressures as manifested in the rival claims of enterprise and heritage in the 1980s. The third case focuses on the mass media, particularly the tension between the opposed principles of the market versus public service, and consumer choice versus democratic citizenship. In each case we will be asking: *How have the competing pressures for change and order been manifested and contested in different forms of cultural regulation?*

In one sense the study of the regulation of culture has always had an important place in sociology because it is closely related to sociology's central focus, which is the regulation of social relations, particularly the institutionalized processes by which social order is produced and reproduced. Since its birth in the nineteenth century, many of sociology's key issues have been concerned with the tensions between the pressures for change ('modernization' or 'progress') and the demands to maintain order and continuity. According to the nineteenth-century inventor of the name 'sociology', Auguste Comte, the French Revolution had made it possible to think in terms of a theory of social progress and not just a static social order (Thompson, 1976). However, the accompanying social crisis meant that the task of sociology, according to Comte, was to combine theories of progress and order, giving particular attention to the role of culture in binding societies together. Hence the interest of early sociologists such as Max Weber and Emile Durkheim in analysing the part that religious values and symbol systems had played in developing and reproducing social order; hence, too, their concern about the need for new cultural bonds that would facilitate orderly social change and reduce the disturbing effects on social order of the industrial and political revolutions, and of pressures from urbanization and individualization. Subsequent generations of sociologists have continued to develop theories and analyses of the changing forms of cultural regulation and their relationships to economic, political and social structures in specific periods.

The early sociologists placed culture on an equal footing in its historical relationship with economic and other structures, but in the most straightforward theory of cultural regulation, the crude historical-materialist version of Marxism, culture was simply a superstructure whose shape is determined by the economic base. According to this theory, changes in culture automatically reflect economic changes, because the interests of the dominant economic class are paramount. The state's role in regulating culture is to act as the 'executive committee' of the ruling class. This crude view of the relationship between culture, economics, politics and the social, was contested by the Italian Marxist Antonio Gramsci, who stressed the need to analyse the complex relationships between the economy, politics and ideology in each specific historical case:

> The claim, presented as an essential postulate of historical materialism, that every fluctuation of politics and ideology can be presented and expounded as an immediate expression of the structure, must be contested in theory as primitive infantilism, and combated in practice with the authentic testimony of Marx, the author of concrete political and historical works.

> (Gramsci, 1971, p. 407)

To illustrate the complexities of this kind of historically based analysis, in section 3 we will examine how changes in economic, political and social structures may have had varying effects on cultural regulation in a series of specific periods of British history, focusing on the *politics of leisure.* The general argument will be that culture is not directly determined by economic forces. Culture enjoys some relative autonomy and is the site of struggles over meanings.

Relevant theoretical developments to be kept in mind in our study of cultural regulation include the following:

- Althusser's claim that ideology represents the 'imaginary relationships of individuals to their *real* conditions of existence' (Althusser, 1971, p. 162, emphasis added) by constituting them as 'subjects', in other words giving them identities, such as subjects of the 'imagined community' of the nation.

- Gramsci's insistence that ideological leadership (hegemony) is only achieved when different cultural elements are articulated together to appeal to the widest possible spectrum of opinion, like a 'popular religion' – of which the best examples are 'patriotism' and 'nationalism'.

- Foucault's focus on discourses rather than ideology. Whereas Althusser emphasized the ways in which individuals were constituted as subjects by discourses in an imaginary representation that distorted their real conditions of existence, Foucault refused to equate discourses with ideology (see the discussion in **Hall**, 1997). Foucault does not distinguish knowledge from ideology, arguing that what is truth is defined by the particular discourse, such as health and disease, madness and sanity, sexuality, justice and punishment. His discussions of the ways in which these discourses are constituted and have their effects will be worth keeping in mind when considering contemporary discourses about 'de-regulation' and 'customer' choice in the media industries. However, unlike Althusser and Gramsci, he does not offer any conception of overall unity in the social structure, or of why one group rather than another is in a position to impose its truth.

- It is this pessimism and extreme cultural relativism that has been attacked by critical theorists, such as Jürgen Habermas, as post-modernist and politically neo-conservative. Whereas the Enlightenment philosphers had believed modernity was characterized by universal progress based on scientific rationality, theories of post-modernity claimed such meta-narratives' are no longer credible. Habermas's theory of communicative action, by contrast, aims to continue the Enlightenment's unfinished project to create a public sphere in which ideology is critically exposed and undistorted rational communication can take place and so establish true knowledge (Habermas, 1989/1962).

In section 5, we will examine the arguments between supporters of public broadcasting and advocates of de-regulation and privatization over which system offers the best hope of securing such conditions. We will also consider the arguments of Jean Baudrillard and others, who present a picture of a media-and-consumer society – 'post-modernity' – where reality disintegrates altogether into images and spectacles, epitomized by television and the tabloid press. According to this view, far from the media presenting the conditions for rational communication, as Habermas argued, their values are those of entertainment and sensationalism, sometimes giving rise to 'moral panics'. This view, at least in its more restricted form concerned with 'media distortion' in relation to media organization and practices, has figured prominently in the sociology of mass media. In its broader sense, insofar as it addresses the question of how cultural institutions regulate knowledge and values, and reproduce an unequal social order, it has been a central concern of sociology since it took up the Enlightenment project of the eighteenth century.

1.2   Outline of the chapter

In section 2 we review some of the theories that might have something to offer in explaining the relationship between the regulation of culture in different periods and economic, political and social forces. The seminal theorist of regulation and of ideology is Gramsci, but we will also consider the contributions of other theorists – such as Althusser on ideology and Foucault on discourse – which address questions of subjectivity and identity, as well as sociological theories of communication and the public sphere, such as those inspired by Habermas.

The usefulness of these theoretical ideas should become evident when we look at some examples of studies which have been informed by them. In section 3, we will begin by considering one line of study that has given a great deal of attention to questions of cultural regulation: it is that concerned with the politics of 'leisure', which comprises a wide range of activities that we tend to think of as cultural. It provides an accessible way into the study of changing forms of cultural regulation because it focuses attention on the state regulation of leisure, which is what most people think of when the term 'regulation' is used. We will be asking the question: *To what extent do economic developments seem to have determined the direction taken by cultural regulation in the sphere of leisure?*

In section 4, we focus on discourses and ideology, comparing different views on whether the New Right ideology of the 1980s managed to articulate together the discourses and practices of national heritage and enterprise culture. The key question here is: *To what extent were the competing pressures of market forces and the desire to preserve a sense of national cultural heritage reconciled in the ideology of 'conservative modernization'? Or is 'heritage' itself a site of contestation, and open to different interpretations?*

Finally, in section 5, we will focus on questions of regulation concerning the institutional forms of the mass media and their effect on the 'mediazation of society' – 'the general process by which the transmission of symbolic forms becomes increasingly mediated by the technical and institutional apparatuses of the media industries' (Thompson, 1990, pp. 3–4). For example, *do the mass media as presently organized provide the necessary public sphere for undistorted rational communication and debate that are said to be essential in constituting a modern democracy? Or do the economic forces in the global culture industry mean that the kind of rational discourse described as characteristic of modernity is now giving way to 'figural' media that offer only entertaining spectacles, typical of 'post-modernity'?* The examples to be considered include the debates about public broadcasting and about whether the popular press tend to create 'moral panics' rather than facilitate rational discussion. Both examples raise important issues about regulation. Two of the key opposing theorists are Habermas and Baudrillard.

The overall story-line uniting these separate topics runs something like this:

Culture has always been reciprocally related to economic, political and social factors in the making of modern society. The question at issue, however, is: Have the competing demands for change and order meant that, although culture has certainly been affected by the economy, the outcome in each historical period has also been shaped by a conjunction of other important factors? We will find tensions between the economic, political, social and cultural spheres – for example, between global economic forces, the nation-state, social groups, and national cultures. In recent times culture seems to have become increasingly important and central to these conflicts. In one sense this is not surprising, as the increasing spending power of people in industrialized economies has meant they have more to spend on the products of the culture industry. However, the culture industry has also become more oriented towards a 'global media space and market' (Robins, 1995, p. 247) and the globalizing media corporations have begun to search for new sources of income beyond their own national borders. Western governments have been torn between pursuing policies of 'de-regulation' to attract investment and increase their economic competitiveness, and 're-regulation' to defend their national cultures and social orders. We will argue that even some of the 'de-regulation' policies might be better described as really 're-regulation', because they have merely shifted from regulatory principles based on notions of the national public interest and citizenship towards those based on the idea of people as customers and the public as consumer markets (Robins, 1995, and **Negus**, 1997). The trend is evident in the prominence of discourses and ideologies associated with such terms as 'enterprise', 'heritage', 'customer', 'the market' and 'de-regulation' from the 1980s onwards. These discourses were powerfully, if uneasily, linked together in the New Right ideology that was promoted as a solution by the governments of Margaret Thatcher and Ronald Reagan, and had an impact on cultural policies in areas like recreation and leisure, heritage and conservation, broadcasting and mass media. However, the tensions between some of these tendencies, as well as resistance to them, meant that they had varying effects, as we will discuss in the three 'case studies' – leisure, heritage, and the mass media.

The development of the chapter thus proceeds from a discussion of *culture* and its relation to economic and political structural forces in different historical periods, to an analysis of the constitution of subjectivity and *identities* by and through discourses and ideologies, to a debate about changes in *media* organization.

The general argument is that cultural regulation is to some extent a response to economic and other structural changes, but is not simply a unilinear or direct reflection of those structural changes. For example, sociologists have discussed the shift from cultural regulation involving religious values and institutions, to secular cultural regulation involving institutions of the state (education) or civil society (popular culture, leisure and mass media). For much of the modern industrial era, the state government at national and local level seemed to be intent on maintaining social stability by the regulation of culture through legislation and bureaucratic institutions. More recently, some would argue, under the impact of global economic developments, social pluralization, and the rise of market ideologies, the shift has been towards 'de-regulation' (reduction of rules and regulatory bodies) and in the direction of 'self-government' for the individual. An alternative view is that it is more a matter of 're-regulation', with a shift in the ideological balance from notions of the public interest (open to rational debate in the public sphere) and citizenship, towards those based on discourses of people as consumers and the public as consumer markets. However, even if such a shift is occurring, there is usually a mixture of symbols and discourses in play, and we need to remember that they do not have fixed meanings, and that consumption is not passive. The process of cultural regulation is always a site of contestation.

2   Regulation theories

cultural regulation

As mentioned earlier, the most clear-cut answer to the question about the factors affecting **cultural regulation** appears to be that contained in Marx's statement that the mode of economic production determines culture in each epoch or period: 'The mode of production of material life determines the general character of the social, political and spiritual processes of life' (Marx, 1963/1859, p. 67). However, Marx showed that he was aware of the complicated and reciprocal nature of the relationship between the economy and culture in any historical period: 'Unless material production itself is understood in its specific historical form, it is impossible to grasp the characteristics of the intellectual production which corresponds to it or the reciprocal action between the two' (Marx, 1963/1905–10, pp. 96–7). It was the Italian writer, Antonio Gramsci, in the *Notebooks* he wrote in Mussolini's prison between 1929 and 1935, who adapted Marx's ideas in such a way as

regulation theories

to inspire the development of **regulation theories** that focus on these complicated and reciprocal relations. Gramsci's most obvious linking of economic production and the culture of consumption, in the article 'Americanism and Fordism' (1971), maintained that the system of assembly-line mass production and the high-wage strategy practised by the Ford Motor Company was translated into a general transformation in the culture and consumption of the working class, involving moral regulation in matters as apparently distant from the concerns of capital and the workplace as alcoholic consumption and sex. This rather mechanical version of regulation theory is not the main lesson that we will draw from Gramsci. In the rest of this chapter, the emphasis will be more on his theory of ideology, but the 'Fordism = an American way of life' argument has had an influence on some of the more economistic regulation theories.

economic regulation theory

regime of accumulation

mode of regulation

Economic regulation theory, developed in the late 1970s and 1980s (Aglietta, 1979; Lipietz, 1987), took forward Gramsci's argument by proposing that every form of capitalist production requires a complementary form of consumption. Taken together, the two forms constitute a **regime of accumulation**. The maintenance of this regime, it was argued, requires a set of non-economic (i.e. cultural) institutions, such as schools, mass media, a welfare system, which are called a **mode of regulation**. For these regulation theorists, advanced capitalism requires an interventionist state to manage aggregate demand (i.e. to maintain economic order) and create the right moral and political framework for the maintenance of moral and social order. Corrigan and Sayer (1985) have attempted to develop regulation theory into a social history of moral behaviour and state formation. They argue that **moral regulation** attempts to 'normalize' historically and socially specific forms of behaviour as universal. Where moral regulation is successful, people accept certain forms of identity, practice and association as 'natural' or 'inevitable' and reject other forms as 'deviant' or 'impossible'. Thus, each regime of accumulation has its corresponding cultural forms. The nineteenth-century 'rational recreation' movement in Britain and the USA (to be discussed further in section 3) is quoted as an example of an attempt by the state to exert a 'civilizing influence' over the lower classes. Although voluntary organizations were prominent, regulation theory identifies the state as the central regulating mechanism – codifying the programmes developed through voluntary initiatives and constructing or legitimating normality.

moral regulation

In one respect this regulation theory resembles that of Foucault in viewing the development of the modern order of things as a movement from external constraint to self-discipline. 'By "voluntarily" keeping ourselves in order, morally and socially, the moral and social order of modernity is cemented' (Rojek, 1995, p. 44). However, Corrigan and Sayer's regulation theory has been criticized on two grounds. Firstly, it has been criticized for underestimating the degree to which the subjects of moral regulation are creative actors who contest and disrupt the agencies of regulation, as in the case of resistance to attempts to control popular leisure forms in the nineteenth century (Cunningham, 1980). Secondly, critics have charged that this moral regulation theory insists on seeing the role of the state as the pre-eminent controlling force in society and underestimates other relations of power (Rojek, 1995, p. 45). It is on this ground that some critics have found Foucault's approach (see below) to be more fruitful.

As we will see in section 3, the Industrial Revolution, urbanization, and the threat of social unrest did seem to stimulate an increased regulation of leisure activities from the early nineteenth century onwards in Britain. In some respects these developments can be seen as simply an accentuation of long-term trends that the sociologist Max Weber had characterized as typical of modernity – the increasing rationalization and bureaucratization of social life in all spheres. In modern society the state reserved to itself a monopoly of the legitimate use of violence and force, and such force was kept as a last resort. In all other respects public order depended on the promulgation of sets of rules, developed according to formally rational criteria, and internalized by participants in the various social activities. Weber's description of modernity as characterized by increasing rationalization in all spheres, to which the individual was subjected not by force but through a sort of voluntary contract, was developed further by Foucault (1975, 1981). The difference is that, whereas Weber focused on formal rationalities and regulations (institutions), Foucault is concerned with a wider range of discourses and discursive practices. In discussing how the voluntary contract was engineered, Foucault wrote of **carceral networks** of power in society.

carceral networks

By this he meant webs of control which both empower and regulate behaviour. In Foucault's sociology the idea of carceral networks is indissoluble from the idea of the individual. The forms of speech, writing, received ideas and law, the forms of discourse, associated with carceral networks are also the forms by which we recognize the individual as a separate subject possessing specific needs and rights.

(Rojek, 1995, p.60)

According to Foucault, there are three types of power: *institutional power,* exercised through rules and regulations; *economic power,* as in the class system; and *subjective power,* in which the individual struggles against discourses organized around the self. On the whole, he maintains, the course of development in modernity is from the first two types towards the increasingly pervasive third type – from external regulation and external discipline towards self-regulation and self-discipline. (To some extent, in section 3, we will be able to trace this development through Henry's description of leisure policy in different periods.) Rather than seeing leisure and cultural activities as a 'realm of freedom' and 'authenticity', Foucault's theory stresses how discourses and practices in modern society generate in us a sense of what constitutes a natural and healthy self, so that we constantly fret about using our free time wisely, having healthy or attractive bodies, and engaging in creative or improving activities without having to be directed by some external authority. The spread of health and fitness clubs and the concern about dieting and healthy eating provide good contemporary examples of this (see **Benson**, 1997). However, Foucault does not see power in 'preventive' terms, unlike many theorists; he presents carceral networks as 'productive', as a source of both regulation and empowerment – they motivate us to strive in certain directions that are judged natural and healthy, and so desirable. For example, the so-called Victorian values that Mrs Thatcher was keen to revive in 1980s Britain were precisely concerned with developing the healthy, enterprising self, that would 'work hard and play hard' – encouraging individuals to take responsibility for themselves. (See the discussion of enterprise values and the enterprising self in **du Gay**, 1997.)

Foucault is less helpful when it comes to conceptualizing how discourses relate to each other and perhaps form an ideological whole, despite their apparent differences, as in the case of the ideology referred to as 'Thatcherism' in Britain or, more broadly, the New Right ideology in the USA and other countries, combining neo-liberal economic doctrines with conservative social and cultural values. Whereas Foucault substitutes difference for unity, maintaining that nothing ever fits with anything else, the French structural-Marxist theorist, Louis Althusser, stresses the necessity of thinking how differences exist within a complex unity. 'Articulation' has become a key theoretical term in understanding how different levels of practice or different discourses relate together. As Stuart Hall puts it:

> The function of the State is, in part, precisely to bring together or articulate into a complexly structured instance, a range of political discourses and social practices which are concerned at different sites with the transmission and transformation of power ... for example, familial life, civil society, gender and economic relations.

(Hall, 1985, p. 90)

I believe this view of politics as involving the *articulation* of discourses to produce ideological effects, such as winning support and consent for certain ideas and practices that sustain relations of power, can offer a useful framework for analysis. It is particularly appropriate for situations in which ideological effort is required to reconcile apparently divergent discourses and forces. The attempt to articulate together the discourses of national heritage and enterprise culture in the New Right ideology of the 1980s, which we will examine in section 4, provides us with a good example on which to test this out.

Before turning to this more contemporary case, however, we will look at a longer historical account of cultural regulation as it relates to the politics of leisure.

3 Cultural regulation and the politics of leisure

Regulatory policies in various fields of culture and leisure activity, whether conceived by public or private agencies, aim to foster or control practices in these fields and so have an important influence on the behaviour of members of society. The state at central and local level has long been involved in developing cultural and leisure policies. For some writers, *leisure* is seen as a distinctive category of social activity that is a product of industrialization, and the separation of work and non-work is viewed as a function of work-time and work discipline (Myerscough, 1974; Murphy, 1981; Clarke and Critcher, 1985). For Britain, as the first industrializing nation, this process is said to have begun in the late eighteenth century. Other writers stress the separation, in the nineteenth century, of the production of cultural forms from their consumption, as the logic of capitalism became applied to leisure markets, represented in an urbanized and concentrated population – thus, leisure industries developed as a specialized sector of the economy (Henry, 1993; Bailey, 1987).

According to Henry (1993) the politics of leisure policy in Britain can be seen as falling into seven distinct periods since the eighteenth century. Each period is characterized by a typical form of regulation of culture and leisure, bearing a close relationship to social and economic trends at that time. Henry's account gives priority to the effect of basic economic and political factors in the history of cultural regulation. In this respect it most resembles the classic Marxist approach, emphasizing economic and political structural factors in determining culture, but without reducing this to a crude economic determinism. The key question is: *To what extent do economic developments seem to have determined the direction taken by cultural regulation in the sphere of leisure in different periods?*

READING A

You should now read the extracts from Ian Henry's account of these historical periods, *The Politics of Leisure Policy*, provided as Reading A at the end of this chapter. You might also bring to mind any personal knowledge you have about these matters in your own lifetime.

After you have finished reading, and allowing for the fact that this is a very condensed history, can you describe the main features of the cultural regulation characteristic of each period and relate them to economic, political and social structural trends?

You may feel that this historical outline is just too sketchy to draw any firm conclusions about the different forms of regulation and their relationships to social and economic changes. Nevertheless, it does give us some ideas about the changes that were taking place, even if the division into periods can only be tentative and there may be trends that stretch over more than one period. Bearing in mind these qualifications, I would pick out the following key points.

The period 1780–1840 is sometimes referred to as the Age of Revolutions – including the Industrial Revolution and the French Revolution – and there was a great fear of working-class revolt and public disorder. The developing industrial economy entailed the institutionalization of work- and time-disciplines, making possible a sharper distinction between work and leisure time. Regulation of cultural and leisure practices has been described as being concerned with 'civilizing' the working classes, legislation being introduced to prohibit the more disorderly activities and to make them more 'regular' in their work habits. However, the working classes were not passive in the face of this legislative and institutional regulation; some unregulated popular activities continued in clandestine form, with the support of commercial interests such as publicans.

Regulation in the next period, 1840–1900, is often characterized by the term 'rational recreation' and was marked by the beginning of a more positive approach to state intervention in the form of fostering the activities of individuals and groups, including legislation to allow local authorities to use public funds to capitalize on gifts, such as land, books or exhibits. The ideology of 'muscular Christianity' was propagated; games and sports were codified and organized; hygiene and education became public responsibilities. Perhaps the most important economic factor was that the working class had more disposable income and spare time, so they had more

FIGURE 1.1

Teetotal demonstration at the Great Exhibition, Crystal Palace, 5 August 1851: Rational recreation was also fostered by the Temperance movement, reflecting a concern with the evil effects of drink on the working classes.

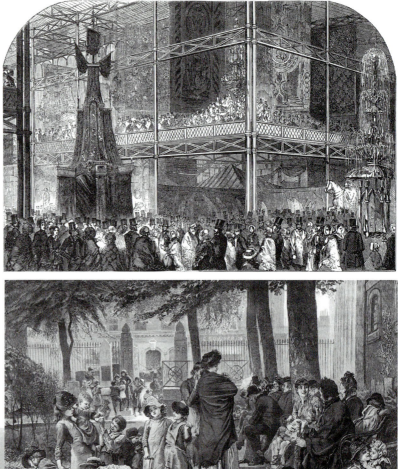

FIGURE 1.2

Scene in the Churchyard of St John's Church Waterloo Road, London, thrown open to the public in 1887: part of the increase in leisure facilities in the interest of the health of urban workers.

FIGURE 1.3

Wakes Week in Blackpool, July 1955, 'presents an example of unrestrained pleasure-making on a mass scale' (*Picture Post*): a rational solution to enable working classes to take holidays with the least disruption to factory production.

opportunities to choose their recreational activities, and these attracted commercial investment.

The period from the beginning of the twentieth century until the Second World War saw the growth of direct state involvement in the leisure field, rather than merely state support for voluntary initiatives as in the previous period. Legislation was enacted to incorporate organizations that had previously been voluntary or independent. It marked the gradual build-up of a Welfare State in which the state has a duty to provide facilities that are conducive to the health and welfare of its citizens.

After the Second World War, until economic circumstances produced cutbacks in state spending from 1976 onwards, there was a gradual shift from 'traditional pluralism' to 'welfare reformism'. However, it was not a smooth development. There were struggles between various political and ideological tendencies: for example, the conservationist tendency was concerned to maintain cultural standards, whilst fostering some increased access ('democratization of culture'); by contrast, critics of such policies wanted 'cultural democracy' in which groups were allowed to promote their own cultural forms. This split was evident in the debates about the role of local government in this field, which continued well into the 1980s. The Greater London Council (GLC), before its abolition in 1988, tried to develop policies which would combine both 'welfare reformism' and 'cultural democracy'. Its political opponents and sections of the Press claimed to be outraged at some of the minority culture groups and activities that it subsidized.

FIGURE 1.4
Corporate sponsorship of the arts: an event from the BOC Covent Garden festival, 1997.

From the late 1970s into the early 1980s, there was a shift in leisure policies as part of the restructuring of the welfare state, from an emphasis on rights of citizenship and reducing inequalities, to that of promoting social order, and to fostering self-reliance on the part of the individual, the family and community groups. The 1975 government White Paper, *Sport and Recreation,* spoke of the need to promote active recreation to reduce hooliganism and delinquency, whilst the 1977 White Paper, *A Policy for the Inner Cities*, aimed to promote leisure services in areas of deprivation as a means of offsetting expenditure on policing and vandalism, illustrating the tension between leisure as an end and leisure as a means of social control.

Increasingly in the 1980s and into the 1990s the Conservative government used its powers to promote free market pluralism and enterprise, whether through voluntary bodies or commercial organizations. This did not mean that government had lost interest in culture and its regulation. The opposite was the case. It was extremely active in implementing policies that fitted in with its ideology of preserving social order and pursuing economic regeneration in areas such as leisure, education (e.g. instituting the National Curriculum, and prescribing the content of History, English, Religion and Sports), and the regulation of broadcasting.

Table 1.1 summarizes the development of leisure policy and legislation.

TABLE 1.1   Development of leisure sectors over time

Chronology	Illustrative social and economic policies	Illustrative leisure policies	Emphasis in role of state in leisure	Emphasis in role of commercial sector in leisure	Emphasis in role of voluntary sector in leisure
c. 1780–1840 Suppression of popular recreations	Poor Law Amendment Act 1834	Suppression of Bloodsports Act 1833; Enclosure Act 1836	Attempts to control and suppress 'disruptive' leisure forms	Small-scale entrepreneurs (publicans) replace squirearchy as patrons of popular recreations	Formation of organizations to control working-class organizations
c. 1840–c. 1900 Erosion of *Laissez-Faire* approach to social/ economic policy	Factories Acts 1847, 1867; Education Act 1870	Public Baths and Washhouses Act 1846; Museums Act 1849; Libraries Act 1850, Recreation Grounds Act 1852	State support, particularly for voluntary effort, promoting 'improving' leisure forms	Increasing scale of capital investment, e.g. rail, larger music halls, sports stadia, mass production of leisure equipment	Sector reflects paternalism of middle classes but control of leisure organizations (e.g. Working Men's Clubs movement)
c. 1900–c. 1939 Social reforms, laying the foundations of the Welfare State	Education Act 1902; Old Age Pensions 1908; National (Health) Insurance 1911; Unemployment Assistance 1934	National Trust Act 1907; Town Planning Act 1909; Forestry Commission founded with recreation role 1919; Physical Recreation and Training Act 1937; Access to the Mountains Act 1939	Increasing recognition of leisure as a legitimate concern of government in its own right	Importation of leisure forms from the US, cinema, music, etc. New technology provides leisure equipment, e.g. radio, cinema, car, motorcycle. New investment attracted by the discretionary income of those in work	Institutionalization of the voluntary sector with establishment of national organizations and pressure groups, e.g. National Trust, Central Council for Physical Recreation and Training, National Playing Fields Association, mass trespass movement

TABLE 1.1 (cont.)

Chronology	Illustrative social and economic policies	Illustrative leisure policies	Emphasis in role of state in leisure	Emphasis in role of commercial sector in leisure	Emphasis in role of voluntary sector in leisure
1944–1976 Growth and maturing of the Welfare State	Education Act 1944; Family Allowances 1945; Distribution of Industries Act 1945; National Insurance Act 1946; NHS launched 1948	Arts Council established 1946; National Parks and Access to the Countryside Act 1949; Sports Council founded 1965; Countryside Commission founded 1968; White Paper *Sport and Recreation* 1975	Leisure added to the portfolio of welfare services, 'one of the community's everyday needs'	Demise of traditional manufacturing industries, growth of service sector. Growth of multinational investment in UK leisure industries. Major growth areas are home-based leisure and tourism	Growth of voluntary leisure organizations, particularly for the higher socio-economic groups. Break-up of working-class communities fuels need for formal organization, especially in 'new' communities
1976– c. 1984 New Economic Realism and the re-structuring of the Welfare State	1976 onwards pressures on local government spending; 1977 White Paper, *A Policy for the Inner Cities*	Squeeze on local government and Arts Council spending: growth in inner city schemes, 'Football and Community', 'Leisure and Unemployed'; Countryside Commission given quango status and marginalized	Emphasis on leisure expenditure as 'social consumption' gives way to leisure expenditure as 'social expenses'	Concentration of leisure investment in few multinationals, diversification of companies across leisure sector; vertical integration	Restricted corporatism: 'voluntarism' within the state as voluntary groups deliver services previously supplied by the state
1985–1990s State flexibilization and disinvestment (the post-Fordist state)	Centralization of powers to achieve decentralization or marketization (i.e. flexibilization) of provision. Establishment of Urban Development Corporations, Enterprise Zones, commercial management of public leisure facilities; abolition of GLC and Metropolitan counties; community charge and rate/charge capping; Education Act 1988	Reduction of local government budgets; compulsory competitive tendering; local management of schools (and control of educational curriculum)	Marketization of service provision; leisure (and tourism) employed as a tool for economic rather than social regeneration; residual provision with leisure as social policy tool in the inner city	Flexible accumulation strategies adopted by corporate organizations: management buy-outs, disinvestment, divisional autonomy as a reaction to diseconomies of scale, and lack of flexibility in large-scale organizations	Free market pluralism: voluntarism 'outwith the state'; voluntary organizations, governing bodies of sport, arts organizations pushed towards sponsorship as alternative to state subsidy

Source: Henry, 1993, pp. 24–5.

This historical sketch has been concerned with Britain (similar periodizations could be carried out on other industrialized countries) and for some periods it might appear to provide evidence to support the kind of economistic regulation theory that posits a correspondence between the forms of production and consumption (and so culture). In other periods, economic changes may have been less important than political, social or cultural developments. The case of Britain is interesting because it was the first country to begin the process of industrialization, involving the separation of work and leisure, and the commodification of leisure activities, resulting in successive efforts to regulate such activities. Perhaps because Britain was the first to industrialize, it was also one of the first economies to experience pressures to switch from ageing manufacturing industries, and Fordist production processes, to 'post-industrial' services, including leisure services, and post-Fordist forms of work organization (discussed in **du Gay, 1997**). The commodification of culture has accelerated with the growth of service industries, such as entertainment and tourism, whilst at the same time, the use of cultural techniques in production and marketing has also increased in prominence. Finally, technological developments in communications, both mass communications and person-to-person, have brought about some fundamental cultural changes.

However, as we suggested earlier when criticizing the more economistic regulation theories, historical accounts that posit a mechanical relationship between economic base and cultural superstructure fail to do justice to some of the other factors that intervene, such as those involving political and cultural contestation. Even an economically and politically focused historical survey such as that by Henry emphasizes that developments in culture cannot be explained as 'functional requirements' of changes in the economic system:

> Regulation theory represents an attempt to escape the notion that capitalism has a single inevitable logic of development. Politico-economic systems develop their own trajectories, influenced by the political, economic and ideological actors and historical alliances within those systems, and the emergence of a New Right-led Conservative government with an ideologically driven political programme provides a major element in the impetus to seek a new set of economic and social relations.
>
> (Henry, 1993, pp. 176–7)

Consequently, in the next section, we will focus on the question of how economic developments relate to the politics of culture as seen in struggles over the discursive and ideological construction of subjectivities and identities.

4   Heritage and enterprise culture

Some of the processes and tensions involved in combining different discourses in an ideology can be seen in the efforts made by Thatcherism and the New Right to reconcile neo-liberal doctrines about free markets and consumer choice with conservative social and cultural values about the arts and national heritage. Whereas neo-liberalism depends on a view of freedom as non-interference, particularly by the state, conservative values tend to rest on notions of community and authority. Conservative politicians have sometimes been found on different sides of the argument, some defending a particular aspect of heritage, others viewing it with indifference or as an obstacle to modernization. Such tensions occur not just on the political Right, but also on the Left. In the latter the split tends to be between those who describe heritage and conservation in negative terms as elements in a strategy of ideological hegemony promoted by an elite in defence of vested interests and conservative social values, and those who see it more positively in sophisticated 'populist' terms as representing authentic grassroots values and local interests, reacting against capitalist globalization and cultural homogenization. However, the actual positions advanced are often quite complex, and do not fall easily into polarized positions.

The key question here is: *To what extent were the competing pressures of market forces and the desire to preserve a sense of national cultural heritage reconciled in the ideology of 'conservative modernization'? Or is 'heritage' itself a site of contestation and open to different interpretations?*

READINGS B AND C

You should now read the articles by Patrick Wright and Raphael Samuel about heritage and cultural policies, provided as Readings B and C respectively, at the end of this chapter. (The extracts have been edited so as to emphasize the differences; Wright's position in his later writings on heritage is more nuanced than appears here.)

After you have read both readings, consider the following questions:

- What are the main differences between these writers in their interpretations of the ideological character of heritage and conservation?

- How do these differences reflect the tensions between globalization and localism, economic change and national culture?

Patrick Wright's position is that of a critic of the conservative 'heritage' view of national culture as something that has to be preserved in the face of constant threats. He begins his book *On Living in an Old Country* (1985) by describing how, after returning to Britain from living in Canada in 1979, he felt that: 'I had come back to a country which was full of precious and imperilled traces – a closely held iconography of what it is to be English – all of them appealing in one covertly projective way or another to the historical and sacrosanct identity of the nation' (ibid., p. 2). And yet, as he makes clear, conservative attitudes to that epitome of national identity, the National Trust, since its foundation in 1895 were not always so unequivocal. For the first twenty years of its existence, when it worked as a campaigning pressure group with a view to protecting the public access to open spaces, it was in conflict with private capital and government. However, in 1907 the Trust was made a statutory body by Act of Parliament, giving it the right to hold land 'inalienably'; as a result, Wright says, it could claim to reconcile the apparent conflict between private property and the national and public interest. Despite the National Trust's preoccupation with the preservation of landscapes and monuments, which seems to have an affinity with a conservative concern to preserve the social order, Wright points out some of the inherent conflicts between conservative 'preservation' and capitalist 'modernization'. 'Capitalist property relations can only be preserved if they are reproduced through new accumulative cycles, and preservation of these relations seems in this sense to necessitate the constant transformation of life in both town and country' (ibid., p. 53). Capital periodically enters into conflict with the preservation lobby, even though the conflict may be concealed behind the 'publicly maintained serenity of "our" national heritage' (ibid.). There is also a potential for conflict between the public's interest in access and amenity, and the interests of those more concerned with the preservation of land and monuments .

Wright also analyses the articulation or coalescence of the discourses of 'historic interest' and 'natural beauty', which has produced 'a merger in which a conventional realism can be used to naturalize a bourgeois interpretation of history and society'. In this way, members of the heritage lobby can sometimes speak of the country house as the 'soul' of the nation. He relates this coalescence of discourses around the National Trust to the rhetoric which surrounded the passage of the National Heritage Act (1980), and describes this national heritage view of history as 'entropic decline'.

Finally, Wright emphasizes the staged or constructed images of the nation and its history presented by the heritage perspective, in which 'sites exist only to provide that momentary experience of utopian gratification in which the grey torpor of everyday life in contemporary Britain lifts and the simpler, more radiant measures of Albion declare themselves again' (ibid., p. 76).

Raphael Samuel provides a contrasting analysis of heritage culture, even though he is also on the Left of the political spectrum. Essentially, he disagrees with critics of heritage like Hewison about their main accusations that it represents:

1   reactionary chic;

2   the triumph of aristocratic and reactionary nostalgia over the levelling tendencies of the Welfare State;

3   an aristocratic plot hatched by beleaguered owners of country houses;

4   an example of post-modern capitalist consumerism, commodifying the past, and creating a simulacrum of a past that never was;

5   an 'expressive totality', projecting a unified set of meanings, a 'closed story' or fixed narrative allowing for no other readings, in which politics, culture and economics reinforce each other;

6   a project or strategy of 'collective recollection', 'a bid for hegemony' and a way of using knowledge in the service of power;

7   a way of shoring up national identity in face of uncertainty, compensating for the collapse of British power.

According to Samuel, none of these accusations which associate heritage with conservative reaction are borne out by the chronology of events, as many of heritage's enthusiasms were in place long before 1975, when the term entered general circulation. He gives the examples of vintage car rallies and railway antiquarianism, which began at least a couple of decades earlier. The cry 'Heritage in danger', he says, may have been more a reaction to the modernizations of the 1950s than to economic decline. While accepting that business may have profited from notions of 'period' in commodity marketing, he suggests we should pay more attention to 'molecular processes' in which culture takes shape, such as small entrepreneurs and craftsmen (sic) retailers. In other words he claims to be presenting a view of bottom-up cultural change as a corrective to 'top-down accounts of the heritage industry which see it as a kind of ruling-class conspiracy' (Samuel, 1994, p. 244).

The most intriguing aspect of Samuel's analysis of heritage is where he refers to recent theories of identity and representation as a corrective to the view which sees it as a direct reflection of economic interests and class domination:

> A sociological perspective on heritage, which took into account the hybridization of contemporary social identities, the mixing and mingling of what were formerly class preserves, or a Marxist one which looked for a dialectical relationship between the imaginary and the real, rather than a reductive and reflective one, might be even more unsettling to currently accepted negative stereotypes than an economic one.
>
> (ibid., p. 246)

He suggests that the popularity of heritage may be due to its representing less a restoration of old class values and more an attempt to escape from class identities into more pluralized and hybridized identities. This conjures up an image of Britain as a post-modern culture in which people construct or imagine for themselves different identities, by dressing up in various costumes, or tracing their family history so as to give themselves a second identity or to 'indulge in a romance of otherness'. At this point, you might think, Samuel comes close to the people he is criticizing, such as Wright and

Hewison, picturing heritage as a kind of post-modern cultural phenomenon. The difference seems to be that Samuel emphasizes the creative, grassroots variety of heritage culture, whereas Hewison especially (and, to a lesser extent, Wright) emphasizes the ways in which heritage culture reflects the economic interests of landowners and capitalists and the political interests of a government concerned to preserve a nostalgic and conservative notion of national identity. You may conclude that the difference between the perspectives on heritage comes down to definitions and the perception that Samuel's focus on heritage culture is a lot broader and more varied than that of Hewison, and less critical than that of Wright. But is this an accident? If not, is it due to political differences over what heritage represents as far as cultural regulation is concerned?

The protagonists have at times suggested that there *are* differences of political emphasis behind their views on heritage. Patrick Wright, reviewing Samuel's *Theatres of Memory,* in *The Guardian* (4 February 1995), argues that:

> Heritage may be 'people's history' in one manifestation, but it is also quango-culture and tourism paraded as an alternative for industrial policy ... Conservation is certainly not responsible for Britain's relative economic decline, but in the public symbolism of recent decades, a partial and backward-looking conception of heritage has been squared off against modernization in a manner that has constrained our ability to imagine a future, and that, contrary to Samuel's assertions, can reasonably be connected to the question of decline.

FIGURE 1.5   Cultural nostalgia and tourism: Wigan Pier, a former industrial site, now a tourist attraction.

So, for Wright, heritage can have some reactionary political effects if it takes the form of cultural nostalgia fostered by powerful elites. Samuel prefers to stress their politically positive and populist connotations – as a 'magnet for cultural dissidents', making 'utopianism feasible', 'the most potent of mobilizing forces', 'a popular cause' (Samuel, 1994, p. 292), whilst noting that the terms 'heritage' and 'conservation' are 'shifting signifiers' with varying connotations. He believes conservation, especially, has a 'predilection for direct action' and 'the politics of the personal, giving space for the unilateral action of the individual' (p. 293). These are very different characteristics of heritage to those singled out by Wright, Hewison and other critics and you might think it makes it impossible to draw any conclusions. However, Samuel does give some clues as to why and how these differences might arise.

ACTIVITY I

1   On the basis of your reading of the Samuel extract, can you pick out some of the factors that might cause people to draw different conclusions about heritage?

2   What are your own conclusions about heritage, in the light of your experience and what you have read?

Samuel shows that heritage, like conservation, draws on a nexus of different interests, and that it takes on different meanings in different circumstances, such as: different periods and national cultures; the extent to which the public arena is open to initiatives from below or the periphery; responsiveness to technological changes; the existence of earlier social movements (e.g. 1960s environmental campaigns); economic developments (e.g. heritage as a style-setter for post-Fordist small-batch production); cultural nationalism and the revival of religion in some places. He also stresses the chameleon ideological character of heritage, which means that it is constantly metamorphosing into something else. That is why he regards the focus on the 'invention of tradition' with respect to the commemorative arts as misleading. He believes that focus is too directed at the 'strategies' of elites and does not take account of 'the great mass of pre-existing sentiment which underpins sea-changes in public attitudes and revolutions in public taste' (Samuel, 1994, p. 307). It is not surprising that he takes this approach, because as a long-standing 'people's historian' and founder of *History Workshop Journal,* he revels in the variety and creative effervescence to be found in grassroots activities such as some of those associated with his broader definition of heritage and conservation. The focus of Wright, Hewison and other critics of heritage in the 1980s has been on its use for cultural regulation on behalf of powerful political interests, and this has led them to focus on certain aspects and not some of those listed by Samuel, which they regard as merely cultural resistance by minorities in the face of more powerful forces.

These more powerful forces, they allege, promoted a particular idea of 'enterprise culture', which came to prominence in the 1980s with the ascendancy in Britain and America of New Right political ideology. The British version came to be called 'Thatcherism' because it was Prime Minister Margaret Thatcher who gave powerful expression to this particular mixture of ideas. According to her former minister, Nigel Lawson, 'The right definition involves a mixture of free markets, financial discipline, firm control over public expenditure, tax cuts, nationalism, "Victorian values" (of the Samuel Smiles self-help variety), privatization and a dash of populism' (Lawson, 1992, p. 64). It has been described as a moral and ideological project that set out to release new energies and produce cultural change. The authority of the state was to be used to free the economy, sweeping out of its path centres of opposition in local government, the Church and education, whilst a new consensus was to be constructed on themes of law and order, the traditional family and patriotism. Thatcherism, wrote the political commentator David Marquand, was about 'British (or rather English) nationhood as well as the profit motive; about history, identity, and above all, authority as well as economics' (Marquand, 1991, p. 226). To critics such as Wright and Hewison, the rhetoric of shared heritage and a conservative definition of the nation were part of a hegemonic strategy to secure consent for policies that favoured certain powerful interests and legitimated increased inequality. For Samuel, heritage and conservation referred to much longer and more varied popular efforts to preserve distinctive local and grassroots cultures in the face of modern global tendencies towards standardization and mass consumption.

Samuel's position might seem to have some similarity to that of earlier critics on the Left, such as George Orwell and Richard Hoggart, who shared the horror of many cultural conservatives about the threat of cultural homogenization or 'mass culture', linked in the post-war era with the onset of 'Americanization'. However, whereas they were anxious to defend an 'authentic' working-class culture against the 'shallow' values of the mass consumer culture of modernity emanating from the USA, Samuel uses 'heritage' to refer to what he sees as the rich variety of people's cultural recreations, reviving old arts and styles in defiance of massification, modernization and standardization. It is not surprising that some commentators have likened this to post-modernism. And Samuel is quite happy to defend the post-modernist character of 'retrochic' and the blending together of enterprise and heritage, even though his populist sympathies are not really post-modern in origin.

ACTIVITY 2

As you read the extracts from Samuel's discussion of retrochic in Box 1.1, make notes on how he blends together heritage and enterprise in a positive interpretation and sees these developments as socially progressive.

BOX I.I   RETROCHIC

Retrochic enjoys an uncertain place in the cartography of taste, making a fugitive appearance in a whole succession of style wars and taking its bow now on the catwalks of the fashion trade, now on the stalls of the flea markets (like retrochic itself, a term imported into this country from France in the 1970s), now in the installations of pop art. Aesthetically it is double-coded: 'olde worlde but ultimately modern' (Galliano, 1988). ... More futuristically, as in the punk style of installation sculpture, retrochic gives free play to some of the more utopian elements in national life, of what a recent writer has called 'England's Dreaming' (Savage, 1991). ...

Retrochic trades on inversion, discovering hitherto unnoticed beauties in the flotsam and jetsam of everyday life; elevating yesterday's cast-offs into antique clothes and vintage wear; and treating the out-of-date and the anachronistic – or imitations of them – as though they were the latest thing. ... [Figures 1.6 and 1.7]

According to the theorists of post-modernism, retrochic differs from earlier kinds of period revival in that what it does is parodic. It is irreverent about the past and only half-serious about itself. It is not concerned with restoring original detail, like the conservationist, but rather with decorative effect – choosing objects because they are aesthetically surprising, or 'amusing', rather than because they are authentic survivals of the past. ...

All this is certainly true of pop art, one of the crucibles of the cultural revolution of the 1960s, as also, if more obliquely, of retrochic. Breaking with both figurative painting and abstractionism and creating new forms out of debris, it juxtaposed past and present iconoclastically – using historic pop-ups or parodies of Old Masters as well as more contemporary images, to cock a snook at the pretensions of the salons and show high art's affinities to kitsch. ...

Retrochic in the 1970s and 1980s was one of those fields where enterprise culture came into its own, ministering not only to the tourist trade but also to the 'alternative' consumerism of the counter-culture; to teenage 'outlaw' fashions (notably punk); and to the new narcissism of health, epitomized by the Body Shop. ...

It is argued against retrochic that it is dazzled by surface appearances; that it is more interested in style than in substance, and that it is obsessed with the language of looks. It is also charged with fraud – creating copies, as Baudrillard puts it in *Simulations* (1984), for which there are no originals, using hyperreality to camouflage the absence of the real (Eco, 1987). Then – in a residue of 1960s jeremiads against consumerism – retrochic is charged, like heritage, with 'commodifying' the past, instrumentalizing it for the purposes of commercial gain, exploiting the sacred in the interests of the profane. ...

A more positive reading of retrochic might register its success in animating the inanimate. It would look with interest at the way in which it ministers to the appetite for objects of fantasy and desire, and in particular at the excitement which it generates from the juxtaposition of old and new – according to one school of pedagogy the crucial element in awakening an interest in the past.
(Source: Samuel, 1994, pp. 83, 85, 95, 100, 113.)

Clearly, Samuel sets out to give a much more positive and optimistic reading of heritage and enterprise than his critics. He certainly highlights some of the cultural trends of the last two decades that are said to have been brought about by economic and political changes, such as increased choice, democratization and pluralization, the collapse of traditional elites and authorities, including hierarchies of values that were enshrined in canons of taste in literature and the arts. He sees retrochic as giving free play to utopian cultural elements. It inverts traditional hierarchies of taste and value, making something out of the flotsam and jetsam of everyday life, and out of cast-offs. It is post-modern in its parodic attitude, playful rather than striving for authenticity.

All original '60s & '70s fab gear, get your clued-in clothing at:
The Cavern
Now even bigger & better at
154 Commercial St, London, E1 6FU
tel: 071 247 1889
wholesale, retail & mail order
10% discount with this issue

FIGURE 1.6
Advertising '60s and '70s clothing in the 1990s.

FIGURE 1.7 A 1950s kitchen recreated in a Leicester home in the 1990s, including authentic 1950s kitchen cabinets, a 1957 New World cooker, an American-style fridge and ceiling fan, a Horlicks maker, round Swan kettle and Kenwood chef.

The point at which the authoritative status of high art was undermined by the collapse of the boundary with popular culture is identified as the 1960s, when pop art was welcomed into the art galleries and auction rooms. The rise of enterprise culture in the 1980s is viewed as allowing space for alternative consumerism of the counterculture and teenage outlaw fashions such as punk, not just mass consumption. The final positive claim for it is that it caters to fantasy and desire.

Although Samuel's critics agree with him about the desirability of the break-up of some of the old structures and hierarchies of culture, including the conflict between high and popular culture, their view of post-modern forms such as retrochic have tended to be more pessimistic. As Hewison puts it, 'Playful post-modernists did not appear to have found anything substantial to put in modernism's place, for they lacked a radical social vision of their own' (Hewison, 1995, p. 222). The only criterion of value became that of exchange value – what something would sell for in the market as a commodity, rather than as judged against agreed aesthetic values. The problem for governments seeking to exercise cultural regulation with an ideology which combines enterprise and heritage is that the two elements are difficult to articulate together for very long, because they are inherently in tension. The commitment to enterprise and the rigours of unconstrained global market forces sits uneasily with a desire to preserve backward-looking symbols of national heritage. For, often, the cultural institutions that had preserved the national cultural heritage were thought to stand in the way of enterprise and economic reconstruction. This was the fate of the universities, the Arts Council, the British Council and the BBC, in the 1980s.

In Britain, cultural institutions had traditionally operated on the quango model, at arm's length from government, with their governors, trustees and board members drawn from the ranks of the Great and the Good. But this instrument for administering consensus was not acceptable to a government committed to radical economic restructuring (Hewison, 1995, p. 230). According to Richard Hoggart: 'Quangos emerged from more than the consensus idea; they emerged from and could only work where there was an assumed pattern of values about the nature of the good society and the good life' (Hoggart, 1990, pp. 271–2). Margaret Thatcher saw them in a different light, expressing her view that 'broadcasting was one of a number of areas – the professions such as teaching, medicine and the law were others – in which special pleading by powerful interest groups was disguised as high-minded commitment to some greater good' (Thatcher, 1993, p.634). Her solution was to keep the quangos, but to change the people, putting in a new breed of entrepreneurs, public relations experts, and financial managers. (We will consider the impact of this on broadcasting in the next section.) The use of quangos to maintain the arms-length principle of the British system for regulating culture and the arts, was being honoured formally but not in practice. Some of the new appointees, such as William Rees-Mogg (who served on the Arts Council, the BBC Board of Governors, and the Broadcasting Standards Council), claimed that they were honouring the arms-length principle. The critics replied that their 'true distance from government policy seems questionable, but the ideology of power is such that hegemony is best maintained by the appearance of independence, and is even more effective when those who exercise it believe that they genuinely are independent' (Hewison, 1995, p. 260).

It is doubtful if the ideology behind these cultural policies ever became completely dominant, but the impact of the discourse of enterprise culture should not be underestimated. In some respects it was an idea whose time had come. It coincided with a loss of confidence in the principles of the more collectivist ideology of the post-war consensus, and the emphasis on large-scale planning and standardization that reduced flexibility and choice, which were not suitable to the new post-industrial conditions. However, although the new populist appeal to people as 'customers' and patriots had some success, as did the attacks on 'permissive society' and the assertions of 'family values', many groups in the increasingly pluralist society were left out or antagonized – not only racial, sexual and other minorities, but also many of those who worked in the cultural institutions. Yet it is these institutions, in the long term, which provide the 'leadership and a sense of identity, legitimizing customary ways and values and organizing consent' (Hewison, 1995, p. 293). The contradictions of enterprise and heritage, international capitalism and national solidarity, customers and citizens, exchange values and moral-aesthetic values, were not resolved.

We have focused on the relationship between heritage and enterprise culture as an example of a cultural politics that involves attempts to articulate together different sets of discourses and practices in order to produce ideological effects, such as securing consent or legitimation for particular values and policies, in the face of conflicting pressures. No one would deny that cultural politics, in this sense, involves ideological work – articulating discourses in order to win the widest support and to unify different interests. But what are we to make of cultural institutions which claim to be ideologically neutral, either because they simply intend to entertain or because they offer a democratic platform to different views? As we have already seen, Foucault would argue that what counts as truth is dependent on the 'regime of truth' established by the terms of the discourse around a particular subject. He would also direct our attention to the ways in which modern discourses increasingly seem to give us a sense of being free from external constraint – self-determining and self-governing – even though the terms of the discourse restrict choice. Although we now turn to other theorists in examining issues concerning the mass media, this Foucauldian approach should be kept in mind.

5   Mass media and the public sphere

In this section we turn to the question posed in the Introduction: *Do the mass media, as presently organized, provide the necessary public sphere for undistorted rational communication and debate that are said to be essential in constituting a modern democracy? Or do the economic forces in the global culture industry mean that the kind of rational discourse described as characteristic of modernity is now giving way to 'figural' media that offer only entertaining spectacles typical of post-modernity?*

Some critics of the discourses of enterprise culture and heritage see these as part of a dominant ideology (e.g. the New Right ideology, Thatcherism), which acted as a **social cement** binding the existing social order together and facilitating its reproduction by misrepresenting or obscuring reality and therefore securing consent to that social order. This view derives from the development of Marxist theory of ideology by the theorists Gramsci and Althusser, which had an influence on cultural studies and media studies in the 1970s. However, there were a number of criticisms of the more mechanistic version of this theory. Its logic was said to be rather circular: in order for capitalism to continue it needs certain functions to be fulfilled, such as a dominant ideology to exist, and therefore any prevalent culture must be serving those functions. But other studies in Britain and western Europe in the 1970s showed that there was not a high level of consensus, particularly among the working class (Mann, 1973), and many working-class people rejected key capitalist values and thought there was too much power in the hands of the rich (the evidence is summarized in Abercrombie et al., 1980).

social cement

An alternative explanation of the reproduction of the social order is that:

> individuals are embedded in a variety of different social contexts, that they carry out their lives in routine and regularized ways which are not necessarily animated by overarching values and beliefs, and that there is a lack of consensus at the very point where oppositional attitudes might be translated into coherent political action.

> (J.B. Thompson, 1990, p. 90)

cultural atomism

To that explanation, which we may describe as **cultural atomism**, we can add the possibility that people become cynical about the chances for bringing about real change or they are not presented with plausible alternatives. Michael Mann (1973) distinguishes between 'normative' acceptance of the status quo and 'pragmatic' acceptance. Normative acceptance occurs when dominant social groups manage to mobilize consent in order to legitimize their social position. Pragmatic acceptance is where people comply because they cannot see a realistic alternative. Similarly, it can be argued that stability in modern societies is more likely to be produced through cultural atomism and fragmentation than by externally induced consensus (Held, 1989).

A variant of the 'social cement' theory of ideology was developed by Adorno and Horkheimer (1979), members of the Frankfurt School of critical theory, in relation to the **culture industry** of mass media (see the discussion in **Negus**, 1997). The term 'culture industry' refers to the commodification of cultural forms, such as film, television, radio, newspapers and popular music. Adorno and Horkheimer use the term 'ideology' in a very broad sense, distinguishing the ideological character of the 'culture industry' or 'entertainment industry' from the narrower sort of ideology, such as political doctrines (e.g. the New Right ideology and Thatcherism). The products of the culture industry do not provide clearly articulated doctrines that comment on reality; as purely objects of exchange and sources of pleasure, devoid of any independent critical faculty, they are more pervasive and obscure. It is in the act of pleasurable consumption that individuals are bound into the social order, and this provides the social cement. Clearly, some of the same objections apply to this version of the 'social cement' theory of social reproduction as were advanced against the 'dominant ideology thesis' discussed above. It overestimates the extent to which individuals are absorbed into a consensual set of values and lose their independent critical faculties. The theory of the 'culture industry' runs the risk of portraying individuals as merely passive consumers, rather than as active protagonists in a contested cultural field, as Samuels argues. However, it would be pushing these arguments too far if we ruled out the possibility that the mass media do have significant ideological effects. Politicians such as Margaret Thatcher and Ronald Reagan clearly believed they do.

I would now like to consider another variant of the critical theory of the Frankfurt School that has been important in studies of the role of mass communications in modern society – the work of Jürgen Habermas on 'the public sphere'.

culture industry

ACTIVITY 3

Before considering this approach, I would like to pose three questions that might indicate why it is important. Make notes of your responses to these questions:

1   Do democratic societies need a public service broadcasting organiza-tion, independent of government and of commercial pressures?

2   What are the implications of thinking of ourselves primarily as 'customers' or, alternatively, as 'citizens', in relation to broadcasting?

3   Do the broadcast media and the Press provide a forum enabling all sections of society to participate in debates about important issues?

Answers to these questions are likely to draw on ideas about democracy that have a long history. Habermas's contribution has been to offer a theoretical and historical framework in which to place issues about democracy and the mass media. In his early work, *The Structural Transformation of the Public Sphere* (1989/1962), Habermas concentrated on the development of media institutions from the seventeenth century to the present, tracing the emergence and subsequent disintegration of what he calls '**the public sphere**'. The story begins in the late seventeenth and early eighteenth centuries in the salons and coffee houses of Paris and London, which became centres of discussion and debate, where private individuals could meet to discuss issues of public concern. These discussions were facilitated by the publication of news sheets and newspapers, which themselves became the forum of political debate where people (provided they were middle-class and male) could criticize the actions of government. Despite the fact that it tended to represent only middle-class, male interests, Habermas argues that this bourgeois public sphere embodied the idea of a community of citizens, coming together as equals in a forum within civil society distinct from the authority of the state and the private sphere of the family, which was capable of forming public opinion through rational debate. Unfortunately, says Habermas, this early promise was lost as the institutions of mass communication became commercialized and their contents became personalized and sensationalized, treating their readers or audiences more and more as customers. In addition, they developed new techniques of 'opinion management'. Habermas refers to this as the 're-feudalization of the public sphere', because the manipulated presentation of events resembled the spectacles of the feudal courts, staged to endow public authority with a kind of aura. The mass media turn politics into a stage-managed show in which the mass of the population is excluded from public discussion and media techniques are used to elicit sufficient assent to legitimate the status quo.

the public sphere

Habermas's early work suffers from some of the same weaknesses as that of Adorno and Horkheimer, overemphasizing the extent to which culture acts as a social cement, integrating individuals into a social order which is thereby reproduced. His more recent works, such as *The Theory of Communicative Action* (1987), by contrast, give little attention to the notion of the social order being reproduced by an overarching ideology, emphasizing the fragmentation of everyday consciousness, rather than its integration by ideology. He also talks about the 'colonization of the life world', by which he means the domination of the cultural sphere by the economy and the state. However, Habermas's earlier work on the public sphere has been taken up in debates about the future of mass media and their potentiality for providing a public forum for rational communication and debate, more closely approximating his ideal of 'undistorted communication'. As John Thompson puts it, 'the idea of the public sphere does retain some value today as a critical yardstick; it calls our attention, for instance, to the importance of a sphere of social communication which is neither wholly controlled by the state nor concentrated in the hands of large-scale commercial organizations.' (J.B. Thompson, 1990, p. 119).

Public service television has been defended on these grounds. As Stevenson explains:

Most of the literature that has taken up Habermas's arguments on the public sphere has sought to utilize his work in terms of a defence of public broadcasting. The argument presented by a number of authors is that the de-regulation of national public services is a threat to democratic citizenship, in that it delivers control of our information into the hands of international conglomerates. According to this scenario, this will eventually lead to the erosion of a 'quality' universal service to which everyone has access, and the abandonment of special interest programming that cannot secure the backing of advertisers. The rise of the New Right has made it necessary to intellectually restate the need for a democratic public sphere. The New Right have denounced state-organized broadcasting because it is high-cost, prevents the free flow of information by restricting advertising and disallows choice. It is probably the restraint upon choice that has ideologically been the most compelling argument. Members of the New Right suggest that the state-protected media are able to impose their elite tastes upon the rest of us. In a free market, according to this perspective, the market would be able to respond to the actual preferences of the public. This ideological offensive has stolen some of the Left's traditional clothing. Lord Reith, the first Director-General of the BBC, argued that public service broadcasting had a duty to educate and inform. However the defence of these norms became entangled within a cultural strategy that sought to impose an elite high culture on a diverse national community. Since Reith's time a multitude of excluded voices have criticized the BBC for imposing a certain version of Englishness upon the audience. This has entailed the emergence of a number of perspectives around the themes of ethnicity, gender and class, which have sought to criticize Reithian paternalism. The problem with the New Right's claim to represent these voices is that it remains blind to the division of interest that exists between a universal public service and the private ownership of the means of communication.

Public service broadcasting, according to those who wish to preserve a notion of the public sphere, remains important for three main reasons: (1) historically it has occupied an institutional space that has some independence from both the economy and the state; (2) public broadcasting potentially provides a national arena for a diversity of social groups to communicate with one another; (3) it addresses the public as citizens rather than consumers.

(Stevenson, 1995, pp. 62–3)

This is an ideal type view of public service broadcasting. Actual public broadcasting organizations, such as the BBC, have often fallen short of these ideals. They have been charged with being patronizing and arrogant, of being run by an elite with values that do not correspond to those of the majority in their audience, and of having too close a relationship to the ruling circles (especially when, as in the BBC, the Board of Governors is hand-picked by the Government). At the theoretical level, both the advocates of public service and the proponents of market competition claim to be on the side of

FIGURE 1.8 Sir John Reith (later Lord Reith): official portrait issued by the BBC, 1927.

FIGURE 1.9 Broadcasting House, c.1932.

freedom and democracy, differing only about the best ways of achieving these values. Market theorists argue that 'free' market mechanisms at least free individual consumers to express their preferences to suppliers (in this case, broadcasters and newspapers) through the price system, and thus provide more variety of choice. Public service advocates argue that the market model of equal and atomized customers camouflages the disparity in power between large corporate entities and individuals, and also neglects to provide for people's needs as citizens (needs such as education, enlightenment, and the development of critical faculties).

The most fully elaborated rationale for public service broadcasting put forward in Britain was contained in the Pilkington Committee's Report in 1962. Its vision was rooted in the traditional ethos of British broadcasting, stemming from Reith's BBC and Matthew Arnold's view of culture in his *Culture and Anarchy* (1869) as 'the best which has been thought and said', as defined and maintained by an elite. Pilkington held that broadcasting was 'the main factor in influencing the values and moral standards of our society', and it needed to be organized so as to protect viewers and listeners from some of their own tastes and desires, which might not be in the public interest. This view prevailed to some extent in public broadcasting until the 1980s, despite the changing attitudes brought about by the growth of commercial broadcasting. As a result of economic and political changes, an alternative view of public service broadcasting was put forward by the Peacock Report on *Financing the BBC* in 1986, which wanted it to be run more like a commercial business organization. Although proposals for introducing subscription viewing were not taken up by the Thatcher Government, changes in the BBC ethos were brought about by obliging it to operate more along commercial and market criteria, forcing it to raise more of its own money, and through the government's appointment of more figures from the private sector to the Board of Governors. The influential ex-editor of the *Times*, Sir William Rees-Mogg, who had been appointed as vice-chairman in 1981, expressed the opinion that the BBC was 'not an enterprise culture but a spending culture' and it had to change (quoted in *The Stage*, 9 October 1986). As a result of these changes, it can be argued that public broadcasting has become more like its commercial rivals, even down to the 'enterprise culture' of its management.

At the same time, paradoxically, whilst the Thatcher Government introduced more competition by encouraging satellite broadcasting and a market-led commercial system through the 1990 Broadcasting Act, which introduced an auction system for commercial television licences, this 'de-regulation' was to be accompanied by closer regulation of 'morals, taste and decency' in broadcasting. Once again, the New Right ideology sought to articulate both enterprise and heritage (or 'traditional') values. The 1990 Broadcasting Act gave the Independent Television Commission and the newly-created Broadcasting Standards Council (first chairman, William Rees-Mogg) the task of regulating 'morals, taste and decency'; the BBC set up its own Complaints Unit in 1994. Libertarians feared that these regulatory organizations would be dominated by moral crusaders, such as Mary Whitehouse's National Viewers and Listeners Association, which had lobbied for the setting up of the BSC. However, most of the complaints they receive seem to come from individuals unattached to any organized pressure group, although certain sections of the population are over-represented, such as people in the south of England, clergymen, schoolteachers and retired members of the armed forces . They are also more likely to complain about the BBC than commercial television, on the grounds that they believe the BBC has a public responsibility to uphold standards (Gauntlett, 1995; Bocock, Sharma and Thompson, forthcoming).

The defenders of public service broadcasting in the 1980s recognized that they needed to change the grounds of that defence from the Reithian paternalistic assumptions about what was good for people. Habermas's ideas about the public sphere became the major theoretical point of reference through the mediation of two articles by Nicholas Garnham, 'Public service versus the market' (1983) and 'The media and the public sphere' (1986). However, there are a number of problems with using Habermas's ideas in this way. Habermas's theory of the public sphere was focused mainly on participation in face-to-face conversation, discussion and debate and in the written media, such as the press and magazines, and he held out little hope for television providing a forum for rational debate. He would probably tend to agree with those critics who maintain that the 'entertainment bias' of television is so strong that it trivializes everything it touches (Postman, 1985). And even where there are 'good journalistic programmes', they are surrounded by programming and advertising whose chief aim is to capture and hold our attention by providing escapist pleasures. The sociologist, Zygmunt Bauman has argued that Habermas describes a 'society shaped after the pattern of a sociology seminar, that is, there are only participants and the one thing that matters is the power of argument' (Bauman, 1992, p. 217). As another critic notes:

> No more than life is broadcasting reducible to the condition of a sociology seminar and it was the earnest attempts of European public service broadcasters to shape broadcasting to a condition of a seminar that gave their competitors the opportunity to offer viewers a more demotic and carnivalesque programme diet, to tempt audiences away from the seminar to the funfair.
>
> (Collins, 1993, p. 251)

FIGURE 1.10 The News Bunny and a Smurf in attendance during a Live TV news broadcast.

Collins concludes that, if we leave aside the irreconcilable theories of the pro-public service advocates and the protagonists of a free market in broadcasting, empirical experience might lead us to the conclusion that the mixed system is best, where a limited amount of regulation ensures that neither public broadcasting nor commercial broadcasting is overwhelmingly dominant. However, this does not mean that we should dispense with the contributions from these theories: 'Both the values – notably the concept of freedom – and the methods – notably its dialectical and iconoclastic character – of Critical Theory will be central to this project' (Collins, 1993, p. 265).

An example of how Habermas's theory of communicative rationality and the public sphere continues to stimulate debate is provided by Scannell's re-statement of the case for public service broadcasting (Scannell, 1989).

READING D

Now read the extract by Paddy Scannell, from 'Public service broadcasting and modern public life' (1989), provided as Reading D at the end of this chapter.

How does Scannell modify Habermas's ideas in order to argue against interpreting broadcasting as ideological and in favour of seeing it as having 'enhanced the reasonable character and conduct of twentieth-century life'?

Scannell rejects the view of the media as ideological, on the grounds that it makes it more difficult to argue the case for seeing broadcasting as a 'public sphere that works to enhance the reasonable, democratic character of life in public and private contexts' (Scannell, 1989, p. 158). On the other hand, he tends to agree with criticisms of Habermas's over-intellectual view of rational communication. Instead, Scannell draws on ideas from Anglo-American sociology and phenomenology about how people in everyday interactions reason together and reach agreement. The criteria are different from Habermas's idea of understanding being reached by marshalling the best argument, which Scannell equates with rhetorical skill. Scannell prefers to view broadcasting as having increased the reasonable, as distinct from the rational, character of daily life in public and private contexts. This is a big claim and he admits that it may be an idealized view of the present system, which is contained within a system of mass democratic politics, where people may have communicative entitlements, but not equality of access to or status in broadcasting.

Although Scannell makes a persuasive case for the capacity of public service broadcasting to enhance rational or reasonable communication in the public sphere, critics might accuse him of being too optimistic and sanguine about broadcasting content and its effects. He does not address the kind of point that Collins makes, which is that the actual existing public broadcasting systems have only been saved from being boring and out of touch with the desires of people because of the competition from commercial broadcasting. This then raises questions about Scannell's sweeping dismissal of the case for analysing broadcasting in terms of discourses and ideology, in favour of seeing them simply in terms of communicative 'reasonableness'. Surely popular understandings and media conventions about what is 'reasonable', just like notions of 'commonsense' and of what is 'natural', are themselves ideologically or discursively constructed, and need to be critically analysed, particularly in relation to the distribution of power and influence.

> ACTIVITY 4
>
> Having considered some of the arguments in this debate about the public sphere and the mass media, you might like to reconsider your initial responses to the questions posed in Activity 3 at the beginning of this section.
>
> ● Have the discussions caused you to modify or add to your ideas on these questions?
>
> ● What are the analytical and practical implications of the different arguments as far as regulation of the mass media is concerned?

5.1   Post-modernism, spectacles and moral panics

We earlier examined the evidence suggesting that there was a New Right ideology that received government backing during the Reagan–Thatcher regimes of the 1980s, combining discourses such as 'enterprise culture' and the more traditionally conservative 'heritage' and anti-permissive moral values. This was reflected in cultural regulation policies with respect to the mass media. However, we have also mentioned the suggestion that 'de-regulation' could have the effect of allowing commercial considerations in the mass media to give predominance to entertainment values. This has been particularly evident in television and the tabloid press (perhaps even in the 'tabloidization' of the serious press). Critics such as Habermas would argue that, although this does not represent the triumph of a dominant ideology, the prevalence of entertainment values does have ideological effects that are socially conservative in that they make it difficult to develop rational, 'undistorted' communication. Habermas levels this charge against alleged 'post-modern' trends in culture and, for this reason, criticizes the fatalism of post-modernity theorists such as Baudrillard. For Baudrillard, the constant stream of television images, and the expanded capacity of the media to seduce us into a strange new world of 'hyperreality', produces a world of simulations which is immune to rationalist critique (Baudrillard, 1981).

Many sociologists would disagree with Baudrillard's thesis that we have now passed from the social epoch of modernity to post-modernity, whilst allowing that it is sociologically warranted to speak of identifiable differences between modernist and post-modernist tendencies within contemporary culture. According to Scott Lash, the cultural forms of modernism and post-modernism can be understood to signify differently – they constitute different **regimes of signification**, which he calls the **discursive** and the **figural**. The modernist mode, associated with discursive processes of signification, in Lash's words:

discursive and figural
regimes of
signification

1   gives priority to words over images;

2   valuates the formal qualities of cultural objects;

3   promulgates a rationalist view of culture;

4   attributes crucial importance to the *meanings* of cultural texts;

5   is a sensibility of the ego rather than the id;

6   operates through a distancing of the spectator from the cultural object.

By contrast, he explains, the post-modernist mode, associated with figural processes of signification:

1   is a visual rather than a literary sensibility;

2   devalues formalisms and juxtaposes signifiers taken from the banalities of everyday life;

3   contests rationalist and/or 'didactic' views of culture;

4   asks not what a culture 'means', but what it 'does';

5   in Freudian terms, advocates the extension of the primary process into the cultural realm;

6   operates through the spectator's immersion, the relatively unmediated investment of his/her desire in the cultural object.

(Lash, 1990, p. 174)

It is not necessary to understand or accept all the details of Lash's thesis, but it is useful for linking discussions of semiotics, discourses, subjectivity and identity, with our present discussion of cultural regulation and mass media in the public sphere. Some commentators would argue that there is a growing tension between the discursive and figural modes within the media and within the public sphere. They talk of 'the informed elite versus the entertained majority' (Dahlgren, 1995, p. 86). Popular mainstream television and the tabloid press are said to lean heavily towards the figural mode of representation, whilst the discursive mode prevails in the serious press and specialist journals (despite the alleged 'tabloidization' of the serious press). Other sociologists refer to contemporary culture as overwhelmingly 'a representation through spectacle' (Chaney, 1993, p. 33, drawing on Debord, 1970).

It is not being suggested that the mass media provide only pictures and no talk (or text). Figural signification through spectacles may well include talk, such as talk shows and 'confessionals' (like the Oprah Winfrey Show) on radio and television, just as the tabloid press features gossip columns and accounts of amazing or scandalous events. (The subject of talk shows and their audiences is discussed in **Moores**, 1997.) The point is that these place their audiences in a voyeuristic position, looking at people making a 'spectacle' of themselves or being paraded in front of us as 'saints' or 'sinners'. Even apparently serious discussion programmes may be set up as confrontations or combats, leading the participants or their supporters to claim that their views were misrepresented. Of course, this may also illustrate the fact that audiences are not passive receivers of mass media messages – they interpret them differently depending on their circumstances and prior assumptions. However, the prevalence of these types of figural signification in the mass media and their preference for certain kinds of subject matter, such as crime and deviance (Sparks, 1992), does raise questions relevant to our topic of social change and cultural regulation.

moral panic

This view of the mass media as providing social participation through spectacles and public drama is particularly relevant to understanding the increasing frequency of 'moral panics' and the part played by the popular press in helping to generate them. The concept of **moral panic** was defined by Stanley Cohen (1972) in his study of the apparent public panic in response to seaside fights between gangs of teenage 'mods' and 'rockers' in the early 1960s:

> Societies appear to be subject, every now and then, to periods of moral panic. A condition, episode, person or group of persons emerges to become defined as a threat to societal values and interests; its nature is presented in a stylized and stereotypical fashion by the mass media; the moral barricades are manned by editors, bishops, politicians and other right thinking people; socially accredited experts pronounce their diagnoses and solutions; ways of coping are evolved or (more often) resorted to; the condition then disappears, submerges or deteriorates and becomes more visible.

> (Cohen, 1972, p. 28)

For Cohen, like the early sociologist Emile Durkheim, panics about deviant behaviour served to reassert the dominance of an established value system at a time of perceived anxiety and crisis, and 'folk-devils' provided a necessary external threat. Hall et al. (1978), in their study of the creation of a British 'mugging' problem in the early 1970s, showed how media representations stressed 'sudden' and 'dramatic' increases in this criminal behaviour beyond what the statistics would justify. They placed this episode in the political context of severe economic crisis and soaring unemployment, noting that it served to divert attention from these problems and against the young, poor and black. (Although there have been some criticisms of the moral panic concept, notably Waddington (1986) and Watney (1987), most of those working in this field have upheld its validity, according to Goode and Ben-Yehuda (1994)). In the 1980s and 1990s there seems to have been a heightening of social tensions and anxieties, if we are to judge by the escalation of media-induced moral panics, which have included (to name but a few): baby-battering and child abuse, dole scroungers and welfare cheats, raves and youth drug culture, pornography and video nasties, 'home alone' children, children who murder, violence in schools, and the availability of knives and handguns.

Although there have been moral panics in other western societies, such as the USA (Goode and Ben-Yehuda, 1994), they seem to have been much fewer or less extensive than in Britain in the same period. One explanation for this might be the combination of a large-circulation national popular press in Britain with a political regime committed to bringing about radical change in the moral–cultural and social fields (Jenkins, 1992; K. Thompson, forthcoming). Whereas in the USA local concerns would only be reported in the local media and so stay local, in Britain they are rapidly projected onto the national stage. This was exacerbated by the transformation of the press that began in the 1970s under the influence of Rupert Murdoch and his mass circulation national dailies and weeklies. Government policies of economic de-regulation, combined with increased regulation of trades unions, made it possible for the most competitive, large media corporations to increase profits. By 1990 the *Sun*'s daily diet of sex, scandal, violence and right-wing populism had brought it sales of nearly four million, and its lead was even followed by hitherto more sober papers like the *Mail* and the *Express*. These changes in the mass media go some way to accounting for the new wave of perceived social problems, and in turn, they offered fertile ground for 'claims-makers' – pressure groups, 'moral entrepreneurs' and opinion-shapers.

FIGURE 1.11
Rupert Murdoch at the launch of a new Sky multi-channel package, September 1993

As we have seen, the New Right ideology is a potent mix of different tendencies. It reacts to global pressures by seeking to bring about radical cultural change to make the economy internationally competitive, whilst at the same time trying to counter social and cultural fragmentation by emphasizing national heritage and a return to Victorian values. It is not surprising that this has resulted in social tensions and cultural battles. A frequent refrain accompanying the moral panics is about moral permissiveness, the loss of values, lack of discipline and respect for authority, and loss of responsibility (particularly on the part of women). The culprits include youth, children (who might also be victims), ethnic minorities, mothers who work, unmarried mothers, foreigners, social workers, and sexual deviants. However, although the mass media construct these public dramas and spectacles, with their cast of heroes and villains, they also reflect deeper anxieties stemming from real social changes. There has been increasing social pluralization and cultural fragmentation, which has undermined traditional social and cultural hierarchies. Developments in communications technology and globalization have also called into question the possibilities for maintaining national cultural boundaries. The way in which these social changes are culturally represented and regulated increasingly depends on the mediation of the mass media. But these representations are influenced by economic, political and social factors, including the activities of individuals, groups and organizations with different amounts of power.

Some theorists have insisted that the study of popular culture should not be about the macro-social issues of political economy, ideology or the public sphere, but about the creative work undertaken by audiences in producing their own interpretative readings and gaining pleasure. John Fiske argues that the tabloid or popular press, unlike the quality or alternative press, deconstructs the opposition between news and entertainment (Fiske, 1989). He maintains that, whereas the quality press claims to present only the facts and so produces a believing subject, the tabloids encourage sceptical laughter and the pleasures of disbelief, of not being taken in. He cites the recurrent tabloid story of aliens landing from outer space. However, one of the few ethnographic studies of the reading practices of tabloid consumers described the mode of address of the *Sun* newspaper as 'heterosexual, male, white, conservative, capitalist, nationalist' (Pursehouse, 1987, p. 2). This meant that those readers who would not normally identify with that mode of address, such as women readers, had to negotiate their way through the paper – for example, by avoiding the page three pin-ups and the sports section. It is true that many of the readers interviewed regarded the paper as a source of fun and relaxation and did not seem aware of the positions it took on social and political issues. Yet there are good reasons to believe that the *Sun*'s stance on such issues did have an effect on its readers, including inducing them to support New Right policies and vote for the Conservative Party until 1997. (The *Sun* is said to have had an effect in key marginal constituencies in the 1992 election, according to *The Independent*, 10 March 1997.)

ACTIVITY 4

Consider your own newspaper reading practices.

From your knowledge of the so-called 'quality' or broadsheet newspapers, do you find that they present the news in such a way as to persuade readers that they are simply presenting the facts, or are you conscious of a slant towards a particular ideological position?

On the basis of your own experience, do you feel more inclined to support the view that readers of the popular press are encouraged to take a sceptical and amused attitude towards social issues, or that the representation of these issues has a determining effect on readers' attitudes, even to the point of creating moral panics?

6   Conclusion

This chapter has been about social changes and cultural regulation, focusing on the politics of leisure, heritage and enterprise culture, mass media and the public sphere. We have drawn on a number of theories to explain how changes in the mode of cultural regulation are related to pressures from economic, political and social structural trends, particularly those associated with modernization and globalization. Because our focus has been on regulatory tendencies, we have given less attention to cultural practices that might be said to escape regulation or be relatively free from it (perhaps some of the local leisure activities discussed by **Finnegan**, 1997). Similarly, there has been less attention to ways in which audiences or consumers create and negotiate meanings (these are discussed in **Miller**, 1997, and **Moores**, 1997).

At several points we have used examples of cultural regulation related to the New Right ideology and its associated discourses that were promoted by governments in the 1980s. This has allowed us to give attention to the most obvious form of the politics of culture, that of political ideology, although we have concentrated on the broader issue of attempts to deal with the tensions between different global and local pressures. However, at other points we have noted that regulation can operate in less obvious ways. It can operate through informal cultural practices and discourses that are not explicitly ideological, although because of asymmetrical power relations they may have ideological effects in reproducing the social order with all its inequalities.

So, what is the answer to the question posed at the beginning of this chapter? Has there been a shift towards de-regulation of culture and in the direction of increased diversity and choice for the individual, under pressures for change from globalization and pluralization? Or is it simply a matter of re-regulation, a shift in the ideological balance from notions of national public interest towards those based on discourses of people as consumers and the public as consumer markets? Or is re-regulation an attempt to restore traditional cultural standards in an era of media commercialization and spectacularization, a way of trying to resolve the tension between heritage and enterprise? In this chapter we have examined some of the theories and debates, but the questions remain open. However, my presentation of the arguments has been influenced by a concern, well expressed by John Thompson (1990, pp. 330–1), that it is possible to be so impressed by the apparent increases in diversity and difference that we lose sight of the structured inequalities of social life in which those differences are embedded. The value of critical sociological analyses of ideology, such as those influenced by Habermas, is that they form part of a broader concern with the nature of domination in the modern world, with the mode of its reproduction and the possibilities for its transformation.

References

ABERCROMBIE, N., HILL, S. and TURNER, B. (1980) *The Dominant Ideology Thesis,* London, Allen and Unwin.

ADORNO, T.W. and HORKHEIMER, M. (1979) *Dialectic of Enlightenment,* (trs. J. Cumming), London, Verso. First published 1944 as *Dialektic der Aufklang.*

AGLIETTA, M. (1979) *A Theory of Capitalist Regulation,* London, New Left Books.

ALTHUSSER, L. (1971) *Lenin and Philosophy and Other Essays*, London, New Left Books.

ARNOLD, M. (1961) *Culture and Anarchy* (ed. J. Dover Wilson), Cambridge, Cambridge University Press. First published 1869.

BAILEY, P. (1987) *Leisure and Class in Victorian England*, London, Methuen, 2nd edn.

BAUDRILLARD, J. (1981) *For a Critique of the Political Economy of the Sign*, St. Louis, Telos.

BAUDRILLARD, J. (1984) *Simulations*, London.

BAUMAN, Z. (1992) *Intimations of Post-modernity*, London, Routledge.

BENSON, S. (1997) 'Body health and eating disorders' in Woodward, K. (ed.).

BOCOCK, R., SHARMA, A. and THOMPSON, K. (forthcoming) 'Moral regulation and television', ESRC Research Project Report.

CHANEY, D. (1993) *Fictions of Collective Life: Public Drama in Late Modern Culture*, London, Routledge.

CLARKE, J. and CRITCHER, C. (1985) *The Devil Makes Work: leisure in capitalist Britain*, London, Macmillan.

COHEN, S. (1972) *Folk Devils and Moral Panics,* Harmondsworth, Penguin.

COLLINS, R. (1993) 'Public service versus the market ten years on: reflections on critical theory and the debate on broadcasting policy in the UK', *Screen,* Vol. 34, No. 3, pp. 249–65.

CORRIGAN, P. and SAYER, D. (1985) *The Great Arch,* Oxford, Blackwell.

CUNNINGHAM, H. (1980) *Leisure in the Industrial Revolution,* London, Croom Helm.

DAHLGREN, P. (1995) 'Cultural studies and media research' in Corner, J., Schlesinger, P. and Silverstone, R. (eds) *The International Handbook of Media Research*, London, Routledge.

DEBORD, G. (1970) *Society of the Spectacle,* Detroit, MI, Black and Red Press.

DU GAY, P. (1997) 'Organizing identity: making up people at work' in Du Gay, P. (ed.) 1997

DU GAY, P. (ed.) (1997) *Production of Culture/Cultures of Production*, London, Sage/The Open University (Book 4 in this series).

ECO, U. (1987) *Travels in Hyperreality*, New York, Harcourt Brace Jovanovich.

FINNEGAN, R. (1997) 'Culture, performance and enactment' in Mackay, H. (ed.)

FISKE, J. (1989) 'Popular news' in Fisk, J. (ed.), *Reading the Popular*, London, Allen and Unwin.

FOUCAULT, M. (1975) *Discipline and Punish*, Harmondsworth, Penguin.

FOUCAULT, M. (1981) *History of Sexuality*, Harmondsworth, Penguin.

GALLIANO, J. (1988) '*Vivat Victoriana*', Guardian, 6 June.

GARNHAM, N. (1983) 'Public service versus the market', *Screen*, Vol. 5, No. 1.

GARNHAM, N. (1986) 'The media and the public sphere' in Golding, P. et al. (eds) *Communicating Politics*, Leicester, Leicester University Press.

GAUNTLETT, D. (1995) *A Profile of Complainants and their Complaints*, London, Broadcasting Standards Council.

GOODE, E. and BEN-YEHUDA, N. (1994) *Moral Panics: the social construction of deviance*, Oxford, Blackwell.

GRAMSCI, A. (1971) 'American and Fordism' in *Selections from the Prison Notebooks*, London, Lawrence and Wishart.

HABERMAS, J. (1989) *The Structural Transformation of the Public Sphere*, (trs. T. Bürger with F. Lawrence), Cambridge, Polity Press. First published 1962.

HABERMAS, J. (1987) *The Theory of Communicative Action*, Vol. 2 (trs. T. McCarthy), Cambridge, Polity Press.

HALL, S. (1985) 'Signification, representation, ideology: Althusser and the post-structuralist debates', *Critical Studies in Mass Communication*, No. 2.

HALL, S. (1997) 'The work of representation' in Hall, S. (ed.) *Representation: cultural representations and signifying practices*, London, Sage/The Open University (Book 2 in this series).

HALL, S., CLARKE, J., JEFFERSON, T., CRITCHER, C. and ROBERTS, B. (1978) *Policing the Crisis: mugging, law and order and the State*, London, Macmillan.

HELD, D. (1989) *Political Theory and the Modern State*, Cambridge, Polity Press.

HENRY, I.P. (1993) *The Politics of Leisure Policy*, London, Macmillan.

HEWISON, R. (1995) *Culture and Consensus: England, art and politics since 1940*, London, Methuen.

HOGGART, R. (1990) *An Imagined Life: life and times 1959–91*, London, Chatto and Windus.

JENKINS, P. (1992) *Intimate Enemies: moral panics in contemporary Great Britain*, New York, Aldine De Gruyter.

LASH, S. (1990) *Sociology of Post-modernism*, London, Routledge.

LAWSON, N. (1992) *The View from No. 11: memoirs of a Tory Radical*, London, Bantam Press.

LIPIETZ, A. (1987) *Mirages and Miracles*, London, Verso.

MACKAY, H. (ed.) *Consumption and Everyday Life*, London, Sage/The Open University (Book 5 in this series).

MANN, M. (1973) *Consciousness and Action Among the Western Working Class*, London, Macmillan.

MARQUAND, D. (1991) *The Progressive Dilemma*, London, Heinemann.

MARX, K. (1963) 'A contribution to the critique of political economy' in T. B. Bottomore and M. Rubel (eds.) *Karl Marx: selected writings in sociology and social philosophy*, Harmondsworth, Penguin. First published 1859.

MARX, K. (1963) 'Theories of surplus value' in Bottomore and Rubel (eds.). First published 1905–10.

MILLER, D. (1997) 'Local production of culture' in Mackay (ed.).

MOORES, S. (1997) 'Broadcasting and its audiences' in Mackay (ed.).

MURPHY, J. (1981) *Concepts of Leisure*, Englewood Cliffs, NJ, Prentice-Hall.

MYERSCOUGH, J. (1974) 'The recent history of the use of leisure time' in Appleton, I. (ed.) *Leisure and Public Policy*, Edinburgh, Scottish Academic Press.

NEGUS, K. (1997) 'The production of culture' in du Gay, P. (ed.).

POSTMAN, N. (1985) *Amusing Ourselves to Death: public discourse in the age of show business*, London, Methuen.

PURSEHOUSE, M. (1987) *Life's More Fun with Your Number One 'Sun': interviews with some 'Sun' readers*, Birmingham, Centre for Contemporary Cultural Studies Occasional Papers, No. 85.

ROBINS, K. (1995) 'The new spaces of global media' in Johnston, R., Taylor, P. and Watts, M. (eds) *Geographies of Global Change*, Oxford, Blackwell.

ROJEK, C. (1995) *Decentring Leisure: rethinking leisure theory*, London, Sage.

SAMUEL, R. (1994) *Theatres of Memory*, London, Verso.

SAVAGE, J. (1991) *England's Dreaming: Sex Pistols and punk rock*, London

SCANNELL, P. (1989) 'Public service broadcasting and modern public life', *Media, Culture and Society*, Vol. 11, pp. 135–66.

SPARKS, R. (1992) *Television and the Drama of Crime*, Buckingham, Open University Press.

STEVENSON, N. (1995) *Understanding Media Cultures*, London, Sage.

THATCHER, M. (1993) *The Downing Street Years*, London and New York, Harper Collins.

THOMPSON, J.B. (1990) *Ideology and Modern Culture*, Cambridge, Polity Press.

THOMPSON, K. (1976) Auguste Comte: the foundation of sociology, London, Nelson.

THOMPSON, K. (forthcoming) *Moral Panics*, London, Routledge.

WADDINGTON, P.A.J. (1986) 'Mugging as a moral panic: a question of proportion' in *British Journal of Sociology*, Vol. 32, No. 2, pp. 245–59.

WATNEY, S. (1987) *Policing Desire: pornography, AIDS and the media*, London, Methuen.

WOODWARD, K. (ed.) (1997) *Identity and Difference*, London, Sage/The Open University (Book 3 in this series).

WRIGHT, P. (1985) *On Living in an Old Country*, London, Verso.

READING A:
Ian P. Henry, 'The politics of leisure policy'

1780–1840: the state and regulative leisure policies; the suppression of popular recreations

[...] [T]he importance of state attempts to control popular recreations during this period cannot be denied. The concern of the landed gentry, and the emerging industrial middle class represented in Parliament and in the local magistracy, was with social stability. The political revolutions of the American War of Independence and the French Revolution were fresh memories at a time when the economic and social fabric of society was being reconstituted. Advances in agrarian production and the associated enclosure of common land provided 'push' factors, reducing rural populations, while the development of industrial technology provided a 'pull' factor in the form of employment in new urban-based factory production. [...]

Given the fear of instability, discipline for the new urban masses was seen as crucial, and it was perhaps in their recreational lives that such groups illustrated least control. Folk football, the gathering of large crowds for spectator 'events' such as prize fighting, racing, public executions, fairs and wakes, animal baiting and so on were not simply brutish and unruly; they were also occasions of considerable damage and potential disorder (Cunningham, 1980; Holt, 1989). However, concern with recreational behaviour was not only related to worries about social disorder, it was also a matter of concern to industrial interests which regarded the instilling of work discipline as essential to the obtaining of a reasonable return on investment (Thompson, 1967) [...] Absenteeism and drunkenness at work were seen as the result of uncontrolled revelry, and resulted in a loss of profit in factories which depended on a workforce being regularly available, compliant and alert. Thus control of recreation was regarded as essential to the maintenance of levels of production.

Contemporary thinking about the role of the state at the beginning of the nineteenth century was reflected in the tenets of Adam Smith, whose book *The Wealth of Nations* (published in 1776) had gone through ten editions by the turn of the century. Smith's liberal economics provided a rationale for a non-interventionist state, arguing that the 'invisible hand' of the market would provide the most efficient allocator of private and public goods. Social policy was also to be minimalist, restricted to easing any obstruction to market forces. [...]

Leisure policy in this period could not, however, be described as non-interventionist since both the national legislature and the local magistracy sought to intervene heavily in the leisure lives of the population. They sought to control mass gatherings of potentially volatile crowds and to curtail leisure forms (particularly those relating to drink) which were seen as a threat to order or to industrial production. [...]

Despite the selective suppression of popular recreations by the state, some commentators argue that these activities were remarkably resilient and survived, albeit hid from public view (Cunningham, 1980). It seems likely that pugilism, wrestling, animal baiting, the 'worship of St Monday' (the unofficial extension of the weekend absence from work) and other recreational forms survived in part with the commercial patronage of publicans (replacing the patronage of the rural gentry) [...]

The erosion of laissez-faire philosophies: state support for middle-class philanthropy and reform (c. 1840–1900)

[...] [T]he mid-century period marks the beginnings of a more positive approach to state intervention in the fields of social policy in general, and leisure policy in particular.

Concern relating to working-class recreation had abated for a number of reasons. First, the spectacular growth of urban populations (by 1851 half the population were urban dwellers) had made it clear that a failure on the part of the state to check the worst excesses of capitalism would generate health and sanitation problems for all sectors of the population, and would do little to enhance the work potential of the workforce. In addition, fears relating to political instability had to some extent been allayed by the mid-century. The year of European revolutions, 1848, left Britain relatively unscathed, generating confidence in the 'responsible' nature of the political aspirations (or apathy) of the working classes (Thompson, 1963). [...]

Thus progressive state intervention was clearly established across a range of activities in the social, political and economic spheres. Leisure policy would be no exception in this respect, although here the state sought largely to foster the philanthropic or self-improvement rationales of middle- and working-class individuals and groups involved in promoting what came to be known as 'rational recreation'.

The support of middle-class philanthropists for rational recreation was, in part, a recognition that the suppression of popular recreations had not been entirely successful, and that their replacement by wholesome leisure forms might prove a more effective 'civilizing' strategy (Bailey, 1987). The Church of England, through Sunday School recreation programmes, sought to provide alternative attractions to the more dissolute leisure forms centred on the public house, with day trips, educational visits, and so on. The provision of public parks, often on land donated by middle-class benefactors, and the development of mechanics' institutes, public libraries and museums, also constituted attempts by middle-class reformers to tame popular recreations. The newly codified games of rugby and football were promoted, influenced by the 'muscular Christian' movement, as a means of propagating appropriate values of self-discipline, teamwork and the subordination of individual interests to the greater good of the team. Wholesome development of the body complemented the wholesome development of the mind in the 'improving' recreations promoted not only by middle-class reformers, but also by elements of the respectable working class.

Marxist analysis might seek to define this middle-class paternalism as simply an extension, but in a more subtle form, of the 'social control' attempted in the suppression of popular recreations in the early part of the century (Donajgrodzki, 1977). However, such a reading of history fails to acknowledge the fact that working-class groups successfully resisted certain forms of paternalism while selectively accepting others. A considerable number of football clubs which were originally founded in the context of religious groups, including many still in the Football League, soon exerted their independence. [...]

During this period the state's role was rather less one of direct provision for leisure than one of fostering the enlightened paternalism of voluntary bodies. The Museums Act 1849, the Public Libraries Act 1850 and the Recreation Grounds Act 1852 sought to allow the use of public funds in order that local authorities could capitalize on gifts of land, exhibits or books from benefactors. The Public Health Acts were complemented by the provision of recreation grounds in the city as 'clean air' zones, and the Public Baths and Washhouses Act 1846, which was not so much inspired by a concern for promoting swimming as with fostering working-class hygiene through bathing. Physical education was introduced into the curriculum in the Education Act 1870, but this simply took the form of military drill. In summary, the health, discipline and cultural improvement rationales which inspired state initiatives clearly reflected the thinking of the rational recreation and muscular Christian movements.

As Myerscough (1974) points out, the disposable income of the working class and their free time increased significantly in real terms during the second half of the nineteenth century. This attracted investment in leisure and related industries in the commercial sector of a considerable order. Bailey (1987), for example, traces the growing market concentration in the music hall business, while Harrison (1971) identifies similar traits in the brewing industry. [...] Indeed, Bailey is able to claim that, despite the attempts of the early century to reform working-class recreation and the subsequent activities inspired by rational recreation, the commercial sector was actually successful in taming working-class recreational habits because it provided other distracting leisure opportunities which satisfied working-class demand. [...]

Laying the foundations of the Welfare State (c. 1900–39)

While the role of government in the second half of the nineteenth century involved aspects of political, industrial and social reform, the aim (in social policy terms at least) was to mediate rather than reform the effects of urban industrial capitalism. It was only with the advent of a Liberal government in 1905, with the support of the embryonic Labour Party (the Labour Representation Committee), and after 20 years of Conservative rule, that a genuine embracing of social reforms (as both desirable and necessary) became evident. [...]

While the second half of the nineteenth century had seen the development of state support for voluntary initiative in the leisure field, the first half of the twentieth century was to be noted for the 'incorporation' of voluntary organizations through legislation such as the National Trust Act 1907, and the Physical Training and Recreation Act. Major organizations such as the National Trust, the National Playing Fields Association, the Central Council for Physical Training and Recreation, and the British Workers' Sports Federation were national in scope. [...]

State involvement in the media also began in the interwar years with the formation of the British Broadcasting Corporation (BBC) out of the commercial British Broadcasting Company in 1926. Its first Director-General, John Reith, shaped its policy, central to which was the aim of elevation (rather than reflection) of cultural tastes. The cultural elitism inherent in this stance continued until the post-war period when three radio services were inaugurated, the Light Programme, the Home Service and the Third Programme, which were seen as broadly reflecting the cultural predilections of the working, middle, and upper classes (Glover, 1984).

The maturing of the Welfare State, 1945–76

If the foundations of the Welfare State had been laid in the various measures of welfare reform between the two wars, the programme of reforms which constitute the Welfare State in modern Britain are largely the product of the post-war Labour government of Clement Attlee. However, although Labour implemented much of the reform, there was an evident interventionist strand to Conservative thinking in the immediate post-war period, even in respect of leisure. [...]

[...] although the general review of the welfare system may have been inspired by reformist

thinking, the nature of state intervention in leisure in the post-war period was rather different. The establishment of the Arts Council in 1946, the National Parks Commission in 1949 and the Wolfenden Report which led to the establishment of the (advisory) Sports Council in 1965 were not inspired solely or even primarily by a concern to provide equality of opportunity through direct state provision.

[...]

There was general agreement across the political parties that the arts should be supported, and the Arts Council received its Royal Charter in 1946. The concerns of the Council were to promote professional rather than amateur art, to limit itself to promotion of high arts, to concentrate on excellence rather than participation, and to involve itself in only very limited direct provision, stimulating provision by others through grant aid. [...] Government's concern with the arts was therefore rather less reformist, in the sense of reducing inequalities through state provision, than it was 'conservationist' or even 'paternalist' in attempting to maintain and improve standards of provision in high cultural forms. There was some attempt at the 'democratization of culture', improving access to the high arts (for some) through subsidy of such cultural forms, but there was little credence given to 'cultural democracy', allowing groups to promote and foster their own cultural forms. The pre-war elitist cultural policy of Reith's BBC was thus reproduced in the activities of the post-war Arts Council.

[...]

Even the establishment of a Sports Council, as advocated in the Wolfenden Report, was not justified by reference to sport and recreation as intrinsically worthwhile and therefore to be positively promoted for all. Instead, the rationale for state involvement was founded on extrinsic factors, such as Britain's failing reputation in international sporting competition and, on the domestic scene, a concern with the emergence of youth sub-cultures and the presumed moral qualities inherent in sporting activity which might provide a useful antidote to counter anti-social tendencies on the part of the young.

[...]

As with sport, promotion of the countryside and of the arts were also motivated to a considerable degree by extrinsic factors, the need to conserve the environment and protect economic activity, and the need to preserve 'Britain's' cultural heritage (usually referred to at this stage in unitary, homogeneous terms). This is a form of traditional pluralism because competing interest groups are seen as meeting their own interests through the market or through voluntary associations, and state intervention is only to be justified where externalities accrue or there are market imperfections or disbenefits generated by the operation of the unrestricted, 'free' market. Traditional pluralism is to be contrasted with 'welfare reformism' which, far from justifying state involvement on the grounds of some extrinsic gain, promotes the rights of the individual to have access to leisure opportunities for their own sake. Welfare reformism seeks to modify the market in terms of social goods, and it was not until the late 1960s and early 1970s that such reformist thinking became evident in government policy.

[...]

[B]y the time the economic problems of the mid-1970s manifested themselves, the welfare framework of leisure provision was subject to criticism as economically unaffordable not only by the New Right, but also by elements of the left, particularly those concerned with race and gender, for its failure to redress social inequalities. State intervention inspired by welfare reformism had failed to enhance the life chances of many of those who constituted its primary targets and, with the advent in 1979 of a Conservative government controlled by the New Right, leisure services (along with other areas of welfare policy) were to be subject to intense scrutiny.

[...]

'New economic realism' and the restructuring of the Welfare State: some leisure policy continuities across Labour and Conservative governments, 1976–84

In the previous [section] an account was given of the resurgence of ideology in British politics in the late 1970s, which resulted in apparently differing approaches to social policy being advocated by the major political parties. This polarization of party politics resulted in major difficulties at the local state level and in terms of central–local relations. However, in terms of central government policy *per se*, leisure was, ironically, one policy area in which strong continuities were to emerge across the Labour administration's approach under James Callaghan, and the incoming Conservative government of Margaret Thatcher. Under this new, restricted consensus the notion of leisure as a right of citizenship was to be replaced by the advocacy of leisure as a social and economic tool, and it was only gradually during the 1980s that evidence of this giving way to a more clearly New Right approach to leisure policy was to emerge.

[...] As Gough (1979) had argued, what was to occur was not the *dismantling* of the welfare state but rather its *restructuring* in particular ways. This shift has been characterized as the supplanting of the hegemony of social democracy, with its emphasis on rights of citizenship and increasing provision to combat social inequalities, by that of 'authoritarian populism' (Hall and Jacques, 1983; John Hargreaves, 1985), which emphasized the use of a reduced state welfare expenditure to promote social order, and to foster self-reliance on the part of the individual, the family and community groups.

The 1975 White Paper, *Sport and Recreation* reflected the beginnings of this restructuring of state expenditure on leisure because, although it rehearsed both the social democratic rationale for leisure provision (i.e. that such services reflect 'one of the community's everyday needs'), it also developed the pragmatic promotion of leisure services on the basis of the externalities which accrue from leisure provision: 'By reducing boredom and urban frustration, participation in active recreation contributes to the reduction of hooliganism and delinquency among young people ... The need to provide for people to make the best use of their leisure must be seen in this context' (Department of the Environment, 1975, p. 2).

This tension between leisure as an end and leisure as a means (i.e. of social control) is reflected also in the White Paper, *A Policy for the Inner Cities* (Department of the Environment, 1977), which promotes the provision of leisure services in areas of deprivation as a means of offsetting expenditure on policing and vandalism. The introduction of such pragmatic forms of justification coincides with the introduction by the Labour administration of public spending limits, which marked the end of the expansion of welfare services.

[...]

State flexibilization and disinvestment: discontinuities in policy, and the emergence of a New Right central government policy agenda for leisure, 1985–1990s

Although we have stressed important continuities between the policy approaches of Labour and Conservative governments, nevertheless significantly New Right-oriented policies began to emerge with the advent of the first Thatcher government and grew in strength and volume in particular from the mid-1980s. Even before the 1979 election, the arts lobby suspected that the New Right might wish to target Arts Council expenditure as part of its strategy for reducing reliance on state expenditure. Shortly before the Conservatives gained power in 1979, the Chairman of the Arts Council wrote to Mrs Thatcher asking for some reassurance that the arts would not be subject to reductions in government subsidy, and specifically that the Arts Council should not have its grant reduced. Mrs Thatcher replied in a letter to the Chairman that, when elected, the new Conservative administration would not be looking to achieve 'candle end' economies by cutting spending on the arts which was relatively insignificant in terms of the overall public sector bill. However, the incoming government did reduce the Arts Council grant by £1.114 million with virtually immediate effect (see Baldry, 1981, p. 32), intending that the deficit be met by increases in private sponsorship.

[...]

The rationale for central government support for leisure in the late 1980s was, then, not simply a less ambitious form of that which obtained during more expansionist times, but was qualitatively different. The social democratic strands in the leisure policy of central government, such as the concern to tackle recreation disadvantage, to 'plug the gaps' in provision in the commercial and voluntary sectors in order to foster cultural democracy or 'recreation for all' (the slogan advocated by the House of Lords Select Committee, 1973), gave way in the late 1970s and early 1980s to the pragmatic cost-benefit analysis of policies based largely on financial savings in other areas. However, throughout the 1980s the evidence of New Right thinking, as opposed to political pragmatism, had become increasingly evident. With the demise of Thatcher and the less stridently ideological approach of the Major government, further progress with the Thatcherite agenda in leisure would seem to have slowed. The Minister's review of the Sports Council's role, published in late 1991 (Department of Education and Science, 1991), for example, stopped short of advocating a reduction of the Council's role and instead promoted the establishment of a UK Sports Commission to be responsible for British international sport, with the establishment also of a Sports Council for England (analogous to those for Scotland, Wales and Northern Ireland) which would take responsibility for domestic and social policy concerns related to sport. This further proliferation of publicly funded sports organizations is not a policy development consistent with New Right thinking. However, the document also signals the government's intention to fund sport increasingly from non-public sector funds, and the paper proposed the establishment of a business sponsorship investment scheme (similar to that adopted for the arts in the mid-1980s) to achieve growth in private sector funding, especially to grassroots sport. A further clue to the impact of the post-Thatcher period on leisure policy was provided by the appointment of David Mellor as Minister for National Heritage with responsibility for sport, the arts and tourism. This emphasis on heritage might be said to signal a re-emergence of traditional 'one-nation' Conservative cultural policy. Perhaps more significant, though, is the bracketing of sport and arts with tourism, which strongly suggests that the commodification strategies of Thatcherite leisure policy are to be continued.

[...]

References

BAILEY, P. (1987) *Leisure and Class in Victorian England*, 2nd edn, London, Methuen.

BALDRY, H. (1981) *The Case for the Arts*, London, Secker and Warburg.

CUNNINGHAM, H. (1980) *Leisure in the Industrial Revolution*, London, Croom Helm.

DEPARTMENT OF EDUCATION AND SCIENCE (1991) *Sport and Active Recreation*, London, Department of Education and Science.

DEPARTMENT OF THE ENVIRONMENT (1975) *Sport and Recreation*, London, HMSO.

DEPARTMENT OF THE ENVIRONMENT (1977) *A Policy for the Inner Cities*, London, HMSO.

DONAJGRODSKI, A. (1977) *Social Control in Nineteenth Century Britain*, London, Croom Helm.

GLOVER, D. (1984) *The Sociology of the Mass Media*, London, Causeway Press.

GOUGH, I. (1979) *The Political Economy of the Welfare State*, London, Macmillan.

HALL, S. and JACQUES, M. (1983) *The Politics of Thatcherism*, London, Lawrence and Wishart.

HARGREAVES, J. (1985) 'From social democracy to authoritarian populism', *Leisure Studies*, Vol. 4, No. 2.

HARRISON, B. (1971) *Drink and the Victorians: the temperance question in England 1815–1872*, London, Faber.

HOLT, R. (1989) *Sport and the British: a modern history*, Oxford, Oxford University Press.

HOUSE OF LORDS, SELECT COMMITTEE OF (1973) *Sport and Leisure* (Cobham Report), London, HMSO.

MYERSCOUGH, J. (1974) 'The recent history of the use of leisure time' in Appleton, I. (ed.) *Leisure and Public Policy*, Edinburgh, Scottish Academic Press.

THOMPSON, E.P. (1963) *The Making of the English Working Class*, London, Gollancz.

THOMPSON, E.P. (1967) 'Time, work discipline and industrial capitalism', *Past and Present*, Vol. 38.

Source, Henry, 1993, pp. 6–23, 60–75.

READING B:
Patrick Wright, 'On living in an old country'

The abstraction of history

National Heritage involves the extraction of history – of the idea of historical significance and potential – from a denigrated everyday life and its restaging or display in certain sanctioned sites, events, images and conceptions. In this process history is redefined as 'the historical', and it becomes the object of a similarly transformed and generalized public attention.

[...]

Abstracted and redeployed, history seems to be purged of political tension; it becomes a unifying spectacle, the settling of all disputes. Like the guided tour as it proceeds from site to sanctioned site, the national past occurs in a dimension of its own – a dimension in which we appear to remember only in order to forget. 'History' is stressed to the same measure that active historicity – the possibility of any historical development in the present which is not simply a matter of polishing old statues with ever increasing vigour – is denied to a consequently devalued and meaningless present day experience.

History as entropy; the new Biedermeier

> Past inner life is turned into furniture just as, conversely, every Biedermeier piece was memory made wood. The interior where the soul accommodates its collection of memoirs and curios is derelict.
>
> Theodor Adorno (*Minima Moralia*)

If temporary endurance stands as some sort of measure of achievement, value and quality, this sense is certainly intensified now that history is widely experienced as a process of degeneration and decline: like people, countries grow old and decrepit. In this perspective the future holds nothing in store except further decline and one can only hope that ingenious stalling measures will be contrived by necessarily Conservative governments.

As that rather embittered stager of ideology Wyndham Lewis put it after the Second World War, Britain is now little better than a rabbit warren on top of a burned-out coalmine (Lewis, 1951). In this vision human dignity and cultural value are non-synchronous residues, sustained only by an anxious and continuously publicized nostalgia not just for 'roots' in an imperial, pre-industrial and often pre-democratic past, but also for those everyday memories of childhood which are stirred by so many contemporary invocations of this better past. In Flann O'Brien's words, 'I do not think the like of it will ever be there again' (O'Brien, 1975).

This sense of history as entropic decline gathers momentum in the sharpening of the British crisis. National Heritage is the backward glance which is taken from the edge of a vividly imagined abyss, and it accompanies a sense that history is foreclosed. With organic history in the last stages of degeneration we enter more than just a commemorative age of dead statues. Under the entropic view of history, supported as it is by High Cultural paradigms, 'the past' is revalued and reconstructed as an irreplaceable heritage – a trust which is bestowed upon the present and must be serviced before it is passed on to posterity. In this process owners are transformed into 'custodians' or 'trustees'. The land or country house owner, for example, emerges as the 'steward' – a public servant who does 'us' and the future a favour by living in the draughty corridors of baronial splendour and tending what he cannot simply consume. [...]

The status quo becomes objective reality in a new sense. All Western Europe is now a museum of superior culture and those citizens who are not lucky enough to be 'curators' of 'the collection' shouldn't worry that they have been left out of the action, for they are still subjects of this new archaism. Their position is to look, to pay taxes, to visit, to care, to pay at the door (even when entering cathedrals these days), to 'appreciate' and to be educated into an appropriate reverence in the process. In this connection it is worth recalling that one of the objectives of the National Heritage Act (1980) was to increase the exhibition of 'the heritage'. In this 'age of dead statues' (Dorfman and Mattelart, 1975) stately display surely provides access enough.

National heritage makes numerous connections with what was initially an aristocratic and high-bourgeois sense of history as decline but it also moves on into new areas. As *The Spectator's* review of Cormack's *Heritage in Danger* announced, 'Physical decay, rather than politics, is Mr Cormack's main theme.'

Comparably, during the second reading of the National Heritage Bill (1980), W. Benyon, Tory MP for Buckingham, made a curious statement in which he defined the national heritage as *that which moulders*. While this remark may have been intended to get preservation funds directed more towards property owners than towards the conservation of landscapes and wildlife, it also testifies to an expansion which has recently taken the national heritage beyond its traditional high-cultural definition. Alongside the customary valuation of artworks, country houses and landscapes, these mouldering times have – as Lord Vaizey said of Calke Abbey – seen fairly ordinary household junk included in the repertoire [Figure 1.12]. Alongside the stately museum and the National Trust mansion there now comes the vernacular pleasure of the junk-shop. Here is an altogether more secular amusement in which worn out and broken rubbish can be appreciated at the very moment of its transformation into something worth saving – a bargain, perhaps, but more significantly something resonant of an ordinary and more hand-made yesterday which is just becoming

FIGURE 1.12   Southeast corner room on the second floor at Calke Abbey at the time the house was handed to the National Trust in 1985; it retains this appearance (although much conserved).

precious as yet another lost world. While the poor have always visited junkshops in search of serviceable items with a little life in them yet, they now jostle with others who are there for more alchemical reasons. These are the ones who pack things over in order to savour the minor pleasure of deciding what shall be allowed to continue on its decline towards the rubbish heap and what will be reinstated in the light of a new attention which values, say, interwar clothes, early synthetic materials or a collection of hand-picked plates and glasses – un-matched but no less newly auratic for that. This, of course, is George Orwell's territory and in due course I will have more to say about his fascination with the modest and cast-off remains of other people's everyday lives.

While the definition of the national heritage has been expanded in the recent sense of decline, this hasn't only involved the inclusion of previously secular contents in an initially sacred repertoire. For if the aura of national heritage hovers over a widening range of objects it has also been relocated, increasingly orientated towards *interiors* and their organization or design. Like the 'technostyle' interior design which became fashionable in the United States during the thirties, this intensification of private space is occurring at a time when public life seems to be in irreversible decline and when doors are surely there to be closed behind one rather than opened onto the world. In his recent suggestion that Britain is seeing the coming of a new *biedermeier*, Roy Strong refers to early nineteenth century developments in the Austro-Hungarian Empire when the '*ancient regime* was reinstated and the liberal middle classes, denied power, turned in on themselves and created a style of living whose basis was the cultivation of domestic virtues in the form of all aspects of family life, the home and the garden (Strong, 1984). Along with Laura Ashley wallpapers and fabrics, Strong cites the success of a magazine called *Interiors* as evidence of this contemporary shift, and high on the list of factors which have contributed to this development we should certainly place both the continuing extension of home ownership and also the rise of television with its transformation of the relationship between 'home' and 'world'.

[...]

Heritage and danger

Given an entropic view of history, it is axiomatic that 'heritage' should be in danger. To the extent that threat defines the heritage as valuable in the first place the struggle to 'save' it can only be a losing battle. The 'stewards' struggle valiantly on behalf of their trust, but a barbarian indifference is all around. It is against this indifference that the urgent tone of the parliamentary conservationist tends to be directed: 'legislation designed to preserve the best of the past has often come too late'. ... Of course the country house is given to decay, but there is a development on this theme which brings in the larger question of property and inheritance: 'The problems of the country house are not only fiscal, but physical. The owner has to do more and more physical work for himself, with the result that a large country house is no place for elderly people: hence the need to be able to hand on to the next generation – and the next generation will need just as much income, and probably more, than at present' (Cormack, 1978, pp. 51–2). Claims such as this leave no doubt that the national heritage is far more than an accumulation of threatened objects. Like Debord's spectacle, national heritage still mediates social relations through its ideas, edifices and artefacts. Quite apart from any matter of physical decay, it is also these social relations which get carried forward and secured against threat. Hence (if only in part) the curious style of presence which is so often characteristic of the national heritage – a presence in which cultural authenticity and a rather more corrupt motivation are closely (if sometimes almost indiscernably) connected. The reality of the national heritage is like that of Bertram's Hotel, an institution of Agatha Christie's invention which survives in the London of the nineteen sixties as an imperilled fragment of High Edwardian life. Intensely and preciously authentic, Bertram's Hotel is also theatrical in atmosphere – real and yet also unreal. The unutterable question has eventually to be asked: 'Could there really be anything seriously wrong with a place that served old-fashioned afternoon teas?' And the answer is that there certainly could be, for behind the manically traditional scenes of Bertram's Hotel there is a multi-national conspiracy going on: 'These people, decayed aristocrats, impoverished members of the

Old Country families' are indeed 'all so much *mise en scène*' (Christie, 1984, p. 11).

National geography: the past which simply exists

Considering the merger of history and landscape which lies at the heart of 'our' national heritage, it is consistent that 'the past' should be treated as if it were a simple existent. This emphasis takes two forms: 'the past' is there both to be dug up and also to be visited.

[...]

A national heritage site must be sufficiently of this world to be accessible by car or camera, but it must also encourage access to that other 'simpler' world when the tourist or viewer finally gets there. This publicly instituted transformation between prosaic reality and the imagination of a deep past is central to the operation of the national heritage. National heritage has its sites, but like amulets to believers these sites exist only to provide that momentary experience of utopian gratification in which the grey torpor of everyday life in contemporary Britain lifts and the simple, more radiant measures of Albion declare themselves again. This publicly instituted lapse into a kind of instinctive neo-tribalism can certainly by understood in terms of Sartre's description of the primitive community of anti-Semitism (Sartre, 1948). As can be seen from the following letter which was sent to the *Birmingham Evening Mail* by an expatriate now resident in Africa, the pleasure of this ideology involves the pseudo-poetry of a 'national' and implicitly racist *gestalt*:

I received a copy of the Evening Mail's Our England special today. A curse on you.

I had just (after 12 months) convinced myself that I was well rid of the rotten weather, football hooligans, unions, dirt, inflation, traffic, double standards of politicians – and suddenly it's back to square one. The grimy facade is lifted, and the real England comes flooding back.

Long winter walks through the Wyre Forest ending at the George at Bewdley, chestnuts roasted on an open log fire and swilled down with a pint of mild, house hunting round Ludlow for the mythical half-timbered home, the

joy of finding one at a price I could afford and trips to auctions to furnish it for £60. ...

Summer evenings at the Royal Shakespeare, scents wafting across the river ... the sounds and scenes of England.

Thanks for helping me regain a sense of perspective.

(*The Birmingham Evening Mail*, 6 May 1980)

The expatriate view has the false and wishful clarity of distance. It is from afar that the 'memory' of woodsmoke and the old counties, of thatch, live elms, threepenny bits and steam engines is most pungent, and no one should be surprised that the most rabidly nostalgic heritage publications are those like the quarterlies *This England* or *Heritage: The British Review* which incorporate an expatriate perspective and which in their reaction seem to assume that the purest Britons are those who simply couldn't stand the decline any longer – superior white subjects who finally realised that the last act of true patriotism must be to take that lucrative job in one of the old colonies. Only from outside can one be the truly loyal custodian of a nation which has declined to the point where it exists only in memory and distant imagination.

[...]

The accommodation of utopia

In its historical repertoire national heritage borrows many of the trappings of the English utopia (of Arthurian legend, of Blake and Samuel Palmer, of Morris, and Pre-Raphaelitism ...), but it stages utopia not as a vision of possibilities which reside in the real – nor even as a prophetic if counterfactual perspective on the real – but as a dichotomous realm existing alongside the everyday. Like the utopianism from which it draws, national heritage involves positive energies which certainly can't be written off as ideology. It engages hopes, dissatisfactions, feelings of tradition and freedom, but it tends to do so in a way that diverts these potentially disruptive energies into the separate and regulated spaces of stately display. In this way, what much utopianism has alluded to or postulated as the challenge of history – something that needs to be brought about – ends up behind us already accomplished and ready for exhibition as 'the past'.

Where there was active historicity there is now decoration and display; in the place of memory, amnesia swaggers out in historical fancy dress.

References

CHRISTIE, A. (1984) *At Bertram's Hotel*, London, Fontana.

CORMACK, P. (1978) *Heritage in Danger*, London, New English Library.

DORFMANN, A. and MATTELART, M. (1975) *How to Read Donald Duck: imperialist ideology in the Disney comic*, New York, International General.

LEWIS, W. (1951) *Rotting Hill*, London, Methuen.

O'BRIEN, F. (1975) *The Poor Mouth*, London, Pan.

SARTRE, J.P. (1948) *Anti-Semite and Jew*, New York, Shocken Press.

STRONG, R. (1984) 'Home is where the art is', *The Times*, 10 November.

Source: Wright, 1985, pp. 69–78.

READING C:
Raphael Samuel, 'Theatres of memory'

Sociology

When Patrick Wright launched his attack on 'heritage' (Wright, 1985), he accused it of reactionary chic and argued that it represented the triumph of aristocratic and reactionary nostalgia over the levelling tendencies of the Welfare State: it was Evelyn Waugh's posthumous revenge on Clement Attlee (Wright, 1991). Robert Hewison, more crudely, puts the appearance of 'heritage' down to an aristocratic plot hatched, it seems, by the beleaguered owners of country houses in 1975. Faced with the prospect of a wealth tax and an incoming and unsympathetic Labour government, they mounted a high-level lobby, raising the cry of 'heritage in danger', and enlisting the support of the House of Lords, the National Trust and the Victoria and Albert Museum (the V&A 1974 exhibition 'The Destruction of the Country House', according to Hewison, is the point at which 'the heritage industry' was born) (Hewison, 1987).

If in one set of discriminations heritage is accused of being crypto-feudal – a vast system of outdoor relief for decayed gentlefolk – in another it is charged with being 'deeply capitalist' (Johnson, 1993), albeit in a post-modern rather than a proto-industrial vein. In a consumer-led society, in which everything has its price, and market values are unchallenged, it 'traffics' in history and 'commodifies' the past (Wright, 1985). It turns real-life suffering into tourist spectacle, while at the same time creating simulacra of a past that never was. Museums are particularly suspect. They are 'part of the leisure and tourist business', and thus intimately linked to the Disneylands and theme parks. They are also, it seems, property's *franc-tireurs*:

> A new museum is not only one of the convenient ways of re-using a redundant mill or factory. It is treated as a form of investment that will regenerate the local economy that has decayed as a result of the closure of that mill or factory. That is why it is relatively easy to find capital to set up a new museum. Museum

projects are a useful means of cleaning up a derelict environment prior to commercial investment.

(Hewison, 1991)

In either of these two cases heritage is an expressive totality, a seamless web. It is conceptualized as systemic, projecting a unified set of meanings which are impervious to challenge – what Umberto Eco calls 'hyper-reality'. In essence it is conservative, even when it takes on, or co-opts, popular themes. It brings the most disparate materials together under a single head. It is what one critic defines as a 'closed story', i.e. a fixed narrative which allows for neither subtext nor counter-readings. Its biases are more or less consistent, its messages coded, its meanings clear. Politics, culture and economics are all of a piece, reinforcing one another's influence, reciprocating one another's effects.

Heritage is also seen by its critics as a 'project' (Corner and Harvey, 1991), if not a conspiracy or plot then at the very least a strategy, 'a complex and purposefully selective process of historical recollection'. It is a 'bid for hegemony', a way of using knowledge in the service of power. It shores up national identity at a time when it is beset by uncertainties on all sides. It is a way of compensating for the collapse of British power.

Chronology alone would put these symmetries in doubt, quite apart from the fact that the country cottage has played an inconceivably greater part in the idea of 'lost England' than the country house. It might suggest that there was not one moment but many from which current retrieval projects and strategies could trace their origin. Using perhaps the Braudelian notion of 'conjuncture', the historian of heritage might want to distinguish between the vintage car rallies – originally, in the 1930s, when no one else could afford to run in them, an aristocratic sport, and later, to judge by the Ealing Studios comedy *Genevieve* (1953) an affair of Home Counties playboys, dressed in cavalry twill trousers and blazers – and the altogether more plebeian 'vintage' engine rallies today where steam ploughs assemble in muddy fields, fairground organs blare out their music, and hobby-horses whirl on the carousels.

Chronology would also call into question association of heritage with conservative reaction. It might suggest that the cry of 'Heritage in danger', or at any rate that sentiment, crystallized, in the first place, in a recoil from the modernizations of the 1950s, rather than as a reflex of economic decline. The post-war mechanization of agriculture, the dieselization of the tractor, and the disappearance of the horseman, might appear as the inspiration, albeit a negative one, for the growth of the idea of the 'folk' or 'working farm' museum – an innovation of the late 1950s and early 1960s. The steam preservation mania of the 1950s is more obviously related to the dieselization of railways, the rationalization of services and the diminution of branch lines. So far as the built environment is concerned, it was arguably the astonishing increase in car ownership – a feature of the 'affluent society' of the 1950s – which set the alarm bells ringing and changed preservation from a rural to an urban cause.

Many of heritage's enthusiasms were in place long before 1975, the year when in Britain, as in the other countries involved in European Architectural Heritage Year, the term entered general circulation. Railway antiquarianism is almost as old as the railways themselves; as Bevis Hillier shows in *Young Betjeman*, in the 1930s it was thoroughly familiar to readers of the *Daily Herald* and the Shell *Guides* (Hillier, 1988), quite apart from the railway modellers running replicas of Puffing Billy, or visitors to the Science Museum confronting – as they had done since 1875 – Stephenson's 'Rocket'. A taste for early industrial buildings and plant goes back at least as far as Nikolaus Pevsner's *Pioneers of Modern Design* (1984/1935), while the gypsy arts – or folk arts as they were called at the time of the Festival of Britain – have had their admirers among the expensively educated ever since, in the 1860s, Francis Groome ran off with his Esmerelda and went off to live with the gypsies on Headington Hill (Groome, 1880).

Economics, and especially economic history, might also put the moment of 1974–5 into question, by drawing attention to the long gestation period of many conservationist projects, and the changes in the material conditions of existence which allowed them to enter the realm of the thinkable. Statistics of car ownership – 2 million in 1949, 17.5 million in 1980 – might help to account for the growth of historic tourism (Blunden and Carrie, 1990, p.114), while attendance figures, if they could be gleaned from the records of places like the Wigan Pier Heritage Centre, or the statistics of school parties, might dispose of the absurd idea that open-air museums are a great magnet to foreign tourists. In another sphere the spread of that most labour-saving and comfort-making of modern household devices, central heating, which can be logged, quinquennium by quinquennium from 1960, might appear as the ghost-in-the-machine of restoration, and the extraordinary increase in the number of 'listed' historic buildings which began in 1967. At a stroke it converted draughty Victorian mansions, fit only for conversion to flats, into desirable period residences.

Economics, disaggregrating such abstracts as 'capital' and 'consumerism' and inquiring into their heterogenous and promiscuous components, might also serve as a useful corrective to those top-down accounts of the heritage industry which see it as a kind of ruling-class conspiracy or plot, or imply that there is some directive intelligence at work. While paying due regard to the ways in which business has been able to profit from, or accommodate itself to, the rehabilitation of old property, or to latch on to notions of 'period' in commodity marketing and design, it might draw attention to those more molecular processes in which any cultural politics takes shape. In heritage-ware, to judge by those who take up the stands when the gift trade holds its annual fairs, the typical entrepreneurs seem to be one-man businesses, female-run franchises and husband-and-wife (or gay) partnerships; the business corporation is a conspicuous absence (NEC, 1990). Heritage supports and is supported by chains of charity shops and armies of flea-market stallholders. Organic farms make some contribution to it; so do the health and whole-food co-operatives.

Heritage puts a premium on the labour and services of the craftsman-retailer, and the maintenance of artisanal skills [...]

A sociological perspective on heritage, which took into account the hybridization of contemporary social identities, the mixing and mingling of what were formerly class preserves, or a Marxist one which looked for a dialectical relationship between the imaginary and the real, rather than a reductive and reflective one, might be even more unsettling to currently accepted negative stereotypes than an economic one. It could begin by pointing out that the rise of the heritage industry, if one chooses to take 1975 as a significant date, so far from heralding an epoch of feudal reaction, coincides, rather, in Britain, as in other European countries, with political dealignment and a collapse of two-camp class divides. [...]

One way of attempting to account for the popularity of heritage, as also the rapidity with which it has spread, is to see it as an attempt to *escape* from class. Instead of heredity it offers a sense of place, rather as environmentalism offers the activist and the reformist an alternative to the worn-out routines of party politics. It may be indicative of this that Covent Garden, that preservationist Ruritania, which emerged in the 1980s as one of the style capitals of the world, is also a Sloane-free zone, where gays are more in evidence than would-be ladies and gents. Heritage allows the Colonel's lady and Judy O'Grady, or at any rate their daughters, to wear the same vintage clothes. It encourages white-collar workers and middle-class men, getting up steam from the boiler, to try their hand at being mechanics; landlubbers, sailing before the mast, to play at being mariners. Heritage offers an ideal home which is defined not by pedigree but by period, and which can be decked out with make-believe family heirlooms. Still more pertinent, through the medium of family history it gives us a second identity and allows the most humdrum and ordinary, so far as present occupation is concerned, to indulge in a romance of otherness.

Heritage might also be aligned with the emergence in the 1960s of what Frank Parkin has called, in another context, 'middle-class radicalism' (Parkin, 1968). It is a familiar feature of the universities in the 1960s, of such newly radicalized groups as social workers and of the new-wave charities of the 1960s. But might it not be applied equally to the formation of amenity societies and 'ginger' groups, the staging of single-issue campaigns, such as those who in London defeated the motorway box (Tyme, 1978), the growth of the country wildlife trusts, and not least the appearance, for the first time, of mass membership environmental campaigning organizations (Cherry, 1982)?

References

BLUNDEN, J. and CURRIE, N. (eds) (1990) *A People's Charter? Forty years of the National Parks and Access to the Countryside Act of 1949*, London, HMSO.

CHERRY, G.E. (1982) *The Politics of Town Planning*, London, Longman.

CORNER, J. and HARVEY, S. (1991) 'Mediating tradition and modernity: the heritage/enterprise couplet' in Corner, J. and Harvey, S. (eds) *Enterprise and Heritage: crosscurrents of national culture*, London, Routledge.

GROOME, F. (1880) *In Gypsy Tents*, Edinburgh.

HEWISON, R. (1987) *The Heritage Industry; Britain in a Climate of Decline*, London, Methuen.

HEWISON, R. (1991) 'Commerce and Culture' in Corner, J. and Harvey, S. (eds) *Enterprise and Heritage: crosscurrents of national culture*, London, Routledge.

HILLIER, B. (1988) *Young Betjeman*, London, Murray.

JOHNSON, R. (1993) 'Heritage and history', cyclostyled paper and presentation, Amsterdam, 2 October.

PEVSNER, N. (1984) *Pioneers of Modern Design from William Morris to Walter Gropius*, Harmondsworth, Penguin.

NEC (1990) International Spring Fair, Official Catalogue and Buyers' Guide, Birmingham NEC .

PARKIN, F. (1968) *Middle-Class Radicalism: the social bases of the British Campaign for Nuclear Disarmament*, Manchester, Manchester University Press.

TYME, J. (1978) *Motorways versus Democracy*, London, Macmillan.

WRIGHT, P. (1985) *On Living in an Old Country*, London, Verso.

WRIGHT, P. (1991) *A Journey Through Ruins: the last days of London*, London, Radius, pp. 45–67.

Source: Samuel, 1994, pp. 242–7.

READING D:
Paddy Scannell, 'Public service broadcasting and modern public life'

VIII

For all its seeming sophistication the Theory of Ideology says something very simple indeed; something not very different from what Leavis was saying in the 1930s: the media are harmful and the function of literary criticism or theoretical critique is to expose them in that light. Such an approach is not reconcilable with a view of broadcasting as a public sphere that works to enhance the reasonable, democratic character of life in public and private contexts. To regard the media as ideological is to regard them as either anti-rational or irrational. But although I reject such characterizations, a major difficulty in discussing the rationality of broadcasting lies in the way that academic debates about rationality are largely contained within the theoretical envelope of the philosophy of consciousness, the so-called western episteme from its provenance in the Greeks to its contemporary terminal state in the aporias of post-structuralism and the intellectual capitulations of post-modernism.

Although Habermas is the most valiant opponent of this latest *trahison des clercs* (this time by abandoning rather than engaging with politics), the terms of his defence of communicative rationality are remote from the actual circumstances of ordinary conversation and mundane social interaction which, I have argued, characterize the communicative domain of broadcasting. I have tentatively tried to ground the communicative ethos of broadcasting in Anglo-American sociology and linguistic pragmatics that take, as their object, mundane daily life, social interaction and talk (Scannell, 1988b). A fundamental kind of human rationality is implicated in this work which attends to the communicative basis of social life and the means whereby it is maintained in ordinary interaction, especially talk. An orientation to co-operation underpins the maintenance of a perspective of normality (Garfinkel, 1984, Ch. 2), the common grounds of intersubjective understanding (Schutz, q.v. Heritage, 1984, pp. 54 ff.) and a communicative intentionality in talk that is grounded in considerations of clarity, sincerity, relevance and informativeness (Grice, q.v. Levinson, 1983, pp. 100 ff.).

Such concerns are closely paralleled in the 'validity claims' that Habermas proposes as the universal grounds of communicative behaviour oriented towards understanding (Habermas, 1979, Ch. 1). My difficulty with Habermas is that he seems to regard consensual understanding as achieved through receptiveness to the best argument (i.e. the most rational one) in ideal speech situations. The ideal speech situation, it appears in John Keane's helpful discussion, is grounded in communicative competence, and the model Habermas has in mind is the classical Greek category of politics as public speaking and acting – 'Socratic forms of communication' (Keane, 1984, pp. 159, 163). But this is to privilege not so much rationality, as rhetorical skill. It is notable about Socrates, for instance, that he always gets the last word and thus always 'wins'. The best argument can be, it is not hard to imagine, a kind of domination and oppression, to which the less articulate must submit. Feminist critiques of how men argue are very much to this point, especially in their observation that listening is as important as speaking (Spender, 1980). For almost all discussion of rational discourse considers it not merely in formal terms (its immanent, logical properties) but as a contestation for the best, the most powerful, the most convincing argument. There is virtually no consideration of rational discourse as social dialogue.

I think Habermas is right to regard communicative rationality as grounded in mutual understanding, but I do not think it is achieved (or achievable) along the lines he proposes, for mutual understanding presupposes cooperativeness as its basis, a willingness to listen, to allow the validity of the other person's viewpoint and, if necessary, a willingness to leave aside what may be the best argument (in terms of clarity, logic, force, etc.) in consideration of the most appropriate decisions in relation to the particular circumstances and the particular persons involved. The skills that are needed for coming to conclusions with which all agree, include tact, thoughtfulness and consideration for others, knowing how and when to listen, etc. Such skills produce agreements that are reasonable (as distinct from rational) and thus acceptable in the eyes of participants. They are the everyday skills that everyone possesses and deploys in ordinary talk and mundane contexts, as distinct from the peculiar communicative competence of philosophers and their peculiar discourses.

Thus, I prefer to characterize the impact of broadcasting as enhancing the reasonable, as distinct from the rational, character of daily life in public and private contexts. In this context, reasonable has the force of mutually accountable behaviour; that is, if called upon, individuals can offer reasons and accounts for what they have said or done. To refuse an explanation, if called for, is unreasonable. To be unable to offer an explanation is unreasonable. Reasonableness is a guarantee and hallmark of forms of private and public life in which people accept mutual obligations to each other, acknowledge that they are answerable and accountable to each other – in short, deal with each other as equals. In such conditions the right to ask for explanations and accounts (where necessary or relevant) is a communicative entitlement.

IX

I have used the term 'communicative entitlement' several times in this article, and it needs clarification. Communicative entitlements presuppose communicative rights. Communicative rights (the right to speak freely, for instance) are enshrined in the written constitutions of some countries, but not in Britain. A minimal notion of guaranteed communicative rights is a precondition of forms of democratic life in public and private. If one party (the state, the police, teachers, parents, husbands) refuse to be answerable for their conduct to the other party (the electorate, suspects, pupils, children, wives), not only is this unreasonable – it denies a communicative entitlement and nullifies a right. Communicative entitlements can be claimed and asserted, within a presupposed framework of communicative rights. Rights of free assembly, to speak freely and (more often overlooked) to listen, contribute to creating formal, minimal guarantees for certain forms of public political and religious life. They seed the possible growth of wider and more pervasive claims from those denied a hearing in manifold public and private contexts, that they should be listened to: i.e. that they should be treated seriously. As equals.

I believe that broadcasting has enhanced the reasonable character and conduct of twentieth-century life by augmenting claims to communicative entitlements. It does this, as I have tried to show, through asserting a right of access to public life; through extending its universe of discourse and entitling previously excluded voices to be heard; through questioning those in power, on behalf of viewers and listeners, and trying to get them to answer. More generally, I have suggested, the fact that the broadcasters do not control the communicative context means that they must take into account the conditions of reception for their utterances. As such they have learned to treat the communicative process not simply as the transmission of a content, but a relational process in which how things are said is as important as what is said. All this has, I think, contributed to new, interactive relationships between public and private life which have helped to normalize the former and to socialize the latter.

In saying this I am not trying to idealize the present system, whose reasonable/rational character is contained within the framework and limitations of mass democratic politics which work, in many ways, to sustain the power of institutional public life over mundane, private life. One way in which the limits of rationality in political debate can clearly be shown emerges from careful analysis of the techniques and protocols of political interviews. [...]

[...] The extent to which politicians can refuse to be answerable and accountable marks the boundaries of open, reasonable and informative discussion on radio and television.

Another way in which those boundaries maintain the inequalities of power between public and private can be seen in the distribution of entitlements to opinions and experiences on radio and television. To have an opinion is to be entitled to comment on events, to have views about them, to assess their significance. To have an experience is to be entitled to describe an event that happened to oneself and to say what one felt about it. In broadcast news public persons are entitled to opinions, private persons to experiences. Public persons (politicians, businessmen, authorities, experts, media reporters and commentators) are routinely called upon to comment on the wider

implications of newsworthy events (what they mean for this country, the government, business, etc.). They speak as representatives of institutions, as agents not as persons, and their views have a generalized weight and authority. They are accredited spokespersons, whose views are legitimated and legitimating. Private individuals appear in news, become newsworthy, accidentally and usually disastrously. They are often the victims or witnesses of catastrophes and are interviewed for what they saw or for how it affected them – what it was like (when the ship sank), what it felt like (on learning their children were/were not safe). They are there to authenticate, to embody, the human consequences of events. They speak as persons, their testimony is particular, their newsworthiness has a one-off, unique character.

This arrangement in news of those who are entitled to express opinions and those who are entitled to experiences reinforces the division between public and private, and maintains them as separate. [...]

[...] More participatory forms of politics and broadcasting are required if people are to play an active part in public life and decision-making, thereby exercising greater control over their own individual and social life. As far as broadcasting goes what is needed are many more properly local radio stations (dozens of stations in London, for instance) and more regional television networks to strengthen rather than vitiate the diversity of identities of place. Moreover, public access and participation in programmes, programming and programme making should be a key feature of decentralized radio and television services.

Such services should enhance but not displace the present system of public service broadcasting in this country and its commitment to properly public, social values. In my view equal access for all to a wide and varied range of common informational, entertainment and cultural services, carried on channels that can be received throughout the country, should be thought of as an important citizenship right in mass democratic societies. It is a crucial means – perhaps the only means at present – whereby common knowledges and pleasures in a shared public life are maintained as a social good for the whole population. As such it should be defended against its enemies.

References

GARFINKEL, H. (1984) *Studies in Ethnomethodology*, Cambridge, Polity Press.

HABERMAS, J. (1979) *Communication and the Evolution of Society*, London, Heinemann.

HERITAGE, J. (1984) *Garfinkel and Ethnomethodology*, Cambridge, Polity Press.

KEANE, J. (1984) *Public Life and Late Capitalism*, Cambridge, Cambridge University Press.

LEVINSON, S. (1983) *Pragmatics*, Cambridge, Cambridge University Press.

SCANNELL, P. (1988) 'The communicative ethos of broadcasting', Conference Paper, International Television Studies Conference, London, BFI.

SPENDER, D. (1980) *Man Made Language*, London, Routledge and Kegan Paul.

Source: Scannell, 1989, pp. 158–66.

CHOICE AND REGULATION: SEXUAL MORALITIES

Robert Bocock

Contents

CHAPTER TWO

1   Introduction

The concept of regulation is wide-ranging, covering, as we have seen in Chapter 1 of this book, on the one hand, state legislation and the law and, on the other, more locally based rules about social and moral conduct, leisure and recreational activities. In this chapter we shall examine another area of regulation: that of morality – more specifically the moral values and rules which regulate the representation of sexual activities in the media in Britain today. Lynne Segal has pointed out that, especially in Foucauldian theory, 'sexuality is the key site of social regulation and control in modern times, primarily in the service of the reproductive family unit' (**Segal**, 1997, section 1.1). In matters of sexual morality, including questions of divorce and abortion, religious discourses, from fundamentalist to reformist, still play a central role in defining moral conduct, attitudes and practice. Religions have traditionally made the family a core moral value. However, moralities can also be grounded in more secular philosophies and world-views, as is the case in feminism or with the gay liberation movement which are discussed in detail below. The tensions between religious- and secular-derived moral attitudes will be examined later in this chapter.

A series of debates and controversies have developed around questions of moral choice and regulation, in Britain as elsewhere, since the end of the Second World War, as older, more traditional patterns have been eroded and as new technologies, in particular broadcast television, video, satellite and cable television, have led to conflicts about who should be 'allowed' to view what on screens. The discourses deployed in these controversies draw on a variety of moral philosophies, but one significant and persistent source appears to be much older traditions of thought, especially sixteenth- and seventeenth-century puritan ideas, which had always opposed theatre, opera, dancing, even church organs, as sinful because they were seen as providing and/or inciting sensual pleasures, inspired by the devil (Weber, 1971/1930). Traditional moral discourses have tended to see sensual pleasure as undermining the monogamous family – which has long been regarded as the proper context for rearing children – and the commitment to work as a God-given duty, or what has been termed 'the work ethic'.

As we shall see in this chapter, these moral values about the dangers of sensual pleasures have retained some of their effectiveness and influence into the twentieth century, especially in the English-speaking cultures where moral debate has long been influenced by puritanical discourses. (Such cultures may be found among some groups in England, Scotland, Wales, Northern Ireland, Canada, the United States, Australia, New Zealand, parts of South Africa, as well as in Germany, the Netherlands, Switzerland, and even parts of France influenced by Calvinism.) Cultures more influenced by Roman Catholicism, Judaism, Islam, Buddhism, Hinduism or other more secular and humanist world-views also contain their own distinctive versions of moral values which seek to regulate conduct and choices, especially in the area of the family, marriage and sexual activities.

Moral debate in modern societies has also been shaped by a variety of secular philosophies. These philosophies drew upon ancient Greek and Roman authors and schools of thought, such as Epicureanism, in which the well-being of people was a central concern. A related secular philosophy, humanism, was a product of the Renaissance and the Enlightenment, and was developed by writers such as Bacon (1561–1626), Voltaire (1694–1778), and the Scottish philosopher David Hume (1711–76). These secular philosophies have continued to play an important role in later debates about what constitutes 'the good life'. From the period of the Renaissance and the Enlightenment, another important secular philosophy, liberalism, emerged, which placed more emphasis on the freedom of choice and action of the individual. Liberal ideas have continued to exert a powerful influence, on, for example, the New Right, the dominant political and moral philosophy of the 1980s and 1990s.

liberalism   **Liberalism**, deriving from the writings of John Locke (1632–1704), John Stuart Mill (1806–73) and Adam Smith (1723–90), has been one of the most important secular philosophies in the influence it exerted on the moral debates in Britain and the United States in the late twentieth century. Values about the freedom of the *individual* to live free as far as possible from state interference, especially in economic matters, and the idea of *equality*, first of all of white male property-owners, then later of women and peoples of colour, who were to be treated as equal citizens, voters, and employees – these values were articulated by different variants of liberal secular philosophies before they became the basis for moral and political practices. The French Revolution of 1789 was perhaps *the* major event marking the start of modernity in the *political sphere*, with its overthrow of the monarchy and the aristocracy and its demand for liberty, equality, and fraternity. In Britain, the growth of modern capitalism in the late eighteenth and early nineteenth centuries marked the move to modernity in the *economic sphere*. At first sight this sphere of economic activity might appear to have little or nothing to do with morality, but Adam Smith wrote of market competition in the context of 'the moral sentiments', and as we shall see when we consider the analysis offered by the sociologist, Max Weber, in his work on *The Protestant Ethic and the Spirit of Capitalism* and in other writings, a certain ethical outlook had a profound influence on economic conduct in the early modern period (from the late sixteenth to the late eighteenth century).

In section 2, the way in which Weber tried to answer the question, 'How are we to understand and analyse the variety of moral discourses which shape economic and related conduct in the modern world?', will be considered in greater detail. Weber provided a major comparative analysis of world cultural values and their effects upon economic and political action. This can still provide a fruitful basis for sociological analysis of more recent developments, albeit with some modifications to take account of late-twentieth-century developments in western societies.

In section 3, we shall look at some concrete examples of moral regulation in Britain in the more recent past – the last hundred years or so. The influence of a variety of moral discourses, from that of religiously-grounded puritanism to liberalism and secular humanism, individual free choice to state regulation, can be seen in these concrete examples of contemporary moral debates. The increasing complexity of modern societies, containing many different groups with differing moral outlooks, and the growth of what has been called moral pluralism have led to a questioning of the hitherto religiously-grounded puritanical morality upon which the state's legal regulation was traditionally based. The effects of the two world wars upon many working men and women's moral outlook have been of major importance in producing questions about the superiority of the dominant moral value system of the British ruling elites. So too has the growth in affluence among many groups, especially among the young of nearly all social classes, with a stronger orientation to mass consumption and pleasure, which has produced a more critical, questioning attitude to the morality of the older ruling elites.

Indeed, those people who supported moral campaigners like Mrs Mary Whitehouse and the campaign to 'Clean-up TV', from the 1960s onwards, thought that the increase in what they saw as 'permissiveness' was leading to a serious moral crisis. One aspect of this crisis concerned the decline in the family – the family defined as consisting of the traditional nuclear pattern of wife/mother and husband/father and their children, living together in one household – in the view of such groups. It came to be widely accepted that without such a stable family life in the lives of most people, there would continue to be more crime among the young, more drug-taking, more sexual promiscuity, more violence like that among soccer fans. Television, in representing such moral breakdown by showing plays and films about unwholesome, 'immoral' people, rather than showing 'decent' people trying to live more normal 'moral' lives, was held to be *a*, if not *the,* major influence in the moral breakdown of family life in post-war Britain. We shall consider these issues in more detail in section 3, looking at both the continuing presence of the religious puritan ethic which Weber had analysed, but also the emergence of new moral voices, new groups articulating different moral values.

Two of these different moral value systems will be considered in greater detail in sections 4 and 5. These are, first, feminism and, secondly, libertarian movements around sexual politics, especially that concerned with homosexual rights. In particular, section 4 will examine the debate among feminists about the role played by pornography in leading to violence used by men against women. Such 'violence' is not only physical but also emotional, verbal and psychic in form, in the eyes of some feminists involved in the debate. For them, pornography either causes, or comes to symbolize, the objectification of women by many, most, or some, men – a process which leads, they argue, to the increasing acceptance of violence against women by men, in films, magazines, television broadcasts, and to the actual brutalization of women in family and sexual relationships. Feminists, as we shall see, have taken up more than one position on this issue of pornography. The moral debates *within* feminism about pornography thus illustrate how complex, varied and difficult such debates about what should or should not be regulated by law in this area of representation have become by the end of the twentieth century.

Further complexities have been added by the movements of sexual politics which seek to gain greater rights for, and to express the concerns and moral viewpoints of, lesbians and gay men. Section 5 will address some of these further complexities in moral debates about what aspects of sexual behaviour should or should not be regulated. These debates have concerned two major areas of moral and/or legal regulation. First, has been the pressure-group activity to produce changes in the laws which regulate male homosexual activities in particular – from decriminalizing homosexuality to debates about restricting the age of consent. Secondly, there have been moral debates surrounding the regulation, by broadcasting authorities, for example, of which (and how many) representations of homosexual men and women and their lives should be permitted screening on television. The pornography debate among feminists has also had some parallels in this area, partly because 'gay' magazines, films, videos, and Internet activities are regulated by law, or by other authorities such as local authorities, school governors, church leaders and other religious groups. Debates about what should or should not be portrayed or represented about lesbians and gay men in various media draw upon a variety of moral value positions. Again, nothing in the contemporary moral culture is as straightforward as it once might have seemed. Complex issues are involved in all these moral debates, as we shall see.

Finally, section 6 will provide an overview of the issues discussed in the chapter about the regulation of sexual activities and representations of women and men as sexually desirable 'objects'. Some tentative conclusions will be drawn about the nature of contemporary moral debate and attempts to regulate sexual conduct and its representations, but these are open to debate.

2   The puritan legacy

In an area as complex as that of moral regulation and choice, it is necessary, in order to avoid confusion, to mark out some basic framework to guide us through the myriad of perspectives. An important perspective about regulation and morality was developed by the German sociologist Max Weber (1864–1920), in particular in his book *The Protestant Ethic and the Spirit of Capitalism* (Weber, 1971/1930).

The relevance of Weber's argument is that it established the importance of the puritanical suspicion of this-worldly pleasures in the moral value system which once dominated, and continues to influence, some western capitalist societies such as those of Britain and parts of the United States. The vocabularies, discourses, moral values and attitudes towards bodily pleasures, which developed in seventeenth-century Calvinism especially, may have declined in terms of organized religious life, but have left a lasting influence in these societies, which has been drawn upon periodically ever since, up to the end of the twentieth century, long after **puritanism** as an   puritanism organized religious force has disappeared. The suspicion of bodily pleasures and associated values is sometimes, in particular political circumstances, so pervasive a discourse that many latter-day politicians, most of whom may be from non-Calvinist religious groups or from none, nevertheless adopt the discourse of 'the suspicion of sensual pleasures' from time to time, as we shall see in the next section. The present and the future are therefore haunted by moral ghosts from the past. Puritanical discourse persists as a moral trace or legacy in large parts of the English-speaking world; its values are, as it were, embedded in the language despite the intentions of individual speakers of that language (see the argument about how language constructs meaning in **Hall**, 1997).

In another essay entitled 'Religious rejections of the world and their directions' (Weber, 1991/1948), Weber was concerned with the effects of different types of religious world-views upon the erotic and the aesthetic. The term 'rational' religious world-outlook is used to refer to the use of the mind to control pleasure-seeking by self and others in what are seen in such religious world-views as illegitimate, immoral ways.

Max Weber identified the processes associated with an increasing use of intellectual, rational modes of thought, as distinct from traditional cultural thought patterns, as the dynamic source of cultural change in western cultures. The roots of '**rationality**', he argued, can be traced back to philosophers in   rationality Ancient Greece and the development of a secular framework for law in the Roman Empire. These processes were further developed when the Catholic West met the world of Islam which transmitted Ancient Greek and Roman culture, together with Arabic algebra, to the West though the Moorish conquest of parts of Europe in the thirteenth century. The Church, however, did not take up the Muslim taboo on pictorial, or sculptural, representations of saints or other sacred figures. Indeed, the Catholic church was a patron of the arts, before the arts became differentiated from religion in the modern period. Weber pointed out that the arts came to flourish in the West, alongside religion, albeit in constant tension with religious messages of an *ascetic* kind:

> Art takes the function of a this-worldly salvation, no matter how this may be interpreted. It provides a *salvation* from the routines of everyday life, and especially from the increasing pressures of theoretical and practical rationalism.

With this claim to a redemptory function, art begins to compete directly with salvation religion. Every rational religious ethic must turn against this inner-worldly, irrational salvation. For in religion's eyes, such salvation is a realm of irresponsible indulgence and secret lovelessness. As a matter of fact, the refusal of modern men to assume responsibility for moral judgements tends to transform judgements of moral intent into judgements of taste ('in poor taste' instead of 'reprehensible'). The inaccessibility of appeal from aesthetic judgements excludes discussion. This shift from the moral to the aesthetic evaluation of conduct is a common characteristic of intellectualist epochs; it results partly from subjectivist needs and partly from the fear of appearing narrow-minded in a traditionalist and Philistine way.

(Weber, 1991, p. 342)

The areas of moral and social conduct which some modern states have sought to regulate by law, or by education in schools, or in medical and social services, have reflected the cultural histories of the nations, ethnic groups, classes and social movements within them. The legacy of puritanism has thus continued to affect moral regulation in the twentieth century in Britain and in some other western countries despite the decline in formal religion. The next section will look at some of these areas of regulation in Britain since the end of the Second World War.

3   Moral regulation in the post-war period

Since the end of the Second World War, Britain has seen a series of conflicts about the legal *regulation* of sexual activities, the family and marriage, and of *representations* of bodies in what some groups defined as erotic or provocative poses, in films, photographs in magazines, on stage or on television. Two areas, in particular, became of such concern that a Home Office Committee, chaired by Sir John Wolfenden, was set up in 1954 to report on what legal changes were needed to regulate prostitution, defined as women selling sexual gratifications to men, and male homosexuality. Wolfenden reported in 1957, and recommended that neither prostitution nor homosexuality should remain regulated by the *criminal* law, but should become redefined as matters of *private morality* between consenting adults (Home Office, 1957). This public/private distinction derives from liberalism's claim to preserve the *individual's choice* of a way of living free from state regulation whenever possible. Wolfenden was therefore seen as initiating a period of 'liberalization' in the sphere of moral regulation. The recommendations in the Report aimed to transfer both prostitution and male homosexuality from the control of the public criminal law to the civil law, and to remove the regulation of both sets of activities from public to private settings, from streets and parks to bedrooms in private houses. The important point here is that these activities were 'liberalized', but remained regulated – prostitutes could still be arrested for openly soliciting in public spaces and gay men could be arrested for importuning in public places, such as public houses and parks, or for having sexual activities with someone under 21 years old. While the recommendations concerning prostitution were enacted in 1959, no changes in law regulating homosexuality occurred until 1967, when sexual relations between two adult males (over 21 years old) in private were legalized, but the changes when introduced applied only in England and Wales. In Scotland and Northern Ireland the laws governing prostitution and homosexuality were not changed until later. The merchant navy and the armed services were excluded from these changes (Weeks, 1977, p. 176).

Another legal event – the trial in 1960 of the publishers of the unexpurgated edition of D.H. Lawrence's *Lady Chatterley's Lover* (first published abroad in 1928) – came to be seen by many moral conservatives as marking another watershed, a sign of the rising tide of 'permissiveness' in sexual morals. The English and Scottish socio-economic class and gender systems were as much issues in the trial as was the printing of the verb 'fuck' – the ostensible reason for the trial. During the course of the trial, the judge asked the jury to reflect on whether or not this was a book they would wish their own servants to read (Lady Chatterley's lover was one of her 'servants', a gamekeeper)! Sexual intercourse between servants and their employers was frowned upon when it involved males in an upper class family having sexual relations with servant girls; but Lady Chatterley broke with the assumption that upper class women should never have sexual relations with a servant. The anachronistic assumption that most people still had servants and that this class-based morality could be used as a guideline to appropriate moral conduct has come to be seen as a key moment in the long and unfinished debate about the rise of permissiveness and the rate of moral decline in Britain. Intriguingly, Professor Richard Hoggart, who defended the novel, complicated matters by arguing that it was Lawrence, with his direct moral honesty and reverence for the body, who was the 'true' puritan. The trial of *Lady Chatterley's Lover* resulted in the full text of the book being allowed to be bought and sold in England and Wales, and it marked a major moment in English publishing, in that more sexually explicit words could be printed and sold to the general public. However, once again state regulation of printed materials, cinema and theatre was not abolished, only altered. Concerns about what may be read in publications, or seen in theatres and on cinema and television screens, continued to be hotly debated in England and Wales. (Scotland and Northern Ireland have their own distinctive legal systems, which legalized male homosexual relations at later dates.)

The 1960s thus came to represent an important watershed in later debates about moral decline. Especially in the 1980s, during the decade of Conservative governments of which Mrs Thatcher was Prime Minister, the 1960s was represented as the decade when permissive values found a foothold everywhere and when traditional Christian family values were mocked and ridiculed by writers and liberal intellectuals and by plays and films seen on BBC television. The 1960s came to be seen as the decade when 'permissiveness' swept through Britain and other societies.

permissiveness

The backlash against '**permissiveness**' began quite early. In 1964, a housewife and headmistress, Mrs Mary Whitehouse, became a leading figure in the 'Clean-up TV' campaign, which later became the National Viewers' and Listeners' Association (NVALA). These campaigns spread from a concern with broadcast television to include the theatre and the cinema. They reflected the legacy of Calvinist puritanism in the thinking of respectable 'Middle England' and its thrust to control others by passing legislation to change not only moral conduct but the *representations* of what the campaigners considered immoral conduct on stage and screen – as though, in an anticipation of the theory of hyper-reality, representations were as 'real', and therefore as morally corrupting, as the actions they portrayed.

At this point it is instructive to read Newburn's account of the post-war period in Britain, as this period has been portrayed in debates upon morality and regulation in a variety of ways, from being seen as a gain in freedom of choice for individuals, to showing a major decline in moral standards, especially in the sphere of the family, marriage and sexual activity. (Newburn's work was written and published in 1992, and thus has some distance from the events it describes and analyses.)

READING A

Now read Reading A, 'Permissiveness: accounts, discourses and explanations', by Tim Newburn, which you will find at the end of this chapter. As you do so, make notes on the following:

1   What were the main approaches to permissiveness which Newburn identifies?

2   Make brief summaries of each of the five approaches.

3   How 'permissive' were the 1960s in your view?

In general, the 'enemy' for those who adopted the view that permissiveness began in the 1960s was liberal intellectual opinion. The main 'folk devils', as far as the NVALA supporters were concerned, included some liberal theologians and church leaders, such as John Robinson, Bishop of Woolwich (in the Church of England), as well as some television producers and controllers, both of whom had neglected their duty to act as the 'moral guardians' of society and to maintain public standards of 'decency'. One significant point to note is that the Church of England contained, as it still does, bishops whose theology is more liberal-Catholic than Calvinist-Protestant in orientation, although the latter tendency does also exist in the Church of England both among clergy and laity. In Scotland, the Church of Scotland has a legacy of less puritanical Calvinism than that to be found in the Free Church of Scotland. Wales has a well-established Calvinist legacy in some parts of 'chapel culture'. Northern Ireland has a stronger, more militant Calvinist tradition, articulated by such leading Protestant Unionist figures as The Revd Ian Paisley.

NVALA illustrates the persisting legacy of the ascetic Calvinism which Weber had analysed. Calvinism was traditionally suspicious of the theatre, opera, dancing, even music – theatres were closed in the Cromwellian period in England in the mid-seventeenth century; organs were removed from many churches, statues and paintings destroyed. The damage wrought by the Calvinist backlash may still be seen in England's older parish churches and cathedrals, reflecting the violent version of the Calvinist world-view which prevailed in the seventeenth century.

In an important trial, in 1977–8, Mrs Mary Whitehouse, who remained a significant figure in mobilizing conservative moralists in the 1970s and 1980s, brought a successful prosecution against *Gay News* for publishing a poem about the erotic feelings of a Roman soldier looking at Jesus of Nazareth being crucified. This resulted in crippling fines and legal costs for *Gay News* and a major victory for Mary Whitehouse. The NVALA engaged in a continuous monitoring, by hundreds of volunteers, of the output of all the main broadcasting organizations for examples of blasphemy, or the portrayal of violence and explicit sex scenes. Mary Whitehouse at first had no connection with the British political elite, but later the famous campaigner, Lord Longford, the then editor of *The Times*, William Rees-Mogg, the writer and broadcaster, Malcolm Muggeridge, and other leading conservative figures in church, state, politics and public life began to take up the 'causes' which she and her movement highlighted.

FIGURE 2.1
Moral campaigner Mary Whitehouse, co-founder (in January 1964) of the 'Clean-up TV' campaign, at a 'Clean-up TV' press conference. In November 1965, the Clean-up TV campaign became the National Viewers' and Listeners' Association.

The early successes of these moral crusades were influential for the ways in which British Conservative governments of the 1980s and 1990s attempted to regulate in the area of sexual morality. 'Morality' came to be equated with a particular way of living sexually – in a monogamous, married relationship, preferably with no extra-marital liaisons by either partner. The traditional patriarchal family was reaffirmed as the moral bedrock of society. In the Thatcher years, 1979–90, the desirability of a return to these 'Victorian values' was often championed by leading politicians. This was taken up again in the 'Back to Basics' policy of the John Major premiership in the 1993–4 period, when personal moral issues relating to people in public life were highlighted in ways which caught out a number of Conservative members of parliament. In the wake of one of these scandals, a *Daily Telegraph* editorial said the following:

STICK TO BASICS

... the problems which 'Back to Basics' seeks to address are anything but simple, and the political dangers of trying to do so in simplistic terms should have been obvious from the start.

When he launched his campaign, the Prime Minister appeared to be harking back to a time when, it was implied, self-reliance, respect for the law and the supremacy of the nuclear family could be taken for granted. Whether or not that was ever really the case, nobody doubts that these are now among the most complicated issues facing society. Compared to the post-war era, there is a lack of consensus nowadays on which to base social policy. Many people do not take marriage for granted. Many regard single parenthood as not only acceptable, but even desirable. Some are prepared to live off benefits indefinitely.

(*Daily Telegraph*, 7 January 1994)

The call for a return to basic moral values, as understood by Conservatives, fitted somewhat uneasily with the other part of what had constituted Thatcherism in the 1980s: namely, the commitment to a free-market, neo-liberal economic approach (Hall, 1988), which also characterized the presidencies of Ronald Reagan in the United States during the 1980s. This paradox at the heart of neo-liberalism was also evident in the countries of Eastern Europe, including Russia, after the fall of communism in 1989. The paradox was that whilst neo-liberalism fostered free-market forces, freedom, choice and deregulation in the labour market and in economic activities generally, in the area of the family, marriage, morality and sexuality, especially in the United States and Britain, firm controls and state regulation were reinforced. For example, in the 1990s, the British Conservative Government, which favoured privatization and deregulation in the broadcasting field, banned the broadcasting by satellite of erotica transmitted from television stations like Red Hot Dutch, TV Erotica, and XXX TV, operating from northern Europe:

PORN TV BAN

The satellite service XXX TV – formerly known as TV Erotica – was effectively banned by the Government. Virginia Bottomley, the National Heritage Secretary, announced an order yesterday outlawing British supply of 'smartcards' to unscramble its signal, listings or any advertising or support for the pornographic Swedish station.

(*The Times*, 15 November 1995)

Free-market choices were to be regulated, at least in this area of media consumption which touched moral and sexual behaviour, by the state.

3.1 The remoralization of Britain

New technological means of representation and communication based upon photography, telephone, radio, cinema and television – first in its *broad*-casting form, and more recently in its *narrow*-casting forms (satellite, cable and the Internet) – have generated new issues about moral regulation. Similar concerns have emerged each time one of the new media has made a technological breakthrough: from concerns with sex and violence in magazines and comics, to worries about photographs of an immoral kind (nudes, or 'rude' pictures), to concerns about the effects which 'suggestive' moving images on film might have on audiences, to the continuing attempts to regulate, censor, and control what is shown in films, broadcast television programmes, on videos or on satellite channels, to current controversies concerning 'pornography' on cable TV, or on the Internet. Policing the newer technologies has become increasingly difficult, and may prove impossible with the Internet, and even with satellite television. One problem is that the electrical impulses which carry such materials can now travel across nation-state boundaries. Whereas, ever since the founding of the BBC as a 'public service corporation', the British state has traditionally been able to regulate what broadcast television stations produce, both by legal processes and by setting up standards which regulatory committees oversee (initially the governing bodies of the broadcasting organizations, more recently such bodies as the Broadcasting Standards Council and the Independent Television Commission), it has been less easy to control either satellite stations (although the European Union has its own laws to regulate these within Europe), or the Internet, which is freely available to all those using computers linked into it.

There has been vigorous debate about the potential for corruption, or for edification, each time a new technological method capable of representing people in sexually 'meaningful' ways has been developed in the last hundred years or so. Some have welcomed and used the new technologies for non-sexually explicit purposes, as Reith did with BBC radio and television from the 1920s to the 1950s. These might be called 'the respectable users' of the new technologies. Others have been suspicious of new technology, virtually *in toto*. These are the suspicious critics, who see the camera itself as intrusive, who reject television as intrinsically trivializing in its treatment of serious news and current affairs, and serious aesthetic materials from literature to music. This is quite apart from what some have seen as television's potentially corrupting influence upon innocent viewers, especially children, who may have little or no knowledge about sexual matters, or be horrified by the frequent use of violence to obtain desired things. A third group, the free-marketeers, have seen new technologies not only as a means by which entrepreneurs may make profits from producing the equipment and the programmes, films, music, or whatever, but also as a means of empowering the choices of 'ordinary people', whatever they choose to see and hear ('giving the people what they want'), as against traditional cultural elites.

During the 1980s and early 1990s, an innovative form of broadcast television was developed in Britain – Channel 4 – in form and organization a public–private hybrid. It was financed by funds from the main commercial television companies, until it became viable as a channel able to sell its own advertising time. However, it was regulated by and required to meet public service criteria. Channel 4 was designed as an editorial channel, commissioning its programmes from independent producers, and carried the remit to provide programming 'alternatives' to those of the mainstream BBC and ITV channels. From the late 1980s into the early 1990s, Channel 4 broadcast some innovative programmes about sexual and moral issues. Women's issues, including lesbian topics, were given broadcasting time, both in a discussion type of format (talking-heads) and in more visually innovative formats such as those which explored new images of women, as in *Dyke TV*. Gay men's issues were discussed too, as were issues around masculinity, especially in a series first called *Out on Tuesday*, and then *Out*. These programmes provided 'positive' representations of lesbian women and gay men, and were viewed by about one million people – 'good' audience figures for Channel 4. BBC 2 tried an explicitly lesbian/gay series called *Gaytime TV* in 1995 and 1996, but the main broadcasting stations of BBC 1 and ITV rarely, if ever, during this period, targeted such audiences and issues outside of current affairs discussion-type programmes. The Channel 4 series *Out* and the BBC 2 series *Gaytime TV* triggered complaints to the broadcasting authorities and articles, editorials and letters in the press condemning such programmes as immoral and corrupting of the young. This remained a major area of contention and debate in moral discourses about the contents of broadcast television, in Britain and elsewhere, during the 1980s and 1990s. One reason is perhaps because such programmes portrayed *difference* in sexual conduct. The very portrayal of some people with non-heterosexual desires on public television was seen by conservative movements as inherently corrupting for young viewers and children, as they reached puberty. Such programmes, by the simple fact of being broadcast, were said to undermine those parents and institutions (schools, churches and youth groups) seeking to socialize young people into traditional, heterosexual, 'normal' forms of sexual morality. The value of tolerance of difference became unacceptable in such circumstances, in the eyes of traditional moralists. This is as much a debate about 'the family' as it is about television. Not all parents control their children's viewing, nor, with new technologies (crucially here, video-recorders and computers) are they all able to control what the young view. Thus, many traditional moralists seek to prevent broadcasts of the kind which explore sexualities of a non-traditional, non-heterosexual, type, as a way of reinforcing a 'family values' morality.

ACTIVITY 1

What do *you* think about these powerfully contested issues?

1   Do you think that public broadcast television should show programmes which portray situations of family breakdown, single parenting or marital infidelity.

2   Should Channel 4 broadcast programmes about gay and lesbian issues?

3   Should BBC 2 broadcast such programmes, or should it be different in this respect from Channel 4?

4   Do you think that women's lives and issues about their dual roles in paid work and in domestic situations are portrayed, or discussed, sufficiently on broadcast television? Try to think of specific programmes in which you recall such issues being dealt with.

4   The feminist debate about pornography

The legal, political and social position of women and the regulation of women's lives have been major areas of moral and political struggle and debate since at least the seventeenth century. The claims that women could inherit property, or have the vote, or be paid the same as men in manual or professional occupations, have all been areas of moral and political contention in the West. **Patriarchy**, in the broad sense of 'rule by men', has been both a widely-accepted set of social, economic, political–legal regulatory practices and a set of cultural moral values, beliefs and symbolic representations, in the West and elsewhere in the world, for centuries.

patriarchy

These practices and values have often been linked to major religious world-views, as in traditional forms of Christianity, Judaism, Islam and Hinduism, for example. Feminism in the West, on the other hand, has also been a multifaceted movement since the seventeenth century. Feminists have expanded the basic liberal idea of equality of all citizens (originally, of course, mainly men of property) so that it has come to be seen as increasingly applicable to women of all social classes and ethnic groups.

The first wave of modern **feminism** as a social movement can be traced back to the late eighteenth and the nineteenth centuries. The work of Mary Wollstonecraft, though critical of the subordination of women in marriage, for example, placed an emphasis upon the rational control of sexuality; there was caution expressed towards abortion, and a general concern for 'fallen women' (Weeks, 1985, p. 207). Second wave feminism, in the first

feminism

part of the twentieth century, often accepted the legitimacy of separate spheres, whilst being concerned with advancing economic and political–legal rights for women, largely within a moral–political framework derived from revised forms of liberalism, with their emphasis upon justice, equality and reform through the legislative methods of parliamentary democracy. More recent forms of feminism, the third wave of the late twentieth century, whilst sometimes continuing the liberal emphases on equality and justice *within* advanced forms of western capitalism, often made a more sweeping and wide-ranging critique of the patriarchal character of society and the many-faceted aspects of women's subordination. This third wave of feminism has been more open to using other philosophical and theoretical frameworks to expand its case for a theory-grounded reconstruction of relations between the sexes, such as some forms of Marxism (in the tendency known as socialist-feminism) and psychoanalysis (as in Juliet Mitchell's seminal, but also much criticized, work, *Psychoanalysis and Feminism*, first published in 1974).

Feminists have also established their own discursive formations which have been developed precisely as critiques of liberalism, conservatism, Marxism and psychoanalysis, all of which have been seen as flawed because they remain reflections of patriarchal values and social–cultural practices to varying degrees. For example, although early Marxism promised a structural change in the economic, political and social position of women, it did so only by subordinating sexual and gender questions to the overarching demands of class politics. In addition, actually existing forms of communist Marxism in various states, such as China, or Cuba, often fell short of the promise of full equality between women and men, consigning women to maintaining the dual role of worker and home-maker.

During the 1980s, some feminists began to develop a critique of one major aspect of western culture which seemed to them to epitomize the oppression, indeed, abuse, of women – namely pornography.

pornography
Definitions of '**pornography**' are themselves always in contention. What might appear to some as erotica – harmless fun – appears to others as an exploitation, in the form of a 'pornographic' representation, of women's already vulnerable position. For some critics of western culture, the use of women in many widely disseminated advertisements, in newspapers, magazines, and on television, was seen as 'pornographic' because of the display of women's bodies in ways designed exclusively to incite, arouse or titillate men. In such pornographic representations, it is argued, men symbolically expropriated women's bodies for their own pleasure in just the same way as, in the home, they exploited the domestic labour of women. The women in such images became objects, subjected to the powerful gaze of the male voyeur, in much the same way as prostitutes were required to serve the sexual needs of their clients. This kind of pornography, it was argued, not only demeaned and degraded women, but was also an implicit attack on marriage and the family. By setting women symbolically within the power of

men, pornographic images licensed the male degradation of, and ultimately violence against, women. Furthermore, the models themselves were seen as exploited – paid less than the market price of the photographs because the photographers, publishers, sellers and manufacturers of the goods being advertised – all principally male – made a profit from women's degradation whilst not adequately compensating them. The careers of the models were also short, for the market in pornography systematically privileged younger, more sexually attractive women.

Although the term 'pornography' appears to refer to the publication in films, videos, magazines, photographs, etc. of sexually explicit or arousing images of women, the term has been extended to include many aspects of what now passes as acceptable forms of advertising in the modern West, much of which makes use of the sexually attractive and inviting female body.

The term 'pornography' might also be used in a third way to refer to visual materials of a more sexually explicit type, involving some form of violence. For not only are 'pornographic' materials available which show explicit sexual intercourse between women and men; there are also materials which contain representations of a sado-masochistic (S and M) type, in which violence of some kind appears to be being perpetrated upon a victim – typically, but not always, the woman in the scene. Different writers, both feminists and others, have taken distinct positions on the desirability of regulating and controlling each of these three main forms of what might be termed 'pornography'.

A powerful case for the regulation and control of all three forms of pornography has been made by the American feminist writers, Andrea Dworkin and Catherine MacKinnon. They argued that legislation to regulate 'pornography' was required on the grounds that: '...pornography is central to the way in which men subordinate women. Pornography, it is argued, both depicts and causes violence against women' (Segal, 1992, p. 5).

The meaning of the term 'violence' in this quotation is not as easy to decipher as one might think. Once one begins to think about the question of why using violence towards another person is morally objectionable, outside of situations of organized warfare, the claim that it is undesirable because it denies the personhood of the victim seems persuasive. It is treating the other as an *object* for the pleasure of the one who observes what is being done, even if this is done at one remove, as it were, by observing a film or a still photograph. The meaning of the term 'violence' is extended from direct physical force of some kind inflicted on another, to include almost any *representation* which has as its main purpose portraying the other as a fantasized *object* for purposes of sexual gratification.

It is worth noting that this kind of argument is often developed from a philosophical basis in secular humanism, where the concept of 'person', as opposed to 'object', derives from the basic notion of a human person as defined in humanism. On the other hand, it could also be developed from

Marxism in which the photographed model is seen as a saleable commodity, sold for profit for the photographer or publisher of the pornographic material. Within Marxism, such material is a form of 'commodity fetishism', where human value has been reduced to exchange value, as distinct from a photograph in a family album, or a family videocassette, which is mainly for personal use – a form of 'use value'. The important point to note here is that the *same* political argument can be derived from very *different* moral and philosophical traditions. Arguments within feminism against pornography could well be – and were – derived from both Marxist and liberal-humanist philosophical and moral premises. The case for regulating and controlling pornographic representations was also advanced by many traditional or morally conservative groups. But in this case, the argument was based on very different moral and philosophical premises from those adopted by the feminist protagonists. Let us explore these complexities of moral debate further.

In 1983, Andrea Dworkin and Catherine MacKinnon put forward a draft bill (an ordinance) for Minneapolis city council based on the idea that pornography causes harm to women, because it frequently reinforces men's view of women as 'objects' and because the pornography industry, which was enormous in dollar terms, exploited the women who worked in it as models (see Chester and Dickey, 1988, pp. 258–60). As Liz Kelly wrote:

> Dworkin and MacKinnon begin from a belief that pornography directly harms women (in both its production and consumption) and that it is a central element in maintaining male dominance. They argue that pornography is a form of sexual discrimination because it is a specific harm which has an impact on all areas of women's lives. The ordinance lists the direct harms to women as: 'dehumanization, sexual exploitation, forced sex, forced prostitution, physical injury, and social and sexual terrorism and inferiority presented as entertainment'. The ordinance also specifies that through the promotion of contempt for women, pornography is also implicated in women's economic inequality, the prevalence of sexual violence and in restricting women's freedom as citizens, i.e. women's equal exercise of rights as guaranteed under the US Constitution.
>
> Pornography is defined in the 1985 draft of the ordinance as:
>
> ... the graphic sexually explicit subordination of women, through pictures and/or in words, that also includes one of the following:
>
> 1   women are presented dehumanized as sexual objects, things or commodities; or
>
> 2   women are presented as sexual objects who enjoy pain or humiliation; or
>
> 3   women are presented as sexual objects who experience sexual pleasure in being raped; or
>
> 4   women are presented as sexual objects tied up or cut up or mutilated or bruised or physically hurt; or

5   women are presented in postures or positions of sexual submission, servility or display; or

6   women's body parts – including but not limited to vaginas, breasts, or buttocks – are exhibited such that women are reduced to those parts; or

7   women are presented as whores by nature; or

8   women are presented being penetrated by objects or animals; or

9   women are presented in scenarios of degradation, injury, torture, shown as filthy or inferior, bleeding, bruised or hurt in a context which makes these conditions sexual.

Drafted as a civil rights law the ordinance empowers individual or groups of women (in very limited circumstances men) to take a case against the producers/distributors of pornography. To take a case the woman has to show that the magazine/book/film/video/photograph is both subordinating and covered by the definition of pornography. She also has to make one of four charges to show that she was directly harmed: that she was coerced into participating in the production of pornography; that she was forced to view pornography; that she was assaulted as a direct result of pornography. In each of these cases the pornography in question has to be specified. The final charge is for trafficking; here the woman appears for women as a group and the case rests on demonstrating that the public availability of pornography constitutes a violation of women's civil rights.

To take account of the complexity of women's involvement in the sex industry, thirteen conditions were cited which *are not* acceptable as a defence in cases brought under the ordinance. They include: previously appearing in porn, signing a contract, that no physical force was used and/ or that payment was received. Because cases would be heard in civil courts, there are no criminal penalties – the only sanctions available to the court are fines and stopping the production/sale of any pornography that is found to be subordinating within the definition, and directly implicated in harm. Where fines are imposed these are to be paid direct to the woman/ women taking the case.

(Kelly, 1988, pp. 54–5)

It is interesting to note that, although Dworkin and MacKinnon agreed on the definition of pornography and the circumstances in which the ordinance could be legally applied, they came from very different philosophical traditions within feminism. MacKinnon is a liberal and 'legal' rights feminist: Dworkin is a radical, anti-patriarchal feminist.

There was an additional point made in the original ordinance which is omitted in Kelly's discussion. This was the following: 'The use of men, children or transsexuals in the place of women ... is pornography for purposes of ... this statute.' How important is this extra provision? Does it matter that it was omitted by some feminists in subsequent discussions?

The role of men in pornography could mean one of three kinds of representation. Men could be shown using, or abusing, women which was included in the original debate about pornography. Men might, however, be shown in submissive roles; for example, receiving the cane from a woman, or as 'slaves' to women mistresses. Thirdly, men could be shown in homosexual pornography in sexual, or sado-masochistic, roles with other men. These types of pornographic representations could be regulated too. Lesbian pornography is a further complicating dimension in the debate among feminists; here the problem is that men are purchasers and viewers of such pornographic representations as well as some women. No viable distinction, therefore, can be made between lesbians' use of pornography (erotica to them) and men's abuse of the same material.

In the debates about pornography, censorship and how best to regulate such material, some feminists became critical of the attempt to regulate pornography at all. They argued that 'erotica' should not be regulated by law, and that one person's pornography, was another person's erotica.

One group of feminists formed the Feminists' Anti-Censorship Task Force (FACT). This group was involved in an acrimonious debate, in the USA, between the pro- and anti-pornography censorship groups. A similar anti-censorship campaign group was organized in the UK. Liz Kelly outlined the FACT disagreements with Dworkin and MacKinnon:

> The FACT brief rests on two fundamental disagreements with Dworkin and MacKinnon: that pornography is not central in maintaining women's oppression and that feminists should not be involved in campaigning for legal reform which restricts freedom of speech. Choosing 'anti-censorship' as part of their name reflects their assumption that the ordinance would result in censorship; ... There are six basic points in the FACT brief:
>
> - Pornography is not central in maintaining gender inequality. The ordinance does not address the more important ways in which women are denied equality. Feminist energies should be directed at acts not images; thus we should focus on the acts of coercion in pornography, rape and battery, which are covered by already existing legislation.
> - The terms 'subordinating', 'degrading' and 'sexual objectification' are not defined in the ordinance; thus judges will be able to define them. FACT suggest that this may result in feminist art, self-help health guides, and so on being prosecuted.
> - The ordinance is sexist, as it represents men and women as fundamentally different. It suggests women are weak, in need of protection, unable to make their own decisions. Women appear as helpless victims who do not seek or enjoy sex and who cannot enter into legally binding agreements. It presumes all men are conditioned by pornography to commit acts of aggression and believe mysoginist myths.

- The ordinance assumes a simple link between words/images and behaviour. Men learn about gender roles in many places; the family is probably more important than pornography. Porn does not explain violence against women which existed before it was widely available.

- Women's experiences with pornography are mixed; some women get erotic pleasure from it. The meanings of pornography are varied, it can be an affirmation – particularly for sexual minorities.

- There are serious dangers in restricting sexually explicit speech. The inevitable alliance with the New Right on this issue is disturbing.

(ibid., pp. 55–6)

Other women however remained unconvinced by FACT's approach. For example, Catherine Itzin, writing in a British, as distinct from a US context, wrote:

From its beginning in the reign of Henry VIII, censorship was concerned with protecting both State and Church against religious and political attack, rather than with questions of good taste or bad language. It was imposed as part of the attempt to stamp out Catholic resistance to the Reformation and to affirm loyalty to Henry as head of Church and State. The stage was feared as a religious pulpit and as a political platform, and that remained the case for over four hundred years.

The purpose of censorship from beginning to end has been *political*: suppression.

...

It is not surprising, then, that the liberal and left position with regard to censorship has always been consistently against it, and in favour of individual freedom of speech and movement. On that level, it is not surprising either, that the 'liberal' Williams Committee (1979) would conclude in favour of the freedom to produce, sell and consume pornography. ...

For myself, I have campaigned in this very same left/liberal tradition against censorship in the theatre in the pages of *Tribune,* and *Theatre Quarterly* in the seventies, and in my book *Stages in the Revolution: Political Theatre in Britain Since 1968* (1981, 1982). Now my views have changed. I will continue to campaign against the censorship of such plays as (Howard Brenton's) *The Romans in Britain*. But I will now actively campaign for the censorship of pornography. I see no contradiction whatsoever in these positions. For I have now had an insight into the *meaning* of pornography, and, significantly, into the *meaning* of Howard Brenton's play in relation to pornography. I can see now that the 'freedom' of pornography is posited on the 'censorship' of women: that the price of the 'freedom' of pornography is posited on the 'censorship' of women: that the price of the 'freedom' given to those who publish and purchase pornography (men) is freedom denied to its objects (women).

...

Pornography is violence. The violence is not just in the exploitation and degradation of real women (and children) in its making, but in the fear induced in all women by the knowledge that such images of themselves as violated objects exist, and in its validation *for* men, *of* men in their role of oppressors.

The images of pornography – whether they are on billboards and television screens (women's bodies used to sell commodities) or come from under the counter (where women's bodies are the commodity) – instruct men in how to see women as dehumanized, as objects; instruct men in the value (lessness) of women, in the exploitation of women, in violence against women.

There still persists an 'illusion' that there is no provable connection between pornography and violence (as the Williams Committee concluded, for example). The truth – the irony – is that pornography *is* violence. Against women by men. The violence is institutionalized and it is internalized (by women, which accounts in part for their 'tolerance' and sometimes 'participation' in it).

(Itzin, 1988, pp. 41–3)

The Williams Committee in the above quotation refers to the Committee set up in Britain in the 1970s under Professor Bernard Williams to examine the issues raised in regulating pornography. The report was published in 1979. It recommended 'the greatest possible freedom from censorship combined with rather stringent restrictions in the open display of material'. This led to the Indecent Displays Act of 1981, which has rarely been used in prosecutions because of the difficulty involved in defining in law the term 'indecent'.

ACTIVITY 2

What do you think about these various arguments concerning the regulation of pornography? Which position most closely reflects your own position and *why*?

The feminist campaign against pornography became somewhat confused in the minds of the general public in the USA and in Britain by the development of a right-wing, Christian campaign against it. This religiously backed campaign drew upon the discourse of puritanism, which has been revitalized in Britain, the USA, Canada and Australia from time to time, as was discussed in section 2 above.

Within religious-based discourses, pornography was seen as either simply immoral, as evil, because it dealt with sexuality, or as falling short of the ideal of sex (i.e. that it should be linked to the purposes of procreation within the framework of the monogamous patriarchal family). Those who define pornography as immoral from within a religious discourse have been vociferous in recent decades in taking political action to try to have its dissemination regulated by law. The moral majority in the United States in the 1980s, and in Britain from the 1960s onwards, in groups like the National Viewers' and Listeners' Association (NVALA), played a significant role in campaigning around such issues. For the reasons outlined above, these religious pressure groups have sometimes been in a tactical alliance with those feminists who were opposed to pornography, albeit for very different reasons and from a very different (i.e. secular) philosophical basis. The movement for the regulation of 'pornography', however defined, has therefore been a complex one. The anti-pornography movement has been underpinned by a *variety* of philosophical viewpoints, some religious, many secular, which have led some women and men to call for more vigorous legislation to regulate 'pornography' in magazines, newspapers, in the theatre, the cinema, on broadcast television, on cable and satellite, and on the Internet.

However, not only have some feminists produced a plausible case for more regulation of 'pornographic representations'. As we have seen, other feminists have argued, equally persuasively, the diametrically opposite case. Some feel that pornography is not so important an issue, nor an area of such significance, that feminists should seek to regulate it by legal–political means to the degree that some have claimed, as we saw above. A debate has developed *within* feminism about how important or otherwise the issue of pornography should be seen to be (Wilson, 1992). Was it a manifestation of patriarchy, the crystallization of men's power over women, typical of a male-dominated culture and built into the power relations between the female models portrayed in these images and the typically male purveyors and purchasers of pornographic materials? Or was it, at worst, a symptom of deeper levels of oppression of women by men, at best, relatively harmless erotic material? The much stronger anti-regulation case advanced by feminists was derived from two other, more powerful, moral premises. The first is the libertarian argument based on freedom of speech, which is deeply suspicious of any attempt to control or censor the free expression of views, however offensive. But the most radical position was the feminist *defence of pornography*, on the ground that women have for centuries been denied the free expression of their sexuality, including sexual fantasies which are not harmful to anyone, which have remained an area of male privilege; and that one of the most subversive feminist demands is therefore to insist on a woman's right to sexual pleasure, including, if necessary, the pleasure of looking at sexually erotic images.

Lynne Segal wrote in her analysis of this major debate within feminism: 'Pro-sex or anti-sex, Western cultures remain sex-obsessed. This is why the issue of pornography just won't go away' (1992, p. 1). She drew upon research, as well as political debate, in her discussion, which you should now read.

READING B

Read Reading B, 'Sex exposed: sexuality and the pornography debate', by Lynne Segal. As you do so, make notes on the following questions:

1   What are the main positions identified by Segal which have affected the debate about pornography since the 1960s in the English-speaking world?

2   Does the evidence Segal describes in her piece support the claim: 'Pornography is the theory, and rape the practice'?

3   Why do you think that, as some studies found, states which were relatively tolerant towards soft pornography, had a better record on equal opportunities for women?

4   What weight do you think should be given to some sex workers' claim that the anti-pornography campaign is based in the life experiences of white, middle-class feminists, which ignores the economic, cultural and legal problems of people with a different social position and life-experience?

One area, of 'pornography' not discussed very explicitly thus far is that of the regulation of homosexuality and of representations containing gay sex in the cinema, on TV, cable, satellite and the Internet. The moral panic about AIDS during the 1980s led to calls for greater regulation of gay sexuality (see Weeks, 1985) and for increased regulation and vigilance towards gay pornography in Britain and parts of the USA, even though it was argued by some gays that pornography was needed more, not less, in the changed circumstances brought about by AIDS. The next section will examine the regulation of homosexuality in Britain and the representation of lesbian, gay and bisexual issues on British television in particular.

5   The regulation and representation of homosexuality

Since the debate about the Wolfenden Report (1957) and the subsequent changes in the law regulating male homosexuality in particular, which followed in 1967 (discussed in section 3 and in the associated Reading A by Tim Newburn), there have been some important changes in general public awareness of, and even tolerance towards, homosexuality. This increase in awareness has been in part due to newspaper coverage of the issues, often of a negative, critical kind. The increase in tolerance towards homosexuality has been more evident in broadcasting on radio and television, partly because broadcasters, unlike newspaper journalists, are regulated in ways which aim to ensure that a *balance* is maintained in political and current affairs programmes. Newspapers are regulated by the Press Council, but ensuring *balance* is not part of its brief as it is for publicly broadcast television (including the commercial channels).

As Newburn described in *Permission and Regulation* (1992), there have been social movements and pressure groups such as the NVALA, as well as some church leaders and politicians in all the political parties, all of whom have pressed for varying degrees of legal regulation of 'erotic' or 'pornographic' representations in the theatre, cinema, magazines, television, videos, and on the Internet. In particular, representations of gay men and lesbian women have frequently been the focus of calls for legal regulation in the media and the theatre. In 1980, for instance, there was an outcry over Howard Brenton's play, *The Romans in Britain*, which was performed at the National Theatre, mainly because it contained a scene in which Roman soldiers raped a young man, a Celt. The Greater London Council threatened to cut off its grant to the National Theatre, and did reduce it in the following year (Itzin, 1988).

The debates about the legal changes regulating male homosexuality and prostitution in the 1950s and 1960s, and those about what should or should not be represented in various media, involved a conflict between two broad philosophical positions – *conservatism* and *liberalism*.

Those who objected to legalizing male homosexual acts in private for adults over 21 years, and subsequently for those over 18 years, did so on the whole from a conservative moral-philosophical position. For example, in the 1950s, the then Lord Chief Justice, Lord Devlin, argued that most ordinary people found male homosexuality abhorrent and that the law should reflect such widely held values (Devlin, 1959). Some church leaders, particularly in the Church of England, the established church, some of whose bishops sit in the House of Lords, held the view that the law should uphold what they saw as Christian values, which condemned homosexuality as sinful. Moral conservatives held that the church, the law and the state had a duty to uphold as far as possible the family, marriage and monogamy. This also entailed making some acts, such as divorce, which undermined the moral basis of society, more difficult if not impossible. The same principle was applied to homosexuality – it was sinful and this should be reflected in the laws of a Christian nation.

The Wolfenden Report (1957) had been based upon a different philosophical position, that of liberalism, which held that the laws of the state should not be based upon, or uphold, one increasingly contentious moral philosophy. Furthermore, the state had no right to interfere in the *private* lives of adults. The argument in Wolfenden rested upon the distinction between the public sphere and the private (Hall, 1980).

These two philosophical positions – conservatism and liberalism – may be seen at work in the debates and conflicts over what should or should not be broadcast on public television, or shown in cinemas or theatres. The NVALA was influenced by the conservative view that the state had a duty to maintain Christian moral standards, and that media representations of homosexuality in particular should be regulated. Those in the media – television, cinema, the theatre, book and periodical publishing – typically held a more liberal position. This entailed that, within the limits of 'decency' sexuality in all its forms, heterosexual, gay and lesbian, could, indeed should, be explored in these media (Weeks, 1995).

There have been other philosophies at work in the area of what the media may explore, as we saw in the debate about pornography. Feminism, Marxism, radical lesbianism and, more recently, 'queer-theory' are examples of such alternatives, and these voices may be found too in debate over the issues we shall explore below. These positions have, however, been less influential at the level of policy-making for broadcast television than conservative and liberal moral values. The major debates about broadcast television programmes which have addressed lesbian and gay issues have been between liberalism and conservatism.

Overall, it has been various forms of liberalism which have underpinned much of the work of broadcasters on lesbian and gay issues, mainly because conservatism would not explore such issues on public television. However, in its coverage of the debates about decriminalizing male homosexuality in the 1950s and early 1960s, BBC television tried to balance the studio discussions about the desirability or otherwise of legal reform by having someone to represent the conservative, no change, position. In the early days of BBC radio, a Reithian, conservative, Christian philosophy had been hegemonic. It was the development of television, from the 1950s onwards, which began to move the BBC towards a less Reithian, more liberal, position. Lord Reith had been the first Director-General of the BBC (1927–38), in an era dominated by radio, and had set conservative, Christian moral standards for the new organization to uphold. After the war, a tension arose between the BBC Governors, symbolized by Broadcasting House (the home of the national radio networks), and the upstart television service, based first in Alexandra Palace, and then in a purpose-built Television Centre in West London.

Indeed, it could be argued that the early period of television broadcast by the BBC, before commercial television developed in the late 1950s, had played a role in building up a realization of the need for a change in the law regulating homosexuality between men. For example, in 1954, Lord Boothby, in a debate on BBC television, had called for the setting up of a Royal Commission to look into how the law regulating homosexuality between men might be changed. This may not seem very radical to later generations, but it was a daring debate to hold in that period, just over a year after the Coronation of Queen Elizabeth II, in which family values and Britain as a Christian country had been ritually celebrated.

The BBC continued to broadcast other discussions about homosexual law reform until the 1967 legal change occurred in England and Wales. From that time onward, more plays and films about lesbians and gay men were broadcast, although some programmes had included lesbian and gay characters before that date. For example, *A for Andromedia* (1961) and *Woman in White* (1957) had included references to lesbianism and homosexuality.

With the change in the law, both Independent Television and BBC TV began to broadcast more plays, films, and comedies which featured lesbians and gay men. Examples included *Are You Being Served?*, with John Inman playing a comic role as an openly gay shop assistant, and Kenneth Williams as a 'camp' character in the *Carry On* films.

The legal change of 1967 had legitimated public, broadcast television not only covering political debates about homosexuality, but allowing an exploration of male homosexual characters, frequently represented as comic camp characters or as 'drag queens' (such as John Inman, in his role in *Are You Being Served?*, and Dame Edna Everidge). One of the first programmes in which a gay man was featured as a break with this tradition of camp, or drag, was *The Naked Civil Servant* (1975; BBC 2). This 'starred' Quentin Crisp and was based on his life-history in which he talked about his life since his move from London to live in New York. The programme was neither a comedy show, nor a drag show, nor a current-affairs style of documentary. It broke new ground by portraying an entertaining, if somewhat eccentric, gay man talking about his way of life as a whole in a sympathetic way. It placed his sexuality in the wider context of his approach to living, as in his enjoyment of walking around New York compared with 'up-tight London'. However, the programme did not fully break with the stereotypical representation of the 'camp' gay, and could be viewed as confirming it in part.

It has been the television soaps, in particular *Brookside* (Channel 4), which included a scene of two lesbians kissing, and *EastEnders* (BBC 1), which portrayed an 'ordinary' man, Colin, who happened to be gay, in a relationship with a younger man, which have moved away from camp, or butch lesbian, representations, and introduced characters who are not 'larger than life', but are regular characters who happen to be gay or lesbian. They are not portrayed as sick, or any more immoral than other people.

The arrival of HIV and AIDS in the 1980s led to both documentary-style television programmes for a general audience, and debates about the issue on youth and schools television. In 1996, for example, *EastEnders* had a male character who was HIV positive, and was portrayed telling people around him about his condition. There were also government-sponsored advertisements about the possibility of catching the AIDS/HIV virus which were broadcast on television in the 1980s. Other programmes more specifically oriented to a gay and lesbian audience also emerged in this period. The advertisements about AIDS and HIV were also included in youth programmes, not only in the emerging gay/lesbian television programmes. Television played a more educative role in the AIDS debate compared with the more sensationalist style of the popular press, with its headlines, for example, about a 'gay plague' hitting Britain.

The first main television series which was advertised as being a programme explicitly for gay people (men and women) was broadcast by London Weekend Television (LWT) in 1980. It was produced by the London Minorities Programme Unit (LMU). This series called *Gay Life* was studied as part of a research project at the Open University, funded by the Economic and Social Research Council, which began in 1995. The research involved tracing press and public reactions to television programmes which address sexual issues, including representations of lesbians and gay men. The *Gay Life* programmes, being the first explicitly gay and lesbian broadcast television series, albeit in the London Weekend Television area only, attracted substantial national press coverage.

The series of eleven programmes began on 11 February, 1980 at 11.30 p.m. They were described as 'topical programmes which reported on gay life rather than trying to explain it' (LWT spokesperson, *Daily Star*, 17 January 1980). One tabloid referred to the programme as a 'TV Shocker' which had scenes of 'homosexuals kissing, cuddling and dancing together in gay clubs and discos' (*Daily Star*, 17 January). Mary Whitehouse stated that 'homosexuals had a right to be heard, but the programmes had to be closely monitored to make sure that there was no attempt at converting people to that way of life' (*Daily Express*, 4 July 1978). A gay newspaper gave the series a more positive reception, stating that it was a 'candid look at the realities of gay life' and a 'pioneering move' since it was the first of its kind in Britain, Europe and most of the world.

The producer, Michael Attwell, felt that the series would have all the major TV companies keeping a close watch on its progress, and assessing the potential future for such programmes (*Gay News*, 20 February 1980). The opening programme looked at lesbians and gays in the Civil Service, followed by programmes on gay parenting, the nature of stereotyping, as well as items on gay lifestyle. Attwell explained that 'the philosophy underlying *Gay Life* is that homosexuality is not a disease or a weakness. Homosexuals form a substantial part of London's population and are entitled to live their lives without becoming the victims of prejudice' (*Now*, 14 February 1980).

There were some problems, however. For example, some lesbian feminists threatened to boycott the series due to the use of a male voice-over in a particular programme dealing with lesbian issues. They wanted women's views and positions presented without being negated by 'patriarchal comment' (*Gay News*, 20 March 1980). The Campaign for Homosexual Equality, along with other organizations, also met with the London Minorities Unit to express concern over the series which they felt needed to give a truer representation of their lifestyles and problems. A gay newspaper, commenting on the brouhaha surrounding *Gay Life*, rather pragmatically pointed out that, before they boycotted the first ever British series produced for them, gays and lesbians should realize that this would affect other TV companies' attitudes to similar enterprises (*Gay News*, 20 March 1980).

Ratings for the series showed that over 350,000 homes were tuning in – the London Minorities Unit were amazed by the high audience figures for a late night 'current affairs' programme. By the end of six of the eleven programmes the LMU had received over 160 calls – the ratio of congratulations to abuse being three to one. Letters to LWT were also mainly supportive, one third being negative or abusive.

In May 1980, at the end of the series, Barry Cox, Head of the Current Affairs Unit at LWT, stated that *Gay Life* had forged a highly disciplined and objective style. The wider implications for the future of minority TV, he maintained, would and could only reach full expression when video, cable, satellite and disc so fragmented the broadcasting industry that it became as pluralistic and commercial as print (*Listener*, 8 May 1996). However the development of Channel 4 in 1982 provided a new national television station, set up to cater for specific minority groups, not as a mass audience station.

Following a great deal of discussion about whether to launch a magazine programme dealing with homosexual concerns, Channel 4 started its first season of programmes for gay/lesbian audiences in August 1986 with a major eight-week season of Films On Four, initially due to be called *In the Pink*, although some days before it started the title was dropped. The programme-makers were critical of the move which they saw as a cowardly one: that is, Channel 4 were going to have a gay season but without the public realizing (*Guardian,* 20 October 1986). By November 1986, Channel 4 ran another film season, this time titled *Six Of Hearts*, representing profiles of six people who were gay. Mary Whitehouse reacted to this decision by writing to Jeremy Isaacs, then Chief Executive of the channel, expressing her anxiety about showing positive images of gay people which could undermine attempts to deal with the serious threat of AIDS. Both Isaacs and the programme-makers attacked Mrs Whitehouse's criticisms as 'mirroring the prejudices that the media relies on' (*Gay Times*, September 1986).

In February 1988, Channel 4 used an interactive process to derive ideas from its prospective audience for a new and original gay series. Readers of *Gay Times* were asked to contribute any ideas they might have for a magazine programme. *Out on Tuesday*, as the series was originally called (this was subsequently shortened to *Out*), began broadcasting on 14 February, 1989. The emphasis was more on the aesthetic than on political debate in studio, and the series articulated cultural differences that existed within the gay community itself. The latter were not seen as an homogeneous minority but as a group with their own different and distinct identities and prejudices.

Produced by an independent production company, Abseil Productions, all the producers and editors of *Out on Tuesday* were women. Celebrities like Ian McKellen and Beatrix Campbell were used to introduce each programme, which took the format of a magazine programme with three or four slots on different topics. The female team stated that they detested the 'freemasonry and exclusiveness of gay politics' and therefore sought to speak to as many groups as possible (*Capital Gay*, 27 January 1989). Producer Clare Bevan emphasized that the series was about the complexity of people's experiences of being gay and would challenge the idea that there is only one kind of gay person, politics or sensibility. The series editor, Mandy Merck, pointed out that the key move was away from victimology towards a more cheeky, exuberant and less self-pitying approach (*Capital Gay*, 27 January 1989).

Following the first programme of *Out on Tuesday*, Channel 4 received over 200 telephone calls from viewers about the programme – 160 welcomed the programme while only 40 found fault with its being broadcast. In March 1990, *Out on Tuesday* went into a second series which was shown at the earlier time of 9 p.m. This series attempted to redress some of the faults found with the first series – it tackled AIDS in two short films and looked at bisexuality. A third series, simply called *Out*, followed in June 1991, a fourth in 1992, a fifth in 1994 and a sixth in 1995.

BBC 2 broadcast a special evening of television in November 1991 called *Saturday Night Out*, that devoted four-and-a-half hours of a Saturday evening to documentary and entertainment pieces about homosexuality (e.g. *Gay Rock -'n'-Roll Years*, and *The Naked Civil Servant* – first shown on BBC 2 in 1975). One tabloid said, 'Remember it was our money that paid for the first hours of gay propaganda' (*Sun,* 18 November 1991). Another said, 'Is it necessary for a major channel to devote a whole evening to lauding a minority sexual taste? At the very least on moral and medical grounds, shouldn't a brief announcement precede this gay gala on the box?' (*Daily Star*, 16 November 1991). The Controller of BBC 2, Alan Yentob, stated that he did not see his job as chasing ratings and that he wanted the channel to provide a distinct alternative to BBC 1 (*Daily Express*, 18 November 1991).

Later, in 1995 and 1996, BBC 2 broadcast a series of six programmes about issues of interest to lesbians and gay men – *Gaytime TV*. These programmes produced some protests from Mary Whitehouse and other moral campaigners, partly on the grounds that the BBC in particular had a duty to spend licence fees more carefully, and to protect and uphold decent, family moral values. According to the Head of the Documentary Unit, the series was designed to expunge the idea that the BBC reacted badly to *Saturday Night Out.*

Channel 4, on the other hand, was not open to these kinds of criticism because of its alternative minority remit. It was funded by advertising, not by a licence fee. Furthermore, the 1981 Broadcasting Act explicitly stated that Channel 4 should be a channel of 'innovation and experiment in form and content'. It was also to cater for minorities not covered by the main broadcasting channels. The 1981 Act thus paved the way for the first public broadcast television programmes for gays and lesbians, as distinct from the cable or satellite systems which were set up for a time in the 1980s in the USA and parts of Europe.

In the last six series from 1989–94, Channel 4's *Out* covered issues which ranged from AIDS to Gay Olympics, to lesbians' growing interest in country and western music, to homophobia in Hollywood. The commissioning editors of *Out* have always emphasized that it was a series created by gay people, and essentially for the gay and lesbian community. Some viewers objected to homosexuality being given air-time or, in their eyes, being 'celebrated' on television; most responses by telephone, letter or fax, however, were positive in so much as they either applauded the series and the issues covered, or offered suggestions for further programme features.

A multitude of issues have been covered in the *Out* series which allowed the gay and lesbian community to share their diverse experiences and feelings with a wider audience. Some of the more celebratory items of the series picked up on different lifestyles and interests of groups within the gay/ lesbian community and mass celebrations of gayness. For example, two items, one in 1991 and the other in 1994, focused on the Gay Pride March in London and how it had united and liberated gays and lesbians by giving them a day/event to celebrate their sexuality. In 1991, a feature on Gay Olympics showed the globalization of gay and lesbian consciousness via Olympics and sport. A feature in 1992 showed lesbian appreciation of country music as performed by female singers like Tammy Wynette, Patsy Kline and K.D. Lang.

FIGURE 2.2 A scene from *Shades of Desire*, featured in the *Dyke TV* series on Channel 4.

A number of features in the series over the years have also examined the problems faced by gay/ lesbian people within their own communities. The item titled 'Walk on bi', from the 1990 series, dealt with the issue of bisexuality. Another item highlighting conflicting moral values and prejudices was the feature on disability in 1992. This dealt with being gay and disabled and featured an Asian man in a wheelchair. In a further development in 1995 and 1996, Channel 4 broadcast a series of programmes called *Dyke TV* which marked a differentiation of the target audience which *Out* had sought to combine.

Both the *Out* and *Dyke TV* series received negative criticism in much of the national press when they were first broadcast. The gay/lesbian press was usually more supportive in its comments, but there were critiques of some of the items, either for being too uncritical of commercialism of the gay scene, or for being too political in the conventional sense of pressure-group politics at international, national and local levels. The national press criticisms were typically less discriminating in tone, and were based upon opposition to having such material on public broadcast television at all. For instance, Paul Johnson wrote in the *Daily Mail* that there is a 'real division in our society'. He explained this claim in a way which graphically polarizes the opposed moral climates:

> On the one hand are the great majority of the people, contemptuously excluded from all decision-making but decent, law-abiding, respectful of strong moral codes, bringing up their children to the best of their ability to be useful citizens, respectful of duly-constituted authority, kind to their neighbours, doing an honest day's work and content with a modest reward. On the other hand there are those in power over our screens with their six and seven-figure salaries and share options, their golden handshakes and platinum payoffs, their bowing doormen and saluting chauffeurs – a table at the Savoy, a battery of secretaries to keep the hoi polloi at bay, and PR flunkies to make all things smooth and arrange a Patsy interview when required to 'answer out-of-touch critics'.
>
> (*Daily Mail*, 16 June 1995)

Johnson's distinction between these two groups, a media elite and the 'moral majority', is presumably intended to highlight a contrast between these groups' moral codes. A distinction is made between the moral values of the broad majority of people and those of the elites who control what we see on our television screens. It is interesting, however, that Johnson's target is the controllers of *television*. Another important component of the media, namely the press, is omitted from Johnson's notion of the elite. Newspapers, however, have played a very different role. The press, especially popular and tabloid newspapers, have played a leading role in articulating a conservative moral code, in attacking lesbians and gay men, and in the critiques of broadcast media for being too liberal on the issue.

For example, there was another article alongside the one by Johnson in the same issue of the *Daily Mail* which quoted Channel 4's Commissioning Editor, Caroline Spry, who commissioned items for the *Out* series, as saying: 'I have attempted to open up British TV to a diversity of visions of gay and lesbian culture and experience.' This would seem to be a relatively straightforward claim. Yet the *Daily Mail* ended its article with the following question: 'Who could be more unrepresentative of British society as a whole than Caroline Spry?'

The use of the phrase 'British society as a whole' in this context is one which is open, of course, to many questions. The most important question is: Who is to be regarded as articulating the moral voice of British society? Is this to be politicians? Right-wing journalists, or liberal television producers? Church leaders? Campaigners and pressure groups? Leaders of the Muslim community in Britain? There is no such entity as British society as a whole, for it is made up of a myriad of distinctive groups, each with their own moral outlook and world-view. Late-modern social formations, in the era of globalization, contain many diverse viewpoints on issues such as those concerning sexual moralities, which range from various types of religiously grounded moral codes to libertarianism, with many intermediate, relatively unformalized, positions which blend aspects of several moral outlooks. Certain people may make a claim to speak, or write, on behalf of the British people, but there is no such entity existing prior to, or outside of, the play between contesting discourses. It is only by addressing the people as a nation, by constructing their social diversity as 'a people', that they become constituted as such. Those who hail 'the people' or the 'society as a whole' create that which they seek to address, by the very words, representations or images which they use.

Politicians and broadcasters have attempted to address some of the moral objections to programmes with explicit sexual scenes or with presentations of gay and lesbian issues by introducing the '9 o'clock watershed'. The 9 p.m. watershed was a practical measure designed to mark the time when younger members of 'the family' were in bed and not viewing television. So what might be appropriate to broadcast after 9 o'clock could be more sexually explicit for 'adult viewers' than what was appropriate to transmit before that time. Parents were assumed to control their children's viewing, certainly after 9 p.m. Programmes such as those aimed at gays, lesbians and bisexuals, it was argued, should be broadcast after 9 p.m., so that 'the family' could view programmes together up to that time, without parents becoming embarrassed or offended by such sexually oriented material in front of the children. Public broadcast television is not only watched by or in family situations, but this is the situation which the regulatory bodies, such as the Broadcasting Standards Council and the Independent Television Commission, both given legislative form in 1990, assume to be typical of the television audience. However, Channel 4 and to some extent BBC 2, are assumed by these regulatory bodies to be catering for a more discriminating audience, and although the 9 p.m. watershed applies to them as it does to BBC 1 and the main commercial channels, after that time they are freer to address issues of interest to 'minorities'. This notion of 'minorities' is complex, for at times it has included women's programmes (who are not 'a minority' and are not subject to the 9 p.m. rule) and programmes for ethnic 'minority' cultural-linguistic groups, as well as lesbians and gays, gardeners, or darts enthusiasts! All viewers may be seen as belonging, some of the time, to one or more 'minority' group of some kind.

Swearing, bad language, violence, as well as scenes of sexual activity have all been objects of regulatory attention by those in broadcasting organizations who have begun to respond to the complaints of some viewers, 'minorities' or otherwise, about these matters. On the more specific issue of lesbians and gays on mainstream television, there has been a slight increase in tolerance of these groups being featured on broadcast television before and after the 9 o'clock watershed. However, *Out* never transmitted any items of sexual activity involving genital contact. Films screened on television were checked for such scenes, and explicit gay or lesbian sexual acts would typically be either edited out, or edited down to be acceptable to the controllers of the broadcasting service, and the regulatory bodies mentioned above.

Television has been a means whereby the horizons of audiences have been expanded and sometimes changed. Some have welcomed this effect, as has been the case, for instance, among those who have had their identities as lesbians, gays, heterosexuals or bisexuals affirmed by the types of programme we have discussed in this section. Others have found the experience of seeing other ways of living, which differ from the one they were socialized into believing was the only morally correct one, to be a disturbing, even an offensive, cultural change. Some of this latter group have formed social movements and pressure groups, to aim to regulate what is broadcast on television, published, or shown in cinemas or theatres. British television has, however, been broadly liberal in its approach, accepting that its audiences hold a wide variety of moral views, not only the traditional or puritan 'Christian' moral view of the family and marriage, and has broadcast programmes which reflect the plurality of moral values in the population. It has broken with the Reithian idea that it should represent only one moral viewpoint, or that it should aim to educate audiences into accepting one moral viewpoint. Rather, it has represented a liberal value of tolerance of differences, albeit within the limits of 'taste and decency'. The question remains, what are the limits on this tolerance of difference, and who sets them? Who defines the boundaries of 'taste and decency'? Are they established by those who are members of the regulatory bodies, the Broadcasting Standards Council and the Independent Television Commission? Or are they set by distinct, differentiated groups of viewers who are involved in communicating with commissioning editors, controllers of channels, and programme-makers? The development of new technologies, of cable, satellite, video and computer-linked programmes may well lead to more specific, differentiated audiences in the future, but something will have been lost compared with the larger, more diverse and less sharply differentiated audiences of the era of public broadcast television of the latter half of the twentieth century. Less mutual awareness and understanding of different lifestyles, of a variety of ways of living human sexuality more specifically, could be the consequence of the greater segmentation of audiences which these new forms of communication may produce.

6   Summary and conclusions

We began by looking at the cultural legacy of the Protestant ethic, as this was analysed by Weber. This has formed the basis of much of the regulation of many aspects of life, where it had influence, especially sexuality. Weber emphasized the unique character of this asceticism – that is a highly disciplined approach to life, found among some of the seventeenth-century puritans and capitalists. This cultural legacy has been reactivated from time to time in some parts of those societies influenced by it, especially Britain and the United States, in the period since 1950. But it has been extensively challenged and eroded by the growth of secular, liberal humanistic and emancipatory philosophies and movements drawing little, if at all, on conventional moralities or on established religious authorities. This has produced a great diversity in the moral cultures of society. It has made the area of moral and sexual regulation a critically contested one. It has also led to a succession of major moral crises and debates from the 1960s to the present. (Some of the main events in this story were outlined in section 3, from the Wolfenden Report (1957) to the 'Back to Basics' initiative in the mid 1990s.)

Two social movements – post-1950 feminism and gay liberation – marked a major shift away from the dominance of the puritan legacy towards the increasing acceptance of a *plurality of moralities*, many of them secular without a specifically religious formation, by many ordinary people who were not influenced by puritan religious morality.

A major area of dispute about how much regulation there should be concerned pornography. As we saw, some feminists argued persuasively for the regulation of pornography. Other feminists, as discussed in section 4 and Reading B, disputed how damaging pornography is to women, in depicting women as objects of sexual titillation, or gratification, for male gazers. The Wolfenden Report (1957) led to changes in the legal regulation of male homosexuality. The role of television in developing the recognition of the need for change away from the criminal law to regulation by civil law was mentioned in sections 3 and 5. The variety of representations of gay men and lesbians in new types of television programme was discussed, and a move from there only being camp, drag queen, or 'sick' representations of homosexuals, to a more relaxed, pleasure-oriented set of television representations was traced in section 5.

A range of philosophical and moral value positions have been involved in the debates about choice and regulation in these areas of sexual activity – that is, representations of women in pornography and of homosexuals on broadcast television. These have included those based on some variant of religious puritanism; those based on a wider political and legal conservatism; those based on liberalism, with its emphasis upon individual choice and freedom from unnecessary state regulation; and those based on a more far-reaching libertarianism. Feminism and the gay movement(s) raised new issues which challenged the patriarchal assumptions of puritanism, conservatism, and liberalism in some of its versions. Broadcast television in Britain has had to try to adapt to the various competing and incompatible regulatory ideas derived from these various moral-political philosophies – with only some degree of success and in the face of a continuing effort of conservative remoralization.

References

CHESTER, G. and DICKEY, J. (eds) (1988) *Feminism and Censorship*, Bridport, Prism Press.

DEVLIN, P. (1959) *The Enforcement of Morals: Maccabean lectures on jurisprudence*, London and Oxford, Oxford University Press.

HALL, S. (1980) 'Reformism and the legislation of consent' in National Deviancy Conference (eds) *Permissiveness and Control: the fate of the sixties legislation*, London, Macmillan.

HALL, S. (1997) 'The work of representation' in Hall, S. (ed.) *Representation: cultural representations and signifying practices*, London, Sage/The Open University (Book 2 in this series).

HOME OFFICE (1957) *Report of the Committee on Homosexual Offences and Prostitution*, Cmnd 247, London, HMSO (Wolfenden Report).

ITZIN, C. (1988) 'Sex and censorship: the political implications' in Chester, G. and Dickey, J. (eds).

KELLY, L. (1988) 'The US Ordinances: censorship or radical law reform' in Chester, G. and Dickey, J. (eds).

MACKINNON, C. (1987) *Feminism Unmodified: discourses on life and law*, Harvard, MA, Harvard University Press.

MITCHELL, J. (1974) *Psychoanalysis and Feminism*, Harmondsworth, Penguin Books.

NEWBURN, T. (1992) *Permission and Regulation: law and morals in post-war Britain*, London and New York, Routledge.

SEGAL, L. (1992) 'Introduction' in Segal, L. and McIntosh, M. (eds.).

SEGAL, L. (1997) 'Sexualities' in Woodward, K. (ed.) *Identity and Difference*, London, Sage/The Open University (Book 3 in this series).

SEGAL, L. and McINTOSH, M. (eds) *Sex Exposed: sexuality and the pornography debate*, London, Virago.

WEBER, M. (1971) *The Protestant Ethic and the Spirit of Capitalism*, London, Unwin (first published in English translation in 1930).

WEBER, M. (1991) 'Religious rejections of the world and their directions' in Gerth, H. and Mills, C.W. (eds) *From Max Weber: essays in sociology*, London, Routledge (first published in English translation in 1948).

WEEKS, J. (1977) *Coming Out: homosexual politics in Britain from the nineteenth century to the present*, London, Melbourne, New York, Quartet Books.

WEEKS, J. (1985) *Sexuality and Its Discontents: meanings, myths and modern sexualities*, London and New York, Routledge.

WEEKS, J. (1995) *Invented Moralities: sexual values in an age of uncertainty*, Cambridge, Polity Press.

WILLIAMS, B. (1979) *Report of the Committee on Obscenity and Film Censorship*, Cmnd 7772, London, HMSO (Williams Committee Report).

WILSON, E. (1992) 'Feminist fundamentalism: the shifting politics of sex and censorship' in Segal, L. and McIntosh, M. (eds).

READING A:
Tim Newburn, 'Permissiveness: accounts, discourses and explanations'

There are essentially five broad approaches to the subject of permissiveness that may be identified. For present purposes these are termed the 'conservative-historical', the 'liberal-historical', the 'Marxist-Gramscian'/Foucauldian, the feminist and the 'Eliasian'. The categories are neither intended to be mutually exclusive nor all-embracing. Not every author who has something to say on the subject of post-war sexual morality is included in the following discussion of each of the five categories, but rather those who are considered to be most representative of each genre are discussed.

At its crudest the conservative-historical approach to permissiveness is but a mourning for a lost 'golden age', an expression of grief for the passing of a time when questions of morals supposedly appeared much simpler, more straightforward and certainly less contentious and open to question. The liberal-historical approach by contrast is more forward-looking in character. The tone is different; it is more optimistic, more likely to assume that the process of historical change being viewed has at least some positive attributes, and less likely to dwell on social 'ills' or problems. It is, in a word, more *modernist*. It would be dangerous to assume from this simplification, however, that the two perspectives can be easily separated by the ideological position each adopts, the former tending to see 'permissiveness' as bad, the latter seeing it as good. This tends not to be the case. Whilst the liberal-historians are less likely to be openly damning of the social changes they identify than are the conservative-historians, this should not be read as a sign of their approval. Permissiveness is used almost universally as a pejorative term.

At the core of the conservative-historical position is the suggestion that the constitution of British society underwent a radical transformation in the 1950s and 1960s, and that this transformation included a significant alteration in the society's moral code. The use of the singular 'code' is important as will become clear. The position is most clearly illustrated by John Selwyn Gummer (1971). The essence of his argument is that, during the course of the twentieth century, British society has been characterized by increasing economic regulation and increasing moral licence. We are, he suggests, much less economically permissive than the Victorians, constraining business enterprise, terms and conditions of employment, advertising and so on, whilst morally and sexually becoming less restrictive. Indeed '[w]e are as restrictive materially as the Victorians were morally', he argues (ibid., p. 5). Gummer takes this argument one step further. The new permissive society differs from its Victorian predecessor not only by virtue of its sexual and moral freedom, but also because it is characterised by lack of agreement over questions of morality, and over the role of the state in the enforcement of morals. This is in direct contrast, he argues, to Victorian society:

> In the nineteenth century, men had a few such worries. They accepted that the state had a duty to uphold morality and that private morality ought to be subject to the law as it affected society. They then experienced little difficulty in deciding of what private morality consisted. There was a consensus – at least among the articulate. People knew what standards were when they and, more particularly, others were falling short of them.
>
> (ibid., p. 7)

For this author, the crucial change has been the break-up of consensus. Even though in the passage above Gummer undermines his own argument (through his use of the phrase 'at least among the articulate', he implies that this consensus is confined to a certain section of society) it is crucial to his thesis that the changes to be identified under the rubric of permissiveness should be viewed against the backcloth of an alleged Victorian moral consensus.

[...]

By contrast, 'moral collapse' or synonyms for such a phrase rarely find their way into the accounts of the period provided by 'liberal-historians'. Much of this is because the changes identified in the 1960s are viewed through different historical lenses. From this perspective the previously existing moral order is not seen as being wholly positive, and consequently its destruction – for both the conservative- and liberal-historians identify such a process – is not necessarily perceived as being problematic. More particularly, different aspects and different consequences of this previous moral order are identified. Bridget Pym (1974) emphasizes the 'joyless morality's' concentration on the integrity of the family and monogamy as the only available form of sexual expression. Fear of promiscuity and perversion, she argues, found expression in laws against abortion and homosexuality, and restrictive attitudes towards contraception. Despite this very different interpretation of pre-permissive morality, there are nevertheless distinct parallels between the conservative- and liberal-historical analyses of cultural change in post-war Britain. Both involve the identification of a previously existing, now largely defunct, set of moral imperatives which have given way to a new order in which control, particularly of sexual conduct, has diminished. Both suggest that in the area of sexual morality the change has been towards less restraint, less control and more choice. [...]

[...] [T]he major changes centred around the family system which prescribed the conditions for sexual relationships, changes which resulted in loosened bonds of matrimony, increased choice and reduced frustration and suffering. In this manner certain aspects, at least, of the process of permissive change are presented as having been positive and beneficial, in direct contrast to the view of the conservative-historians.

[...]

For both the conservative- and liberal-historians legislative change is of central importance to an understanding of the permissive society. The conservative-historical analysis takes certain legislative changes as being fundamentally permissive in outlook, and even suggests that the reforms of the law can be used as a barometer of the times. [...]

[...]

The liberal-historians, on the other hand, whilst being generally more sceptical of the extent of permissiveness, nevertheless argue that 1960s Britain was characterised by a greater degree of freedom [...]. Thus for both groups the major legislative changes of the period – the Obscene Publications Act, the Sexual Offences Act, the Street Offences Act, the Abortion Act, the Theatres Act – are significant for their 'permissive' or 'liberalising' character. Although interpretations differ, particularly ideologically, they share a common thrust.

This is also true of the Marxist, or more strictly, Gramscian approach to the question of permissiveness, taken by Stuart Hall and others, as well as what might be termed the 'Foucauldian' position. It is a considerably more sophisticated approach though, as should become clear, not without its flaws. The authors of *Policing the Crisis* (Hall et al., 1978), although concerning themselves primarily with the 'mugging panic' of the 1970s, also focus on what they take to be the changing moral climate in 1960s Britain. The fundamental change is conceived of in terms of the 'crisis of hegemony' that is experienced by the modern capitalist state when the basis of its cultural authority becomes contested. As the ability of the state to mould popular consensus diminishes, so the argument goes, the method by which hegemony is achieved moves from consent to coercion. This can be seen, they argue, in ever more direct forms of state intervention. More particularly, Hall et al. suggest that the discrete moral panics associated with the permissive age, e.g. those around abortion, VD, drugs and pornography, form the backdrop to the 'general crisis of the state' which was identified in panics around violent conduct like 'mugging'. Little evidence is presented that would support the claim that the moral panics associated with permissiveness were linked to the latter panic over street crime. Having suggested that the 1960s were characterised by a series of discrete panics around moral issues, there is neither an account – other than an essentially economistic one – of the aetiology of such panics, nor an explanation of the way(s) in which they can be considered to be discrete.

[...]

[...] Moral regulation was now more often brought about through coercion rather than consent. Laws which, in the early 1960s, had been 'liberally interpreted and allowed to lapse' were applied with increased rigour. The liberal interlude, as they call it, where laws such as those over obscene publications were allowed to lie fallow, soon came to an end. The laws, they argue, were soon dusted off and exercised to the full.

Stuart Hall employs a rather more sophisticated approach in an article for the National Deviancy Conference on 'consenting legislation' (Hall, 1980). In this he suggests that description in terms of either permissiveness or control would be too simple and too binary, and thus it is to the nature of reformism that one must look. In the 1960s, moral reformism, he argues, was aimed most specifically at sexual practices, and particularly those of women. The role of women from the 1950s on contained an inherent contradiction, he suggests, a contradiction between what have been termed 'the ideologies of consumption and domesticity' (Tolson, 1975). For the new post-war ideology of consumption to be stimulated it was necessary for women to remain in the home, yet at the same time to enter the labour market to supplement the 'main income' to sustain the family's purchasing power. During the 1960s, however, this traditional role was partially disarticulated, and replaced with a recognition of women's sexual pleasure and satisfaction. This shift was largely made possible by the breaking of the tie between female sexuality and reproduction, particularly through new contraceptive techniques. Women, Hall suggests, were the key interpellated subject of the new legislation:

> Overwhelmingly, it was the position of women in the field of sexual practice, which provided the legislation with its principal object/subject. What is proposed, in sum, was a measure of relaxation in the social and legal control of selected aspects of female sexual practice. It meant, in effect, a new 'modality' of control over these aspects – a more privatized and 'person-focused' regulation.
>
> (Hall, 1980, p. 21)

This 'legislative moment' incorporating all the major changes which Hall places under the title 'legislation of consent', lasted roughly from 1959 (Wolfenden, and the Obscene Publications Act) to 1968 (end of theatre censorship and the Wootton Report on drugs). This was followed, the authors of *Policing the Crisis* (Hall et al., 1978) suggest, by two 'waves' of social reaction. The first wave was organised around social, cultural and moral issues, the second around the politicisation of the counter-culture. The major contrast between the two is that in the latter, 'youth' had become more than mere 'agents' of change, and were identified as 'subversive' (Clarke et al., 1976). In terms of concrete events, the first wave of the backlash was associated with Mrs Whitehouse, *The Longford Report*, the Festival of Light and the Society for the Protection of the Unborn Child (SPUC). The second wave included such 'events' as the prosecutions of *OZ, IT* and *The Little Red Schoolbook*. [...]

A slight reorientation of the approach taken by Hall and colleagues is to be found in the writings of authors like Jeffrey Weeks. Weeks' approach is influenced by the French philosopher Michael Foucault [...].

For the Foucauldians sexuality is made meaningful through the discourses which shape it. Sexuality is 'organized' by the state as a technique of social control. Weeks argues that recent history has seen an explosion of speech surrounding sex and that the 1960s in particular 'experienced a decisive, qualitative escalation of the volume' (Weeks, 1985, p. 20). [...]

Although a number of feminist authors have tended to view some of the 1960s legislation as 'liberalising', they have sought to distinguish the identification of such a trend from any notion of 'liberation'. Whilst legislative reforms such as changes in the abortion laws and the law governing homosexuality are viewed as essentially liberal measures, we are not to assume therefore that this was indicative of a period of unproblematically increasing sexual liberation.

For critics such as Sheila Jeffreys the so-called 'sexual revolution' was in fact a counter-revolution. It was a smokescreen behind which the reconstitution of male domination was hidden:

> Behind the baloney of liberation, the naked power-politics of male supremacy were being acted out. The high priests of sexalogic, helped by the pornographers, progressive novelists and sex radicals continued to orchestrate woman's joyful embrace of her oppression thorough the creation of her sexual response ... The 1960s was a period when greater opportunities were open to women and the 'sexual revolution', rather than being liberating, helped to diffuse the potential threat to male power.
>
> (Jeffreys, 1990, p. 2)

It was not until the feminist movement re-emerged with vigour in the early 1970s that a critique of 'permissiveness' was constructed. As feminist writers began to question male sexuality and, particularly, to consider male violence against women, so they questioned the nature of the revolution. The authors who began to write about rape (Brownmiller, 1975) and related it to male power, male supremacy and male sexuality, questioned what they saw to be the essentialist constructions of female sexuality which continued to predominate within the age of sexual revolution.

The critique of male sexuality which originally focused on rape, developed through analyses of child sexual abuse (Meiselman, 1979; Russell, 1984) and non-stranger rape (Brownmiller, 1975; Dobash and Dobash, 1979) - and later pornography (cf. Dworkin, 1981). Such work hit at the heart of the institution which the conservative-historians took to be so much under threat – the nuclear family. Ironically, whilst such a group took the very existence of the family to be in danger from permissiveness, the developing radical-feminist position argued that the 'talk' of permissiveness was a means of disguising the threat that such an institution posed to women's real chances of liberation: 'Rather than posing a threat to traditional patriarchal marriage the sexual revolution strengthened the institution' (Jeffreys, 1990, p. 93).

Feminist authors such as Jeffreys, like the conservative historians, are almost unremittingly critical of permissiveness and its products. Although there is little of essence in common between the two approaches, it is perhaps not hard to see how on occasion unlikely alliances between radical-feminist anti-pornography campaigners and moral entrepreneurs such as Mrs Whitehouse might have been countenanced. Of all the recent authors it is perhaps Jeffreys who has developed the most thorough analysis of permissiveness or what she refers to as the 'sexual revolution'. She looks in some detail at the process by which the counter-revolutionary attack on women's liberation took place. Focusing *inter alia* on the work of the sex radicals Reich and Marcuse, and the sexologists of *Forum* magazine and manuals such as *Joy of Sex*, she details the prescription of male dominance and female submission. As she acidly puts it, 'the liberation was not intended to liberate (women)

from anything but their common-sense and their instinct for self-protection' (ibid.).

An element which is largely missing from both the Marxist and feminist accounts, in contrast to either the conservative- or liberal-historical approaches, is reference to the role of religion in contemporary society. For both the conservative- and liberal-historians, the process of 'secularisation' is identified as a necessary if not sufficient condition for the rise of the permissive society. From the Marxist point of view, a process such as secularisation takes a more secondary role in relation to features more closely associated with the functioning of a capitalist economy, and particularly changes in the class structure. As an example, as has already been suggested, the authors of *Policing the Crisis* (Hall et al., 1978) explain the existence of moral entrepreneurial groups in the 1960s by reference firstly to their common location in the class structure, and only secondly by reference to their religious views, and their perception of the modern 'secular' world. The [...] role of the National Viewers' and Listeners' Association (NVALA) in the 1960s, [...] casts doubt on this order of priority.

The Eliasian approach, as adapted by Cas Wouters, places even less emphasis on changing religious influences on contemporary moral codes than does the Marxist. Indeed notions of moral indignation, moral panic or moral conflict are not used in this perspective at all. The major focus is upon human interdependency, its levels of organisation, and the concomitant balance of social and self-controls that results. [...]

Wouters refers to this process as 'informalisation'. The major example that he gives of informalisation is what he takes to be the decrease of social restraints, particularly in the middle classes, imposed upon sexual behaviour and other connected spheres of conduct. As a result of these changes it has become possible, among other things, to show more of the male and female body. It has become possible to talk more freely and openly both about sexual experiences and other bodily functions such as menstruation. In essence, he argues, certain forms of conduct which were once forbidden are now allowed, and are regulated much less formally than they once were. These areas of conduct have become more subject to self-constraint and less subject to external constraint.

[...]

Wouters project is to build upon Elias' theory of the 'civilising process', and to show how informalisation, far from contradicting Elias' thesis, can actually be incorporated within it. Elias' theory of the civilising process has also been described as a history of manners, in which changing patterns of living are documented, and within which what he refers to as 'affect' becomes increasingly regulated. Emotion becomes ever more constrained by feelings of shame, repugnance or propriety. Changes in standards of conduct in Europe since the Middle Ages have so far generally proceeded, he argues, in the direction of increased civilisation:

> Whatever may be the differences in detail, the overall direction of change in behaviour, the trend in the civilising movement is everywhere the same. The change always presses toward a more or less automatic self-supervision, the subordination of short-term impulses to the commandment of a habitual long-term perspective, and the cultivation of a more stable and differentiated super-ego apparatus.
>
> (quoted in Wouters, 1977, p. 437)

[...]

In defending the theory of the civilising process, Wouters argues that informalisation is not inimical to civilisation, but can in fact be integrated into the overall theory. [...]

[...]

Thus it would be wrong to suggest that the young can behave uninhibitedly in contemporary society. They are, rather, expected to express their impulses in certain ways, ways that do not transgress against the more lenient standards of modern times.

At this point, one encounters two similarities between Wouters' analysis and those of the conservative- and liberal-historians. First of all, he accepts that standards are more lenient than those of the preceding periods. Thus, whilst he has rebutted the charge that permissiveness represents a simple diminution in control, he nevertheless asserts that within the new control structure there are greater possibilities for the expression of emotion. The second point of similarity emerges from the point of his analysis where he talks of changing codes of conduct. With the changing balance of power between the working and middle class, it is suggested that we have witnessed the destruction of traditional codes which have yet to be replaced by a similarly coherent new set.

[...]

Conclusion

All five major approaches to the subject of changes in post-war morality would accept, to a greater or lesser extent, that the term 'permissiveness', whilst not ideal, nevertheless does describe, albeit partially, the changes they identify. [...]

References

BROWNMILLER, S. (1975) *Against Our Will*, New York, Simon and Schuster.

CLARKE, J., HALL. S., JEFFERSON, T. and ROBERTS, B. (1976) 'Subcultures, cultures and class' in Hall, S. and Jefferson, T. (eds) *Resistance Through Rituals*, London, Hutchinson.

DOBASH, R.E. and DOBASH, R. (1979) *Violence Against Wives*, New York, The Free Press.

DWORKIN, A. (1981) *Pornography: men possessing women*, London, The Women's Press.

GUMMER, J.S. (1971) *the Permissive Society*, London, Cassell and Co.

HALL, S. (1980) 'Reformism and the legislation of consent' in National Deviancy Conference (eds) *Permissiveness and Control*, London, Macmillan.

HALL, S., CLARK, J., CRITCHER, C. and ROBERTS, B. (1978) *Policing the Crisis*, London, Macmillan.

JEFFREYS, S. (1990) *Anticlimax: a feminist perspective on the sexual revolution*, London, The Women's Press.

MEISELMAN, K.C. (1979) *Incest*, San Francisco, Jossey-Bass.

PYM, B. (1974) *Pressure Groups and the Permissive Society*, Newton Abbot, David and Charles.

RUSSELL, D.H. (1984) *Sexual Exploitation*, Beverly Hills, Sage.

TOLSON, A. (1975) 'The family in a permissive society', *Working Papers in Cultural Studies*, CCCS, University of Birmingham.

WEEKS, J. (1985) *Sexuality and Its Discontents*, London, Routledge & Kegan Paul.

WOUTERS, C. (1977) 'Informalisation and the civilising process' in Gleichmann, P., Goudsblom, J. and Korte, H. (eds) *Human Figurations*, Amsterdams Sociologisch Tijdschrift.

Source: Newburn, 1992, pp. 1–2; 5–15.

READING B:
Lynne Segal, 'Sex exposed: sexuality and the pornography debate'

Introduction

[...]

Pro-sex or anti-sex, Western cultures remain sex-obsessed. This is why the issue of pornography just won't go away. Its presence has dogged and divided Western feminism like no other. The debate over pornography reflects different views about the nature of sexuality, the forms of its representation and its place in our lives. Definitions of 'pornography' have changed dramatically since the word was first used in the mid nineteenth century to separate off the dangers of 'the sexual' from offensive religious and political material. At that time *any* type of sexually explicit writing or image, whether scientific, medical, poetic or popular, was equally liable to censorship. Throughout the twentieth century, however, recurring obscenity trials resulted in the progressive uncoupling of the 'pornographic' from anything which could be claimed to have 'scientific' or 'literary' value. Yet despite this narrowing of legal definitions, the meaning of 'pornography' remains today as contentious as ever; if not more so (for a history of 'pornography', see Kendrick, 1987).

Moral crusaders have always worried about the corrupting effect of explicit sexuality. Sex should be confined to its only legitimate place, in marriage, and linked at least in some way to its only legitimate purpose, procreation. Liberals, in contrast, have worried about public surveillance and censorship of displays of explicit sexuality which may cause little or no harm to others, especially when consumed privately and willingly. The feminist case against pornography is different. Feminists object not to the sexual explicitness in pornography but to the sexism: to its characteristic reduction of women to passive, perpetually desiring bodies – or bits of bodies – eternally available for servicing men. [...]

[...]

Two ... moves were necessary to push the pornography issue into its present ruling place in the sexuality debates. The first was to insist that sexuality was *the* primary, the overriding, source of men's oppression of women, rather than the existing sexual division of labour, organization of the state or diverse ideological structures (see MacKinnon, 1987, p. 50). The second was to cite pornography as the cause of men's sexual practices, now identified *within* a continuum of male violence: 'Pornography is the theory, and rape the practice' (Morgan, 1980, p. 139). As with rape, the same contradictory assertions were made denying the importance of sexuality altogether in men's consumption of pornography, while simultaneously holding pornography responsible for constructing male sexual behaviour. Men in this type of feminist analysis no longer had a sexuality. What they had was something else: a need for power, expressed through violence but *disguised* as sex.

Sexuality had been significant in British feminist analysis and politics from the beginning of women's liberation. At first feminists celebrated female pleasure, and what they saw as the *similarity* between women and men's sexuality. 'Acknowledgement of lust, acceptance of so-called promiscuity must be recognised as potentially inevitable stages in women's escape from sexual conformity', Beatrix Campbell wrote in 1973 (Campbell, 1974, p. 108). But five years later, many would declare that there is a fundamental *difference* between women's sexuality and men's, with women's sexuality once again the inverse of men's: gentle, diffuse and, above all, egalitarian (Editorial Collective, 1981, p. 29).

With denunciation rather than celebration the new mood of the moment, a type of political lesbianism became the sexual ideal for one influential strand of feminism: 'Women who make love to women are more likely to express their sexuality in a more equal way' (Meulenbelt, 1981, p. 90). Most feminists simply stopped writing about sex altogether, refocusing on the problem of men's violence. Not to focus thus, in Britain, was to court aggressive attack from the 'revolutionary feminist' faction, increasingly active from 1978. Coincidentally, in the United States, Women Against Pornography groups proliferated rapidly after that same year. Not coincidentally, as Ann Snitow was later to write, this was the time when the mood of the women's movement changed – especially in the USA, where the feminist anti-pornography campaigns first flourished (and US

feminism has always had a profound influence on feminism in Britain) (Snitow, 1986).

[...] With poorer women facing greater hardship, welfare services being removed, and the conservative backlash against radical politics in ascendancy everywhere, 'pornography' served as the symbol of women's defeat. From then on, feminists were less confidently on the offensive, less able to celebrate women's potential strength, and many were now retreating into a more defensive politics, isolating sexuality and men's violence from other issues of women's inequality.

The basic feminist anti-pornography argument is that pornography is central to the way in which men subordinate women. Pornography, it is argued, both depicts and causes violence against women: 'Domination and torture is what it's about' (Russell with Lederer, 1980, p. 26). Pornography which does not depict violence nevertheless objectifies women reducing them to sex objects for servicing men. The production of pornography also involves the brutalization and exploitation of women as sex workers. Pornography 'programmes' women into accepting female identities as subordinate 'dehumanized sex objects' (Lederer, 1980, p. 122). More recently Andrea Dworkin and Catharine MacKinnon, the leading feminists seeking legislation against pornography in the USA, have argued that pornography violates women's civil rights because it *is* discrimination against women. It convinces men that women are inferior and do not deserve equal rights; it is 'the essence of a sexist social order, its quintessential social act' (MacKinnon, 1987, p. 154).

Anti-pornography feminism is compelling because it makes intuitive sense. Much of pornography is at the very least complicit in some of the most offensive aspects of our sexist, male-centred culture: it appears to position men as active and powerful, women as commodified – objects, not subjects. Its target audience – at least until recently – is men, not women. Unlike liberals, concerned only with freedom of speech untroubled by questions of whose speech is heard, feminists have always seen cultural production as a site of political struggle. In recent decades they have consistently condemned the sexist use of women's bodies in the marketing of commodities. More provocatively still, pornography caters to men's sexual fantasies of female availability and eagerness for sex in the context of societies which have proved unable, and until recently unwilling, to offer women protection from widespread sexual harassment, abuse and violence; indeed, unwilling not so long ago, and for many men still today, even to acknowledge the existence of these issues.

Nevertheless, problems and contradictions come thick and fast the instant we look more closely at any one of the premises of anti-pornography feminism. On the contents of pornography, for example, so influential has the feminist anti-pornography message been that it is easy not to realize that in most pornography [...] violent imagery is extremely rare. One recent New York survey found between 3.3 and 4.7 per cent of violent imagery in a random sample of pornographic films. Another found around 7 per cent of s/m or bondage imagery with women submissive in pornographic magazines (9 per cent with men submissive) (see Howitt and Cumberbatch, 1990, pp. 7–8). Moreover, contrary to the often-asserted claim that violence in pornography – due to its assumed 'additive' nature – has been increasing, recent research has consistently indicated a *decline* in violent imagery since 1977, suggesting that the feminist critique is getting through (Scott and Guvelier, 1987; Palys, 1986; Dietz and Evans, 1982; Thompson and Annetts, 1990; Howitt and Cumberbatch, 1990).

There is now a mountain of debate, drawing upon psychological and sociological research as well as experiential reports (most of it collected in the USA), about the effects of pornography on behaviour. Empirical research on soft-core pornography has almost without exception failed to reveal *changes* of any significance in the behaviour of its consumers, whether affecting sexual practices, attitudes about, or behaviour towards, women. Indeed, its most characteristic effect, were we to feel confident generalizing from laboratory research on aggression to behaviour generally, has been to *lower* aggression levels (Baron, 1974; Donnerstein et al., 1987; Kelley et al., 1989; Thompson and Annetts, 1990; Howitt and Cumberbatch, 1990).

For this reason, attention has focused on pornographic material which does depict violence against women (in the form of rape scenes where

the victim ends up 'enjoying' it, for example). It may come as a further surprise to many to learn that heterosexual men in general list violence as the least titillating aspect of pornography and, along with most other people, have become less, rather than more, tolerant towards violent pornography (Smith, 1987). [...] In psychological experiments the majority of men react with distress to pornographic violence (Donnerstein et al., 1987; McCormack, 1985).

[...] In the great majority of sociological studies, variations in rates of sex crime do not correlate with the availability of pornography: Japan, for example, has an extremely low sex crime rate despite the existence of extensive and extremely violent pornography (Abramson and Hayashi, 1984; Baron and Straus, 1989).

Against Dworkin and MacKinnon's belief that pornography violates women's civil rights because it increases discrimination against them, one recent study of the relationship between circulation rates of soft-core pornography and levels of gender equality in fifty states in the USA discovered a positive correlation between equal opportunities for women in employment, education and politics, and higher circulation rates of pornography (Baron, 1990). Conversely the researcher Larry Baron found that states with a preponderance of Southern Baptists – followers of the anti-pornography campaigner Jerry Falwell – had the highest levels of inequality between women and men. (This is all the more ironic when one remembers that it was Beulah Coughenour, a Southern Baptist, anti-abortion and 'Stop ERA' activist, with whom Dworkin and MacKinnon worked in Indianapolis to enact their model Minneapolis anti-pornography ordinance.) Baron's conclusion was not that pornography led to more positive attitudes towards women's equality, but that other factors, like greater social tolerance generally, probably explained his findings.

Baron's study is consistent with the far higher levels of overall economic, political and other indices of gender equality in Sweden and Denmark compared to the USA, coupled with far more liberal attitudes towards pornography (Kutchinsky, 1990). This survey also found that gender inequality correlated with the presence and extent of legitimate violence in a state (as measured by the numbers of people trained to work in the military; the use of corporal punishment in schools; government use of violence; and mass-media preferences for violence, as in circulation rates of *Guns and Ammo*).

In contrast to many of these surveys, however, some psychological experiments – including the now often cited work of Donnerstein, Linz and Penrod – have, albeit inconsistently, found that men watching violent pornography are more likely to score higher on laboratory measures of aggression and to display, at least temporarily, more calloused attitudes towards women. These researchers, however, express caution over how far it is possible to generalize from their highly artificial laboratory set-ups to reactions to pornography more generally (Donnerstein et al., 1987, p. 175; see also Brannigan and Goldenberg, 1987; Christensen, 1987). Whatever we conclude from this, three points in their research are salient: first, it was those subjects who had said that they were likely to commit rape if they could get away with it *before* watching the violent pornography who showed more calloused attitudes *after* watching it; secondly, it seemed to be the violence, rather than the sexual explicitness, which correlated with the increase in calloused attitudes and the higher measures of aggressiveness towards women (established after using non-pornographic films involving violence against women) (Maalamuth and Check, 1985; Diatz et al., 1986; Donnerstein et al., 1987). Finally, debriefing subjects after watching violent pornography, with information that all rape is harmful, led to lower rather than higher expressions of calloused attitudes towards women in all subjects. This effect was evident for at least six months, which would seem to point to the significance of anti-sexist educational initiatives in undermining the sexism of pornography.

Donnerstein and his fellow researchers have complained – rather inconsistently, given Donnerstein's own former enthusiasm for public testimony – of the misappropriation of their empirical data by feminist anti-pornographers to strengthen censorship laws (Donnerstein et al., 1987, p. 178). But Donnerstein's own inconsistencies, and those within the wider research data, are dwarfed by the far more troubling contradictions within the feminist anti-

pornography position itself, especially in terms of what should be done about pornography. For instance, the consumers of pornography are here seen as 'almost exclusively men', yet pornography is seen as 'programming' *women* into adopting identities as 'dehumanized sex objects' (Lederer, 1980, p. 122). It seems that women learn to imitate pornographic representations, even though they do not read or view them (except, presumably, from a distance, unintentionally). Dworkin and MacKinnon's assertions of what pornography has done to women really do seem, in themselves, astonishingly offensive and discouraging to women. Dworkin declares that because of pornography a woman literally becomes 'some sort of thing', while MacKinnon maintains that women's lives are 'seamlessly *consistent* with pornography': 'For example, men say all women are whores. We say men have the power to make this our fundamental condition ... Feminists say women are not individuals' (Dworkin, 1981, p. 128; MacKinnon, 1987, pp. 149, 59).

The anti-pornography position of sex workers is similarly offensive and unhelpful to many women. We are exhorted to save our sisters, the 'coerced pornography models', as represented by Linda 'Lovelace'. But of course most sex workers are not looking for feminist salvation. On the contrary, they complain bitterly about the stigmatization of women who work in the sex industry by anti-pornography feminists (Alexander, 1986). Speaking for themselves, both individually and collectively, some sex workers have described why they choose the work they do and the type of control they feel it gives them over their lives, as well as their feelings of victimization caused not so much by how they are treated at work as by their fears of arrest, low pay, poor working conditions, inadequate health care and social stigmatization. These are all dangers they see as *exacerbated* by state censorship and criminalization of their work. Sex workers provide an important corrective to feminist debates around pornography by suggesting that it is the privileges of largely white and middle-class anti-pornography feminists, who are not as exploited or oppressed as many other women, which enable them self-centredly to present the issue of women's sexual objectification by men as *the* source of oppression of all women (Freccaro, 1991, p. 316).

In 'Confessions of a Feminist Porno Star' Nina Hartley describes why she works in pornographic films in the USA:

> Simple, I'm an exhibitionist with a cause: to make sexually graphic (hard-core) erotica, and today's porno is the only game in town. But it's a game where there is a possibility of the players, over time, getting some of the rules changed ... I find performing in sexually explicit films satisfying on a number of levels ... In choosing my roles and characterizations carefully, I strive to show, always, women who thoroughly enjoy sex and are forceful, self-satisfying and guilt-free without also being neurotic, unhappy or somehow unfulfilled ... I can look back on my performances and see that I have not contributed to any negative depictions of women; and the feedback I get from men and women of all ages supports my contention.
>
> (Hartley, 1988, p. 142)

However complex our attitudes to sex workers may be, it is clear that feminists face problems in choosing which women's voices to privilege. However troubled our reaction to pornography may be, it is also clear that feminists face problems choosing to downplay the social *context* of pornographic consumption. When pornography does work to empower men, it works not simply because of the nature of its images but rather because it is being used as a form of male bonding, as in the boys' night out to the strip joint – something quite different from their solitary, embarrassed visits to peepshow or porn arcade.

The problems we face as feminists tackling pornography today, however, are not just those of deciding to which women's voices we should pay most attention, and why. Nor do they reduce to questions of which types of explicitly sexual representation, or which contexts of pornographic consumption, produce the most coercively sexist behaviour from men, why, and what to do about them. They also – at least for some feminists – connect to the fear that the setting of sexual agendas in Britain, as in the USA, is increasingly led by the conservative right, with its traditionally repressive attitudes towards sexuality generally, and towards women and sexual minorities in particular. It is a fear led by the knowledge that, in recent years, moral conservatives interested in

attacking gays and lesbians, as well as in controlling women's sexuality, have become more successful precisely through focusing on pornography and, especially in the USA, using the rhetoric and tactics of the feminist anti-pornography project.

[...] In such a political climate, it is more urgent than ever to rethink the highly charged issues surrounding sexuality, which so frequently take the form of debates over pornography.

References

ABRAMSON, P. and HAYACHI, H. (1984) 'Pornography in Japan: cross-cultural and theoretical considerations' in Malamuth, N. and Donnerstein, E. (eds) *Pornography and Sexual Aggression*, Orlando, FL, Academic Press.

ALEXANDER, P. (1986) 'Response to Andrea Dworkin', *Gay Community News*, Winter.

BARON, L. (1990) 'Pornography and gender equality: an empirical analysis', *Journal of Sex Research*, Vol. 27, No. 3.

BARON, L. and STRAUS, M. (1989) *Four Theories of Rape in American Society*, New Haven, CT, Yale University Press.

BARON, R. (1974) 'Sexual arousal and physical aggression: the inhibiting effects of "cheese cake" and nudes', *Bulletin of the Psychonomic Society*, Vol. 3.

BRANNIGAN, A. and GOLDBERG, S. (1987) 'The study of aggressive pornography: the vicissitudes of relevance', *Critical Studies in Mass Communication*, Vol. 4, No. 3.

CAMPBELL, B. (1974) 'Sexuality and submission' in Allen, S. et al. (eds) *Conditions of Illusion*, Leeds, Feminist Books.

CHRISTENSEN, F. (1987) 'Effects of pornography: the debate continues', *Journal of Communications*, Vol. 37, No. 1.

DIETZ, P. and EVANS, B. (1982) 'Pornography imagery and prevalence of paraphilia', *American Journal of Psychiatry*, Vol. 139.

DIETZ, P. et al. (1986) 'Detective magazines: pornography for the sexual sadist?', *Journal of Forensic Sciences*, Vol. 31, No. 1.

DONNERSTEIN, E. et al. (1987) *The Question of Pornography*, New York, Free Press.

DWORKIN, A. (1981) *Pornography: men possessing women*, London, The Women's Press.

EDITORIAL COLLECTIVE (1981) *Scarlet Woman*, 12/13, May, p. 29.

FRECCERO, C. (1991) 'Notes of a post-sex war theorizer' in Hirsch, M. and Fox Keller, E. (eds) *Conflicts in Feminism*, London, Routledge.

HARTLEY, N. (1988) 'Confessions of a feminist porno star' in Delacoste, F. and Alexander, P. (eds) *Sex Work: writings by women in the sex industry*, London, Virago.

HOWITT, D. and CUMBERBATCH, G. (1990) *Pornography: impact and influences*, London, Home Office Research and Planning Unit.

KELLEY, K. et al. (1989) 'Three faces of sexual explicitness: the good, the bad and the useful' in Zillman, D. and Bryant, J. (eds) *Pornography Research: advances and policy implications*, Hillsdale, NJ, Lawrence Erlbaum Associates.

KENDRICK, W. (1987) *The Secret Museum: pornography in modern culture*, New York, Viking.

KUTCHINSKY, B. (1990) 'Pornography and rape: theory and practice? Evidence from crime data in four countries where pornography is easily available', *International Journal of Law and Psychiatry*, Vol. 13, No. 4.

LEDERER, L. (1980) 'Playboy isn't playing' in Lederer, L. (ed.).

LEDERER, L. (ed.) (1980) *Take Back the Night*, New York, William Morrow.

MACKINNON, C. (1987) *Feminism Unmodified: discourses on life and law*, Cambridge, MA and London, Harvard University Press.

MALAMUTH, N. and CHECK, J. (1985) 'The effects of aggressive pornography on beliefs of rape myths: individual differences', *Journal of Research in Personality*, Vol. 19.

McCORMACK, T. (1985) 'Making sense of the research on pornography' in Burstyn, V. (ed.) *Women Against Censorship*, Vancouver, Douglas & McIntyre.

MEULENBELT, A. (1981) *For Ourselves*, London, Sheba.

MORGAN, R. (1980) 'Theory and practice: pornography and rape' in Lederer, L. (ed.).

PALYS, T. (1986) 'Testing the common wisdom: the social content of pornography', *Canadian Psychology*, Vol. 27, No. 1.

RUSSELL, D. and LEDERER, L. (1980) 'Questions we get asked most often' in Lederer, L. (ed.).

SCOTT, J. and GUVELIER, S. (1987) 'Sexual violence in *Playboy* magazine: a longitudinal content analysis', *Journal of Sex Research*, Vol 23.

SMITH, T. (1987) 'The polls – a review: the use of public opinion data by the Attourney General's Commission on Pornography', *Public Opinion Quarterly*, Vol. 51.

SNITOW, A. (1986) 'Retrenchment vs. transformation: the politics of the antipornography movement' in Ellis, K. et al. (eds) *Caught Looking: feminism, pornography and censorship*, New York, Caught Looking Inc.

THOMPSON, W. and ANNETTS, J. (1990) 'Soft-core: a content analysis of legally available pornography in Great Britain 1968–90 and the implications of aggression research', Reading University.

Source: Segal, 1992, pp. 1–11.

INTERNATIONALISM, GLOBALIZATION AND CULTURAL IMPERIALISM

John Tomlinson

Contents

CHAPTER THREE

1   Introduction

In this chapter I want to explore one of the most prominent critical stances that has been adopted towards the globalization of culture: the discourse of cultural imperialism. The idea of **globalization** and the arguments surrounding it are increasingly part of our lives, and the currency of academic discussion. For example, the complex interplay between economic and cultural aspects of globalization is discussed by Kevin **Robins** (1997). What Robins' account brings out well are the complexities, the contradictions, the ambiguities and the uncertainties in the globalization process. Globalization, as you may have discovered, is a complicated and perplexing process not just in terms of the densening web of interconnections that it establishes at all manner of levels, but in terms of the complexities and uncertainties of the cultural politics it poses for us. But another significant point made by Robins is that globalization is ordinary. Its consequences are matters which confront us every day in our routine lives: when we go shopping, eat in a restaurant, watch television, go to the movies. The cultural 'lived experience' of globalization can thus be grasped as a transformation in the way we experience our everyday local lives as they are increasingly penetrated by distant globalizing forces.

globalization

One general way of describing this is as a process of **deterritorialization**, which the Mexican cultural theorist Nestor Garcia Canclini describes as 'the loss of the "natural" relation of culture to geographical and social territories' (Garcia Canclini, 1995, p. 229). The broad idea of deterritorialization is that we are no longer able to live our lives entirely 'locally': our cultural experiences are pervaded by distant influences – the foods we eat, the music we listen to, the landscapes, images and events we are familiar with on our television screens, our ability to speak by telephone to people on the other side of the world – all make our routine lives more 'open to the world'. As Anthony Giddens puts it, globalization means that 'the very tissue of spatial experience alters, conjoining proximity and distance in ways which have few parallels in prior ages' (Giddens, 1990, p. 140).

deterritorialization

Understanding this change in the texture of lived experience is a difficult task in itself, but it is made more complicated by the need to find appropriate critical responses to the process of globalization. We certainly need to *be* critical of globalization – not merely to stand in awe-struck wonder at the achievements of globalizing technologies, nor to celebrate it as an historical *fait accompli* in the manner of the 'symbolic analysts' of the business world that Robins describes. But finding the critical vocabulary that is adequate to the complexities and ambiguities of globalization is not an easy task – and this chapter will not attempt to construct anything like a critical model. What it will attempt to do is to examine one critical model that is frequently invoked, either directly or implicitly, as a response to **cultural globalization**: the idea of globalization as **cultural imperialism**. By focusing on the strengths and weaknesses of this critical discourse we

cultural globalization, cultural imperialism

should be able to move at least some way towards understanding what an adequate critical response to cultural globalization might look like.

The cultural imperialism argument, as we shall see, is by no means a tidy homogeneous position. It contains some truth about, and useful insights into, the distribution of global cultural power. But it also harbours quite a lot of conceptual confusion, empirical misperception and political-ideological ambiguity. And, although rather less theoretically fashionable than it used to be, the theme of cultural imperialism – and the associated ideas of 'Americanization', 'westernization' and 'cultural homogenization' – still represent a convenient (almost 'ready made') and temptingly simple way of grasping what is going on in the globalization process. As we shall see, it also remains a powerful polemical position in a number of contemporary cultural policy debates, and so, in this respect alone, it is useful to understand what its strengths and weaknesses are.

regulation

de-regulation

However, another important way of reading this chapter is in relation to one of the organizing themes of the book: the idea of **regulation**. Cultural imperialism as a critical discourse on the globalization process can be understood in various senses as a discourse structured around the broad themes of the regulation and **de-regulation** of culture.

When people write about cultural imperialism they tend to employ a number of conceptual moves which frame the complex totality of global cultural flows, interconnections and exchanges as various strategies of regulation or de-regulation. Thus, as we shall see in section 2, for some critics of cultural imperialism, the supposed dominance, worldwide, of a standardized, 'homogenized' consumer culture, emanating from western (and particularly North American) capitalism, represents a form of global cultural regulation. This is the sense of regulation that Kenneth Thompson describes (Chapter 1) as developing (in various complex ways) out of the Marxian idea of the shaping of culture in conformity with the political-economic demands of capitalism. So a commonly made claim is that the loss of cultural diversity and particularity that (it is argued) can be seen across the world is due to the way transnational capitalism imposes commodified western culture as the only available model for us to live our lives. Keith **Negus** (1997) refers to this sort of argument where he describes the critical position that UNESCO (a body that has been at the centre of the cultural imperialism debate) adopted in its 1982 report on the global 'culture industries'. As Negus argues (pp. 77–9), the position of UNESCO was very close to that of the Frankfurt School theorists Adorno and Horkheimer in relating an impoverishment of culture (in this instance, particularly the threat to global cultural diversity) to its commodification and standardization in a transnational capitalist market.

For critics of cultural imperialism then, the increased international traffic in cultural goods that is a prominent feature of (both economic and cultural) globalization is understood primarily as a process of cultural imposition, dominance, regulation. They would have little truck with those on the other side of the argument who claim, quite contrarily, that this traffic is the benign fruit of a 'de-regulated' international cultural market. 'De-regulation' for critics of cultural imperialism is a weasel word. Whilst it suggests freedom of cultural choice and practice, what it really means is the process of clearing the way for the inexorable advance of a 'one-dimensional' capitalist culture across national borders.

Supporters of cultural de-regulation for their part might accuse critics of cultural imperialism of being the real regulators. For the cultural policy options most generally proposed to deal with the encroachment of alien cultural goods and practices are various forms of **protectionism** – which as   protectionism
we shall see (section 2.2) can range from the imposition of tariffs on cultural imports to more radical measures like the banning of satellite dishes that has become a (controversial) feature of cultural policy in several Islamic countries. What can such measures be if not attempts to regulate the cultural practices of a national population?

So thinking about the politics of global cultural flows in terms of regulation/ de-regulation reveals a complex situation. Critics of cultural imperialism from the political left can be oddly aligned with more conservative national forces in their opposition to the de-regulation of culture. And de-regulators are, moreover, by no means all apologists for free-market capitalism. This category would also embrace those who, whilst critical of the commodification of culture, either believe cultural protectionism to be an impractical option in a globalized world or else an inherently undesirable one for political reasons. Just to give one example of the latter view, it could be argued that the attempt to defend national cultural identity against a supposed threat of cultural imperialism involves the representation of a spurious cultural unity in nation-states. The dominant cultural constituency (for example, dominant versions of 'Englishness' or 'Frenchness') thus becomes that which 'needs protecting', and this has the effect of internally regulating cultural identity by suppressing the ethnic and cultural diversity – the 'multiculturalism' – which is in fact a feature of all modern nation-states.

It would be a mistake, however, to try to make sense of all the arguments about cultural imperialism exclusively in terms of the regulation/de-regulation pair. And, in fact, in most of what follows I shall not generally use the terms explicitly. But it will be useful to keep these ideas in mind as you read the chapter and to decide at which points you think they become relevant to the argument.

In moving on to this, though, we can use the idea of 'regulation' in a slightly different way to try to illuminate the way in which, as I mentioned earlier, theorists have been tempted to incorporate the complexities of cultural globalization within the rather more clear-cut critical model of cultural imperialism. We can think about the way in which one already existing discourse – that of cultural imperialism – can act to 'regulate' the way in which we construct a new discourse – that of cultural globalization. In Chapter 1, Kenneth Thompson mentions Michel Foucault as a theorist of regulation, and we can use (if only very briefly) some of Foucault's ideas about the regulation of discourses to understand this tendency.

In his essay 'The order of discourse', Foucault discusses the various ways in which, 'in every society, the production of discourse is at once controlled, selected, organized and redistributed by a certain number of procedures whose role is ... to gain mastery over its chance events' (Foucault, 1981, p. 52). Foucault points out how anarchic discourses potentially are: anything can be said and so discourses are in principle boundless – they 'proliferate to infinity'. In his essay he discusses the range of ways in which social institutions contrive to regulate unruly discourses: for example, by prohibiting what can be said in certain circumstances, by constructing taboos, by elaborating rituals of speech, by restricting the right to speak to certain 'qualified' people. But one of the most interesting forms of the regulation of discourse which Foucault mentions is what he terms **procedures of rarefaction** which are, in effect, ways of regulating discourse from within. The term 'rarefaction' has the general meaning of 'becoming less dense', thus of 'refinement' but also of a 'thinning out' of the dense mass of what can be said about a subject. One of the examples Foucault gives of a procedure of rarefaction is the operation of academic disciplines, which enforce regulation of discourse by establishing rules of what counts as legitimate knowledge – and ways of expressing it – within their boundaries.

procedures of rarefaction

Now we can apply this idea of rarefaction – of 'thinning out' – to the emerging critical discourse of cultural globalization. For the cultural and political complexities and ambiguities that the globalization process throws up can be handled more easily if we contain them within a few familiar critical categories and assumptions about the world: for example, assumptions about the ideological impact of imported cultural goods, about the relationship between capitalism and the West, or about the coincidence of cultural identity with national identity. It is these sorts of assumptions, as we shall see, that structure the discourse of globalization as cultural imperialism. And the point is not that all these assumptions are necessarily false ones, but that they cannot be applied uncritically to the complex and rapidly changing context of cultural globalization. To do this would be to construct a perhaps more reassuringly 'coherent' model of global cultural politics but, almost certainly, a misleading one. As Foucault puts it, 'we must not imagine that the world turns towards us a legible face which we have only to decipher' (Foucault, 1981, p.67); rather we should expect things to be complex and contradictory. In the following section, then, I will try to sketch out how the world looks as it is 'ordered' from the perspective of the cultural imperialism thesis (section 2); I will go on, in section 3, to examine the adequacy of this 'rarefied' account of cultural globalization.

2   Cultural globalization and cultural imperialism: one discourse lying in wait for another?

There is certainly a case for seeing the theory of cultural imperialism as the earliest theory of cultural globalization. As Jonathan Friedman says, the discourse of cultural imperialism tended to set the scene for the initial critical reception of globalization in the cultural sphere, casting the process as 'an aspect of the hierarchical nature of imperialism, that is the increasing hegemony of particular central cultures, the diffusion of American values, consumer goods and lifestyles' (Friedman, 1994, p. 195).

The central proposition of the cultural imperialism thesis is quite straightforward: the idea that certain dominant cultures threaten to overwhelm other more vulnerable ones. So applying this means roughly that the globalization process is seen as the global working through of some familiar patterns of cultural domination: of America over Europe, the 'West over the Rest', the core over the periphery, capitalism over more or less everyone. Viewed like this, globalization becomes instantly recognizable and even predictable. The complex experience of cultural deterritorialization becomes read through an emphasis on the global spread of certain dominant cultural practices, goods, forms and institutions, and this becomes the primary critical concern. This is what I mean by saying the cultural imperialism thesis is a critical position that was 'ready made' for the globalization process.

2.1   The emergence of the cultural imperialism thesis

To understand this predisposition it will be useful to see it in historical context. There is insufficient space here to trace all aspects of the idea (see Tomlinson, 1991), but we can identify two important strands in its development.

First there is a history, dating from the early decades of this century, of perceptions of the malign effects of American cultural exports to Europe. The reasons for this are complex, having to do with various positions of pro- and anti-Americanism that developed in different European countries. These positions were particularly influenced by the increased presence of American culture – sometimes along with the American GIs 'over here' during and after the Second World War (see Hebdige, 1988; Webster, 1988; Shou, 1992). It is difficult to generalize about these perceptions. Whilst some were genuine anxieties about the swamping effect of American culture, others expressed a more basic concern over the economic power of US cultural industries, while yet others represent a generalized cultural conservatism, tied to a suspicion of the 'inflammatory' potential of popular culture itself. A good example of this last is found in a speech made by the Archbishop of Toledo to a Spanish clerical conference in 1946. The problem the Archbishop posed was:

> How to tackle woman's growing demoralization – caused largely by American customs introduced by the cinematograph, making the young woman independent, breaking up the family, disabling and discrediting the future consort and mother with exotic practices that make her less womanly and destabilize the home.

> (Instituto de la Mujer, 1986, p. 375)

As we can see from this quotation, the fear of 'Americanization' is a complex cultural phenomenon which can embrace all sorts of cultural anxieties and politics from the left to – as here – the unequivocal right. Perhaps precisely because it is so loose and accommodating, the idea of the Americanization of culture continues to be the most common formulation of the cultural imperialism thesis.

FIGURE 3.1
Statue in municipal park in Valencia, Spain – the inscription reads 'To Walt Disney [from] the children'.

The other strand is more recent – though it draws on a much longer history of genuine domination – and articulates the problem primarily as a relationship between the 'first' and the 'third' worlds. Although it could be traced back to criticism of the imposition of European culture in the process of eighteenth- and nineteenth-century colonialism, this strand of the cultural imperialism argument really takes off in the late 1960s and 1970s. One important context here was a series of debates in the United Nations and in particular in its specialized 'cultural affairs' agency, UNESCO. These debates originated in concerns about imbalances in the flow of information between the developed and the developing nations and the control of media and communications by the West, and led to the call by UNESCO for a 'New World Information and Communications Order'. But the debates soon developed into much broader attacks on the cultural dominance of the West and were, arguably, influential in the eventual withdrawal from UNESCO, in 1984 and 1985, of both the USA and the UK (see McPhail, 1987; Hamelink, 1994).

At the same time that these policy debates were taking place in UNESCO, a parallel critique was developing in the work of critical media and communications scholars. Thus in 1971 Ariel Dorfman and Armand

Mattelart published in Chile their 'classic' ideology-critique, *How to Read Donald Duck: imperialist ideology in the Disney comic*, in which they argued that Disney comics, widely distributed in the Third World, not only caricatured and denigrated the cultures of these countries, but also contained a covert ideological message: 'Underdeveloped peoples take the comics at second hand, as instruction in the way they are supposed to live...' (Dorfman and Mattelart, 1975, p. 98). As Martin Barker summarizes their argument: 'American capitalism has to persuade the people it dominates that the "American way of life" is what they want. American superiority is natural and in everyone's best interest' (Barker, 1989, p. 279).

However, one of the important features distinguishing critiques like Dorfman and Mattelart's from simple 'anti-Americanism' is the way the USA is made representative of a larger cultural threat: the spread of multinational capitalism. This is also the theme of Herbert Schiller's approach. Schiller is one of the most well-known and prolific writers on cultural/media imperialism and has maintained a more or less consistent position since the 1960s. Herbert Schiller's 1979 paper 'Transnational media and national development', provided as Reading A at the end of this chapter, is a typical example of Schiller's concerns.

As you will see, Schiller focuses on the role of the multinational corporation, in particular the transnational media corporation, in the 'modern world system'. Crucial to an understanding of 'transnational media dynamics', in his view, is the experience of the USA, where 'the utilization of public information channels for the objectives of the corporate business system occurs in its most pure form' (Schiller, 1979, p. 23). The mass media 'have been integrated fully into the marketing system'. 'The apparent effect of saturation, through every medium of the advertising message, has been to create packaged audiences whose loyalties are tied to brand-named products and whose understanding of social reality is mediated through a scale of commodity satisfaction' (ibid.). It is this consumerism that, according to Schiller, has been exported throughout the world by multinational capitalism.

READING A

You should now read the extracts from Herbert Schiller's paper 'Transnational media and national development', provided as Reading A at the end of this chapter.

- Whilst reading this, it may be useful to recall the discussion of cultural 'regulation' in the introduction. How does Schiller implicate global capitalism in the process of cultural regulation?

- The other thing to consider in this reading is where the weight of Schiller's critique falls. Is he primarily interested in the autonomy, development and sovereignty of national cultures or in the nature of capitalism as a global cultural form?

global capitalism

Schiller is concerned with ways in which the capitalist world system is relentlessly expanding and incorporating all societies, including those of the 'developing world', into its ambit. He allocates a key role to the transnational media and communications industries in this process: they are the 'ideologically supportive informational infrastructure' of **global capitalism**, the agents for 'the promotion, protection and extension of the modern world system' which 'create ... attachment to the way things are in the system overall' (Schiller, 1979, pp. 21, 23, 30). So it is in this sense that he sees transnational capitalism as 'regulating' cultures. The destruction of traditional cultures – the 'swamping' theme of the cultural imperialism argument – is seen as an obvious consequence of this process, and yet I do not think this is really the key issue for Schiller. Rather, he is concerned with the *sort* of culture that is being spread: commercialized media products containing the ethos and values of corporate capitalism and consumerism. Schiller therefore provides a particularly strong version of cultural imperialism as a theory of cultural (and particularly media) globalization – and a good example of a critic of the 'regulatory' nature of the transnational culture industries that we referred to in the Introduction. For what is being globalized, according to him, is capitalism as both an economic and a cultural system: a 'way of life' and a 'developmental path' (ibid., p. 31).

This strand in the cultural imperialism thesis clearly differs in a number of ways from the critique of Americanization: in contrast with the more politically ambiguous stance of generalized 'anti-Americanism', it is almost exclusively a critique from the left; it centres on transnational capitalism and consumerism rather than just on the spread of American culture (although, as we shall see, it also tends to conflate these); and it has a particular relevance to the situation of the Third World, providing, in Ulf Hannerz's terms (1991, p. 108), a dramatic, pessimistic 'master scenario' for the absorption of peripheral cultures into a global-homogenized future.

But although these strands are analytically separable, in practice – as these things tend to do – they have become intertwined. Thus arguments about the ideological significance of Disney comics in Latin America tend to shade into concerns over the cultural implications of Eurodisney in France; the 'incorporation thesis' made out in relation to the global distribution of *Dallas* becomes mixed up with the debate about 'elite' and popular culture (Ang, 1985); Schiller's critique of transnational capitalism drifts towards a criticism of 'homogenized North Atlantic cultural slop' (Schiller, 1985, p. 19). What looks, at first glance, like a fairly straightforward critical position turns out to be rather complicated and often contradictory set of claims, issuing from often quite different political-ideological discourses. Partly because of these complications and ambiguities, and partly because of some fundamental theoretical problems which we shall consider presently, the cultural imperialism thesis has come in for sustained criticism across a wide front (Boyd-Barrett, 1982; Fejes, 1981; Schlesinger, 1991; Sinclair, 1992; Thompson, 1995; Tomlinson, 1991; Tracey, 1985; Tunstall, 1977). As a result McGuigan (1992, p. 229) scarcely exaggerates in calling it 'a deeply unfashionable problematic' in the 1990s. But despite all this criticism, some of the broad ideas contained within the cultural imperialism thesis remain influential and there are, in fact, good reasons why it still deserves to be taken seriously today.

2.2   Cultural imperialism up to date

In the first place the idea of cultural imperialism, though it may be academically unfashionable, is by no means universally rejected. Indeed, certain of the assumptions of cultural imperialism continue to find voice in the work of some major, and sophisticated, cultural critics (see, for example, Said, 1993; Hall, 1991). Even thinkers critical of the cultural imperialism thesis recognize its significance. For example, John Thompson, writing about the globalization of communication in 1995, saw fit to revisit Herbert Schiller's work from the 1970s. Though, as we shall see, he finds serious problems with Schiller's account and ultimately rejects it, he nonetheless describes his work as 'probably the only systematic and moderately plausible attempt to think about the globalization of communications and its impact on the modern world' (Thompson, 1995, p. 173). Similarly, the globalization theorist Roland Robertson, whilst criticizing the cultural imperialism approach, nonetheless recognizes its growing importance in focusing issues of global–local culture (Robertson, 1995, pp. 38–9).

Another significant reason for its continuing relevance is that the idea of cultural imperialism has become part of the general cultural vocabulary of modern societies, invoked in all sorts of contexts beyond those of academic debates. For instance, the idea frequently emerges in journalistic treatments of globalization issues. To give just one example, the merger of the Disney Corporation with ABC in 1995 prompted a piece in *The Guardian* by Martin Woollacott which reflects on the implications of the creation of a media conglomerate 'as big as the entire media sector of a large European country'. But from this question, Woollacott goes on to discuss the dominance of global culture by American culture: 'what will it be like when all the globe is Disneyland?' (1995, p. 12). Although he does not simply reproduce the standard arguments of 'Americanization', his article provides a good example of how 'ready to hand' the discourse of cultural imperialism is as a response to globalization issues. For despite its sensitivities to changing contexts produced by recent globalizing tendencies, the article preserves intact certain assumptions about American cultural dominance, and even references to its standard icons – hamburgers, Mickey Mouse, Coca-Cola.

But perhaps the area in which the cultural imperialism thesis remains most alive is in policy debates conducted at the level of the nation-state. As

globalization brings us all into closer cultural proximity, sensitivities about what distinguishes us as national cultures increase, along with ideas that national cultural identity needs 'protection' from alien influences. Cultural imperialism has thus become the threat against which various 'cultural protectionist' policies have been implemented in recent years.

One example is legislation banning the import and use of satellite dishes or decoders which is now quite common in Islamic states. Satellite dishes have been illegal in Saudi Arabia for a number of years and during 1995 similar bans were declared in Bahrain, Egypt and Iran. Such measures are highly controversial within the states involved, extremely difficult to implement and further complicated by the desire of these countries to utilize satellite technology themselves. In Malaysia, for example, legislation banning the use of parabolic antennas passed in 1988 was due to be lifted at the end of 1995 to allow access to the Malaysian government's own Measat satellite (BBC Monitoring, 30th June, 1995, p. 11).

In Iran, the banning order issued in April 1995 followed a year of heated debate and a number of ambiguous government statements demonstrating a reluctance to enact unpopular legislation. With an estimated half a million dishes in homes in Tehran alone (Haeri, 1994) it is entirely unclear how the ban is to be enforced, and there were immediate calls for special provisions to be made for access by journalists, research scholars and others. However, despite the massive practical, technical and political difficulties of this sort of protectionist legislation, its cultural-ideological rationale is quite clear. Hoijat Taqavi, the head of the Iranian Majlis (parliament) committee on Islamic arts and guidance said of the ban: 'This is one way of curbing the cultural assault ... we showed the world that we are against foreign culture, that is we will never be subservient to that culture and invasion by foreigners' (BBC Monitoring, 16th June, 1995, p. 5).

One immediate response to such statements is to ask who the 'we' is. It is quite obvious that speaking on behalf of the government in such a context is not the same as speaking on behalf of the people (see Sreberny-Mohammadi and Mohammadi, 1994). The problem of who represents the national culture is thus one that lies at the heart of the politics of cultural imperialism and protectionism (Tomlinson, 1991, Chapter 1). However, we should resist the temptation to read this issue simply as the desperate attempts of 'fundamentalist' authoritarian states to restrict their people's cultural rights. The situation is more complex and there is certainly a spread of popular opinion about the influence – malign or otherwise – of western culture throughout the Islamic world, just as there is a range of governmental responses to the threat of 'sky invasion'. What is clear is that the technology of globalization – from satellites to the Internet – is something *all* nation-states have increasingly to reckon with simultaneously on an economic and a cultural front.

So this sort of policy is by no means restricted to the Islamic world, or the Third World more generally. Cultural protectionism is very much alive in the West in the 1990s. Perhaps the incident which focused most attention here was the dispute between the USA and Europe at the conclusion of the Uruguay Round of GATT talks in December 1993. GATT – the General Agreement on Tariffs and Trade – is the body which, since 1947, has attempted to regulate world trade and particularly to limit restrictive foreign trade practices such as tariff barriers and quotas imposed on imports. The Uruguay Round refers to the last series of negotiations begun in Uruguay in 1986 and due to be completed by the end of 1993. Following this GATT was wound up and replaced in 1995 by a new regulatory body, the World Trade Organization (WTO). The complexity of economic globalization made these negotiations the most protracted in the history of GATT (van Hemel, 1994). In their closing stages they were principally focused on differences between the USA and the European Union over agricultural issues.

But then, in September 1993, a lobby group from the French audio-visual industry, with the support of EU cultural ministers, succeeded in placing the issue of film and television imports from the USA to Europe at the centre of the GATT agenda, thereby precipitating a last-minute crisis. The Europeans – particularly the French – demanded that trade in audio-visuals be left outside the GATT agreement, allowing them to continue in various ways to restrict the flow of American films and television programmes into their countries. The American position, as might be imagined, was that any such exclusions would contravene the free-trade principles on which GATT rests. The outcome of the dispute – forced largely by the pressure to conclude the negotiations by 15 December 1993 when President Clinton's mandate to negotiate ran out – was that audio-visual products were left out of the final treaty. However, this was not seen as a clear victory for the Europeans but as somewhat of a fudge (see van Hemel et al., 1996). The issue was still unresolved in 1996 but there is every expectation that the audio-visual sector will become included in future world trade agreements.

Now, clearly a major concern in this debate was simply the protection of the *economic* interests of the media industries in Europe against the tide of US imports. However, this interest was presented as closely allied with the protection of European national cultures. But what does the GATT dispute actually tell us about the cultural protectionism/cultural imperialism issue?

READING B

You should now read the extract from Cees Hamelink's book *The Politics of World Communication* (1994) discussing the GATT talks, provided as Reading B at the end of this chapter. Again, it will be useful to read this – particularly where Hamelink sets out the contending positions in the dispute – with an eye to the regulation/de-regulation themes.

- What sense do you get from this discussion of the relationship between the issues of *cultural* and *economic* protectionism as they appear in the GATT dispute?

- Why do you think Hamelink believes the discord between the EU and the USA 'is only of marginal significance'?

At one level this episode clearly *was* an economic dispute like any other about the protection of national industries in a global market-place. As Hamelink shows, there are significant economic interests at stake for the culture industries on both sides of the Atlantic. But I think his scepticism about the affair's wider significance is that he sees it conducted within a discourse of the market-place which fails to problematize the treatment of culture as a tradable commodity within a capitalist totality. When he says the European protectionist position 'is not motivated by deep principles', he implies a certain cynicism in the hitching of the interests of media entrepreneurs to the bandwagon of national cultures. Hamelink has a point here. Statements like that from the head of the French *Gaumont* company that protectionism is necessary 'if France wants to be home to new Prousts in the future' (Godard, 1993, p. 14) surely invite scepticism. Moreover, Hamelink's suggestion that the broader interests of international capitalist trade will eventually find a compromise position also implies that the argument was not one that went to the core of anxieties over cultural identity – and certainly did not raise any uncomfortable questions about cultural imperialism as the spread of commodified culture in general.

As Hamelink also recognizes, the debate is complex at a number of levels and it is not always easy to separate out economic from cultural issues and positions. For example, the question of 'cultural dumping' is, at one level, purely an economic argument. American media producers can generate sufficient income from their large domestic market to recoup production costs and allow them to sell films and TV shows at enormous discounts in overseas markets: one discounted price for Europe, another for the Third World. Though this is sometimes represented by American producers as 'subsidising' world television, it has the obvious effect of squeezing out competition (and in the Third World of inhibiting the development of media production). But dumping also, of course, has cultural implications beyond the culture industries and their immediate interests. For the number of American movies and television shows on European screens is in direct relationship to these economic processes within an increasingly de-regulated market.

The issue of protectionism is therefore also one of how much of the cultural 'space' of Europe will be filled with American products, and this concern is also a genuine motivation for those European film makers – like Bertrand Tavernier or Bernardo Bertolluci – who have involved themselves in the debate. Bertolluci, for example, recently claimed that 'European cinema is dying and may not make it to the year 2000 unless something is done'. At one level this simply voiced the fears for the film industry, but he expressed a wider concern when he went on to claim that 'the world hegemony of American films means moving towards a dreadful mono-culture, a kind of cultural totalitarianism' (Bertollucci, quoted Tornabuoni, 1995).

Bertolluci was speaking at a meeting of the cultural commission of the European Parliament in 1995, and such meetings again illustrate the wider cultural dimensions of the debate. For the 'official' representatives of national cultures do not only speak the language of the market, but have a more direct constituency of interest in the preservation of national cultures.

The position of France, in the GATT talks and in wider cultural policy, illustrates this most forcibly. France has demonstrated the keenest sensitivity of any European country to the defence of its national culture and has been at the forefront of the protectionist lobby (Andrews, 1995). In particular, the French Cultural Affairs Minister, Jacques Toubon, pursued a policy of protecting domestic cultural production with elaborate systems of quotas and subsidies. But his name is perhaps most associated with a piece of legislation in 1994 which attempted to restrict the incursion of foreign – mainly English – words into the French language. The famous 'Loi Toubon' was in fact an attempt to revive and enforce an earlier law, by proposing fines and even prison sentences for the use of foreign words in, for example, advertising, TV and radio output. Although some key aspects of this bill were subsequently rejected by the French Constitutional Court (Ardagh, 1995, p. 12), the legislation continues to influence cultural practices and to divide popular opinion in France. For instance, the latest aspect of the legislation to come into force on 1 January 1996 requires all French radio stations to broadcast a minimum of 40 per cent of their pop music output in French (Burns, 1996, p. 8).

As the French case illustrates, then, cultural protectionist policies relate to a wider politics of national identity. This is by no means without its problems and contradictions, for it raises difficult questions concerning the legitimacy of state intervention in cultural practices: the right by which government can claim to 'speak for France'; the paternalism involved in cultural restrictions; the problems involved in assuming a monolithic or homogeneous French culture that is under threat (Tomlinson, 1991, pp. 11ff.). But it does at least show that protectionist measures are not motivated purely by economic interest.

This 'autonomous' interest of states in the protection of national identity is further confirmed if we consider, briefly, the case of Canada and its broadcasting policy during the 1980s. As Richard Collins says, Canada, because of its proximity to the USA and the consequent high degree of penetration of American programmes into Canadian television, is often taken as 'an exemplary national instance' of media imperialism. But Collins argues, against the general drift of media imperialism critics like Herbert Schiller, that this penetration is not unambiguously and comprehensively contrary to the overall cultural and economic interests of Canadians. Canadian viewers, he points out, have demonstrated a distinct lack of interest in home-produced television drama, manifestly preferring that produced in the USA. What is more, due to the great difference in the comparative sizes of the Canadian and US domestic markets, Canadian broadcasters and cable companies make more money from screening American drama imports than from producing and screening their own (the economics of programme dumping). Collins comments:

> An economically rational policy for Canadian television-program producers would be specialization in a program type undersupplied on the international market in which Canadians have demonstrated competence (for example, live-action and animated children's programming). Yet specialization in such a form would necessitate importation of programs to fill other parts of the schedule (including drama). For cultural-nationalist reasons ... Canada has been reluctant to follow such a policy of specialization. Instead, a major commitment in broadcasting policy in the 1980s has been to compete in a very high-cost section of the international market – drama – against producers in the United States who have demonstrated over a long historical period their capability and competitive advantages.
>
> (Collins, 1990, p. 37)

As Collins goes on to demonstrate, the assumption that drives this policy choice is 'that viewing American television drama threatens Canada's continuing existence as a separate and independent state ... The belief that cultural sovereignty and political sovereignty are mutually dependent is the core assumption on which Canadian broadcasting policy has been based' (ibid.).

One of Collins's purposes in fact is to dispute this assumption – at least in the Canadian case where there are two distinct language communities (English- and French-speaking) co-existing within a single stable overarching polity. Cultural factors, he argues, are less important in maintaining political sovereignty than the defensive posture of Canadian broadcasting policy

FIGURE 3.2
Sheila Copps, Canadian Deputy Prime Minister and Minister of Cultural Heritage, announcing funding to support Canadian-produced televsion and film, September 1996.

assumes. But this is another story and, given developments in Canadian nationalist politics in the 1990s, perhaps a controversial one. At any rate it is rather too specific for us to pursue here. The point for us is that Canadian television policy, though employing what might be called an 'import substitution' approach rather than some of the more robust protectionist measures of the French, has been none the less highly regulatory – and for specifically cultural-nationalist reasons rather than ones of national economy.

To this extent then, and despite their obvious differences, we can see some parallels in the Islamic defensive posture towards the West, and that of Europe and Canada towards the USA. In the case of the Islamic states, there is not the same complicating overlay of economic interests as in the European case, and the measures involved are rather cruder and more dramatic. But in both sets of cases the threat of cultural invasion is articulated at the level of the nation-state without necessarily commanding the support of the population. And in both it is clear that protectionist measures are extremely difficult to implement and unlikely to succeed in the long run.

Now I think these two common factors may be linked. For what makes cultural protectionism difficult to implement is not merely the technological innovations in electronic media that are making national borders more and more permeable, but – more significantly – the divergence between the routine cultural desires and practices of ordinary people (for example, to watch satellite TV) and the state's interest in the preservation of 'the national culture'. This divergence is nicely put in an article which appeared in the Iranian leftist newspaper, *Salam*: 'Please tell the interior minister that the best way of fighting [western] cultural aggression is to erect around Iran walls as high as the sky; to forbid people to go beyond them on pain of execution ...' (Haeri, 1994, p. 51).

This advice might equally apply to the French or the Canadian cases. We might conclude then that the globalization process is revealing both political and conceptual problems at the core of our assumptions about what a 'culture' actually is. Is a culture a set of ideal, stable, definable practices which exist over and above the vagaries of individual cultural practices and consumption choices, thereby legitimating the state's regulatory intervention in its defence? Or is it, in fact, simply a way of describing the predominance of the mass of individual choices and practices in a society at any historical moment? This is a difficult question to answer but one that lurks behind the range of positions people take on the politics of cultural regulation, invasion and protection.

In this section I have tried to show some ways in which the cultural imperialism thesis manifests itself in the cultural politics of the 1990s. And in the process we have also glimpsed some of the political and conceptual problems that surround it. Three things overall might be observed about this continuing debate.

First, the debate is still an active one in policy terms and is no less complex and ambiguous now than it was during the 1970s. Second, despite these complexities and difficulties, it seems clear that fundamental issues to do with cultural autonomy and cultural identity in a globalizing world are embedded in this debate. These issues are likely to endure, partly because the technical and economic processes creating them are intensifying with the advance of globalization, and partly because we don't have adequate critical-conceptual answers to them. And third, the recognition of the impact of cultural globalization in recent years has not yet generated its own distinct critical theory. Consequently, the cultural imperialism perspective, now widely distributed within cultural discourse, tends to be adopted as a ready-made critical position.

In the following sections I want to advance the argument by considering in more detail the strengths and weaknesses of the cultural imperialism perspective as a way of approaching cultural globalization. I shall suggest three broad reasons why cultural imperialism deserves to be taken seriously, but for each of these I will try to show the limitations of the argument for understanding the rapidly changing cultural landscape that globalization is producing.

3   Cultural globalization through the prism of cultural imperialism: three arguments and three responses

3.1   The undeniable spread of western/American cultural goods

The first and most obvious argument in support of the cultural imperialism approach is that there is a wealth of evidence that western (or even American) cultural tastes and practices are becoming global ones. Take any index, from clothes to food to music to film and television to architecture (the list is only limited by what one wants to include as 'cultural') and there is no ignoring the sheer massive presence of western (meaning here predominantly North American, western European) cultural goods, practices and styles in every inhabited area of the world. And one could be more specific. Isn't global mass culture, as Stuart Hall argues (1991, p. 27; see also, Lash and Urry, 1994, p. 127), actually predominantly *American* culture? Certainly if the process *has* to be tied to one national culture there really isn't much competition. And if we agree with Hall in seeing the global cultural sphere as 'dominated by the visual and graphic arts ... dominated by television and by film, and by the image, imagery, and styles of mass advertising' (Hall, 1991, p. 27) then the case for seeing cultural globalization as 'Americanization' is a persuasive one, endorsed as each new Hollywood blockbuster outgrosses the previous one in world box office receipts, or every time the CNN logo appears on our screens superimposed over the latest, most 'immediate' global news footage.

There is, without a doubt, at least a prima facie case to be answered here. Doesn't the sheer material ubiquity of western – and indeed American – cultural products worldwide support the casting of cultural globalization as in some sense the extension of cultural empire? Granted this is a 'soft' imperialism, quite different from the bloody coercive cultural impositions of, for example, nineteenth-century European colonial expansion. But is it not still inescapably 'domination', the wilful displacement of 'weaker' cultures by a more powerful one?

When viewed from this perspective, the complex web of interconnections of globalization takes on more specific features: it appears to have specific points of origin and concentrations of power – to densen towards the centres of cultural production and concentrations of power and wealth in the West. And the complex cross-cutting and overlay of communication paths and flows takes on a less benign aspect: now it appears as a 'web' which enmeshes and binds all cultures. Or take another image of globalization – the idea of 'action at a distance'. As Giddens (1990, p. 19) describes this, it refers to the extent to which 'locales are thoroughly penetrated by and shaped in terms of social influences quite distant from them'. The perspective of cultural imperialism invites us to construct this idea around the issue of the locus of control of lived experience. Thus the 'distanciated' influences (Giddens, 1990) which order our everyday lives can easily appear as those of the culturally dominant 'other': from the McDonald's restaurant that replaces the local café to the multiplex cinema chains that appear like pieces of implanted American suburbia on the fringes of our cities.

Moreover, all this is simply the experience of globalization within the West. If you happen to live in the Third World, the sense of distanciated influences must seem almost total: from the western brand marks which carry the most social cachet, to the transnational that owns the plant where you work, to the World Bank that provides the development loans but also dictates the pattern of that development, and – in extremis – to the foreign aid workers who try to keep you alive at feeding centres and in refugee camps.

When we look at 'world culture' as it presents itself in its most immediate form – the form of the distribution of cultural products and texts – the case for seeing cultural globalization as cultural imperialism appears at its strongest.

3.2   Looking beyond the self-evidence of global cultural goods

However, we really cannot let matters rest here. For perhaps the most important point in the whole cultural imperialism debate is that the sheer *presence* of western or even specifically American cultural products distributed around the world is not a self-evident cultural fact, but something which always needs interpreting (Tomlinson, 1991). It is one of the fundamental conceptual mistakes of the cultural imperialism argument to make unwarranted leaps of inference from the simple presence of cultural goods to the attribution of deeper cultural or ideological effects.

In the first place the 'evidence' itself often turns out to be ambiguous. Take the obvious example of US television exports. There is, first of all, a common assumption that the American film and television industry enjoys a virtually unchallenged position of dominance in the global market – particularly in the Third World. Certainly it enjoys a very strong position, but, as we shall see in section 3.4 below, it is certainly not entirely without competition, which the globalization process may well be increasing. However, it might still be argued that an undeniable case can be made for US cultural imperialism simply from scanning the number of American television shows on the world's national channels. No one denies that there is a lot of US product around. But if we look closer at patterns of viewing, two things emerge.

First, as surveys of 'primetime' scheduling around the world show, it is domestically produced programmes which almost always top the ratings during peak viewing hours, with American imports frequently filling in the less popular times during the day (Dziadul, 1993). When most people are watching television, then, they are watching their 'own' indigenous programmes. And, as Dziadul argues, this is a trend which is growing, particularly in some areas of the Third World, due 'to both local tastes and the growing strength of indigenous television production industries' (1993, p. 52). What this suggests is that the sheer quantity of US televisual texts does not necessarily signal a swamping of the national cultural tastes and a threat to national cultural identity. The argument about programme dumping (section 2.2) may still obtain, but it might simply have more to do with the economics of providing a full daily schedule of TV programmes. So the economic aspects of media imperialism do not translate directly into the 'obvious' issue of cultural influence without raising other, perhaps more interesting, questions. For example, a daily schedule which needs to be 'filled' with cheap imported programmes might prompt the deeper cultural question of why we expect or desire television programming to occupy so many hours in the day – of why the model of continuous television 'flow' is such a dominant one.

Secondly it has been argued that foreign imports generally operate at a 'cultural discount' (Hoskins and Mirus, 1988) in terms of their popularity with audiences. That is to say that cultural differences tend to limit ('discount') the appeal of foreign programmes to domestic audiences, particularly because of language differences and the need either to dub or subtitle. Morley and Robins summarize the implications for the reception of American television in Europe: 'US imports tend to do well when domestic television is not producing comparable entertainment programming – and whenever viewers have the alternative of comparable entertainment programming in their own language, the American programmes tend to come off second best' (Morley and Robins, 1989, p. 28).

Neither is it simply a question of language. As McGuigan (1992, pp. 149–50) argues (following Geraghty, 1991), the cultural specificity of British soap operas like *Coronation Street*, *EastEnders* and *Brookside* – tuned to the everyday experience of a British audience – is what makes these shows consistently more popular than American imports like *Dallas* whose broad 'global' appeal depends precisely on their lack of specific cultural reference.

But it is not just a question of interpreting evidence. The preoccupation with the presence of cultural goods can also lead to another familiar set of theoretical problems with the cultural imperialism argument – its misrepresentation of the cultural agent as a passive, unreflexive recipient of alien cultural goods – and to the associated fundamental misinterpretation of cultural processes as *unidirectional* flows of power. As is evident in, for example, the ideological readings of the Disney comic by Dorfman and Mattelart (section 2.1) the cultural imperialism argument has tended to rest on rather crude assumptions about how audiences 'read' cultural texts, reproducing the much criticized 'hypodermic model' of ideological effects.

The more sophisticated 'active audience' perspective (see, for example, **Moores**, 1997) has prompted some empirical studies on the influence of supposed 'imperialist texts' like *Dallas* (Ang, 1985; Liebes and Katz, 1993). These, unsurprisingly, suggest that just as audiences for domestic programmes are active and critical in their constructions of meanings and negotiations of ideological messages, so audiences faced with imported ideologies, values and lifestyle positions bring their own cultural dispositions to bear on these texts. Watching *Dallas* (or any other cultural import) around the world, then, has been a much more active, complex, ironic and critically aware process than theorists of media imperialism have supposed.

READING C

You should now read the extract from John Thompson's book *The Media and Modernity* (1995), provided as Reading C at the end of this chapter, in which he applies some of these criticisms to the work of Herbert Schiller. It might be worth referring back to the extracts from Schiller (Reading A) as you read this. Notice that Thompson is not entirely unsympathetic to Schiller's broad critical perspective on the political economic structuring of global communications. But here he finds deep problems with his account as a specifically *cultural* theory of domination.

- What do you understand by Thompson's reference here to the 'fallacy of internalism'?

- In what ways do audience research studies like that of Liebes and Katz that Thompson describes pose problems for the Schiller's account?

Thompson's 'fallacy of internalism' refers to a tendency to try to 'read off' the impact of capitalist-dominated media systems at the level of individual cultural experience from an analysis of the structures themselves, without paying attention to the complexities of cultural reception. I think Thompson is correct to say that this line of criticism 'presses to the heart of the cultural imperialism thesis'. The point is that cultural – as distinct from political-economic – criticism of the globalization process cannot rest simply on arguments about the movement of cultural products, but is essentially a matter of understanding the complex meanings generated in the appropriation of these products. This is the hermeneutical nature of cultural processes that Thompson stresses. In focusing on the hermeneutics of reception, studies like that of Liebes and Katz highlight what Thompson describes as the critical 'short circuit' in Schiller's work – the reliance of his theory of cultural domination on the unexamined assumption that 'hegemony is prepackaged in Los Angeles, shipped out to the global village, and unwrapped in innocent minds' (Liebes and Katz, 1993, p. xi).

Whilst we are discussing the issue of cultural reception, we should also note a tradition of cultural analysis emerging from the Third World experience – from Latin America – which insists on the dynamic interaction between external cultural influence and local cultural practice. A key aspect of this tradition (in the work of cultural and media theorists such as Nestor Garcia Canclini (1992; 1995) and Jesus Martin-Barbero (1993)) is the concern with the nature of cultural mixing and hybridization rather than with direct cultural imposition from the developed world. In Martin-Barbero's words (1993, p. 149), what is central to the experience of cultural modernity in Latin America is the way in which 'the steady, predictable tempo of homogenizing development [is] upset by the counter-tempo of profound differences and cultural discontinuities'.

Now this stress on 'transculturation, hybridity and indigenization' (Lull, 1995, p. 153) is important in understanding the *dialectic* involved in the reception of hegemonic cultural influence. But it also has a wider significance. For if we approach the cultural process as a dialectic, it becomes clear that the idea of the emergence of a monolithic global culture universally reproducing one hegemonic national culture is rather implausible. This is because, in James Lull's apposite phrase, global culture is always 'meaning in motion' (ibid., pp. 115ff.). It might be that global culture has its space *between* rather than within cultures and that its 'essential' nature is that of the hybrid.

We have only to think of the complex mutations involved in popular musical culture: for example, 'hip hop' culture, often taken as the essential expression of Black American urban poor – born in the South Bronx, and now something like a global youth movement. But in fact 'hip hop' is not quintessential Black American music but a complex hybrid mix of Afro-American and Caribbean musical cultures. This is a form which, in Paul Gilroy's words 'flaunts and glories in its malleability as well as its transnational character' (Gilroy, 1993, p. 33). So what sort of grasp of the significance of 'hip hop' – as it crosses and re-crosses what Gilroy calls the Black Atlantic – can we have if we treat it merely as an American cultural export? There is, I think, the world of difference between recognizing the global popularity of such essentially hybrid forms – forms which perhaps belong to no particular locality – and the rather grotesque universalism of the late Ithiel de Sola Pool's assumption that the popularity of American mass culture was really 'the discovery of what world cultural tastes actually are' (Pool, 1979, p. 145).

3.3   The centrality of capitalism in global cultural processes

The second argument in favour of the cultural imperialism approach concerns its critique of the cultural implications of transnational capitalism. 'Globalization is really advanced capitalist globalization', write Lash and Urry (1994, p. 280) and, if we don't take this to mean it is *solely and exclusively* a phenomenon of capitalist expansion, it is hard to disagree. For few would not place the dynamics of capitalism near the centre of the analysis of globalization. Indeed, the use of the term 'globalization' itself is common amongst corporate managers to describe their strategies (Robins, 1991, p. 36).

Many of the complex interconnections of globalization both derive from and facilitate an expanding capitalist production system and market. And some of the most striking images of the shrinking world of globalization have to do with the immense power of global markets opened up by information technology: foreign exchange markets, for example, trading hundreds of millions of dollars per minute, dwarfing the trading power of even the largest nation-states. It is this gigantic 'decentred' order of capitalist transnational practices that not only threatens the economic and political autonomy of nation-states (Lash and Urry, 1994, p. 280; McGrew, 1992, p. 91), but also provides some of the most dramatic imagery of cultural globalization.

cultural identity

There is a sense then in which global capitalism is significant not only in terms of its economic power and thus its bearing on the material well-being of everyone of the planet, but also in terms of its impact on our **cultural identity** – the very way in which we understand our day-to-day lives. This is the point at which the cultural imperialism argument engages, urging us to understand globalization as the process whereby all global cultures are inexorably drawn into the sphere of influence of one single 'capitalist culture'. This, as we have seen, is a position consistently argued by Herbert Schiller and broadly supported by others directly associated with the cultural imperialism position (for example, Dorfman and Mattelart) as well as in some more recent neo-Marxist accounts (for example, Sklair, 1991).

Now within this broad perspective there are clearly more and less sophisticated and discriminating positions. Some, like Schiller, tend to elide the capitalist culture argument with the 'Americanization' thesis while others make a point of distinguishing the two. For example, Lesley Sklair claims, with some justification, that:

> to identify cultural and media imperialism with the United States or even with US capitalism is a profound and profoundly mystifying error. It implies that if American influence could be excluded, then cultural and media imperialism would end. ... Americanization itself is a contingent form of a process that is necessary to global capitalism, the culture-ideology of consumerism.

> (Sklair, 1991, p. 135)

The actual cultural implications read off from the logic of capitalism argument also vary – from the straightforward idea of incorporation into consumer culture (Sklair, Schiller) to the corollary (though, in fact, more controversial) claim about cultural homogenization. But, despite such differences, the critical thrust of all these positions for globalization theory remains the same: that, in order to avoid idealism in the analysis of cultural globalization, one must start with a grasp of the 'real foundations' of global culture – the expansionary imperatives of the capitalist production process and market.

3.4   The 'decentring' of capitalism from the West

It would be foolish to underestimate the centrality of the expansionary development of capitalism within the process of globalization. However, this does not necessarily mean that we should approach it in the 'totalizing' way in which, for example, Herbert Schiller has done. Indeed, the globalization of capitalism might have quite contradictory implications for the hegemony of the West.

Returning to our original image of globalization as a complex set of interconnections and interactions and adding the insight that cultural change tends to be 'dialectical' rather than unidirectional, we might form a very different image of the world from that implicit in the cultural imperialism thesis. Instead of settled and confident centres of economic and cultural power exercising global hegemony, a better image may be that of a **decentred network**, in which power is diffused rather than concentrated and the patterns of its distribution are unstable and shifting.

decentred network

Applying this way of thinking to the development of global capitalism points us towards a re-examination of one of the most powerful critical metaphors employed in this connection – that of the **core** and the **periphery**. This model of the workings of the global political economy informs a great deal of critical analysis of the global distribution of political and economic power – including the discourse of cultural imperialism. What the model does, most basically, is to provide a spatial metaphor in which the concentration of capitalist power and interests coincides with the nation-states of the West at the centre of a system which simultaneously keeps the nation-states of the Third World on the periphery: that is 'at a distance' from the locus of control of the capitalist process. This structuring of the global capitalist system assures the continued economic weakness, cultural subordination and conditions for the exploitation of the Third World by the First.

core–periphery model

But as global interconnections and interactions in the economic sphere are becoming more complex, this model is put under increasing strain. Indeed, globalization theorists like Giddens are quite explicit in their criticisms:

> [The global economy] is increasingly decentred, no matter what power western states and agencies continue to hold over what was 'the periphery'. ... However critical one might still want to be of the unfettered processes of capitalist enterprise, the target has now become much more elusive. Conspiracy-style theories of global disparities don't have the purchase they once seemed, to some observers at least, to have.

(Giddens, 1994, p. 87)

And this is by no means simply a view from the First World. The Mexican theorist Nestor Garcia Canclini argues in much the same vein. He criticizes the inadequacy of the core–periphery model as 'the abstract expression of an idealized imperial system' (1995, p. 232) and calls for a more nuanced view of cultural power 'within a transnational system that is diffuse with a complex form of global interrelations and interpretations' (Garcia Canclini, quoted in Martin-Barbero, 1993, p. 207).

It is important to be clear exactly what is being suggested here. The point is not to suggest that global economic, political and cultural disparities are somehow being smoothed out. All available indices of quality of life continue to show the highest levels in the 'core' countries of North America, Europe, Japan and Australasia, while the levels of poverty and immiseration in large areas of Africa, Latin America and Asia scarcely need pointing out. It is also fairly obvious that the distribution of globalizing technologies is hugely biased towards western industrial societies. Not only is it the case that the people of the First World are predominantly the fax-senders and the Internet users, we need to keep in mind that vast proportions – hundreds of millions – of people in the Third World have no access to electricity and have never made a telephone call.

The point, rather, is that the core–periphery model does not adequately grasp the *complexities* of the operation of global capitalism: the way this cuts across and re-figures relations between nation-states and regions within nation-states, and the resulting shifts in the balance of global power. This is not to underestimate the obvious weight of disadvantage suffered by the 'less developed' countries, but it is to argue that they cannot be understood in the rather monolithic terms that the core–periphery dualism encourages. The so-called 'Asian Tigers' – South Korea, Taiwan, Singapore, Hong Kong, Malaysia, Indonesia – are the most obvious cases of Third World economies that have rapidly and 'successfully' developed within the framework of global capitalism. And though of course we have to recognize all the social and cultural costs and contradictions of such 'success', they do represent evidence of shifting patterns of economic power which cannot be ignored.

Of course this raises a whole range of controversial issues which cannot be properly addressed here. But it does seem to me that such developments in global capitalism, viewed in the long term, leave the nation-states of the West without any guarantees as to their continuing position of dominance. As Giddens argues, globalization links the fates of localities in complex ways which do not necessarily reproduce the familiar historical patterns of western dominance: 'The increasing prosperity of an urban area in Singapore might be causally related, via a complicated network of global economic ties, to the impoverishment of a neighbourhood in Pittsburgh whose local products are uncompetitive in world markets' (Giddens, 1990, p. 65).

So what globalization theory calls attention to here is emerging patterns in the distribution of advantage and disadvantage which cut across the North-South, First–Third World, Core–Periphery divides. These new patterns – the result of the dense web of connections which characterizes globalization – disengage the economic fates of regions, cities, even neighbourhoods, from their generalized core or periphery locations, and connect them with globalizing systems which may, in a sense, bring the First World into the Third World and vice versa: 'Two areas that exist directly alongside one another, or groups living in close proximity, may be caught up in quite different globalizing systems, producing bizarre physical juxtapositions. The sweatshop worker may be just across the street from a wealthy financial centre' (Giddens, 1994, p. 81).

Recognizing such emergent patterns clearly places a question mark over one of the grounding assumptions of the cultural imperialism argument: the assumption of the continuing concerted dominance of the West – seen as a coherent cultural-economic-geographical totality at the centre of global processes. This is a theme we will pick up in section 3.6. But for now we can consider some specific instances of the growth of 'Third World capitalism' in the cultural sphere.

READING D

Now read the extract from John Sinclair's paper, 'The decentring of cultural imperialism: Televisa-tion and Globo-ization in the Latin world' (1992) provided as Reading D at the end of this chapter. As Sinclair's punning title suggests, his critique of the cultural imperialism thesis is drawn from an analysis of the rise of new and powerful centres of capital in the cultural field within the (erstwhile) Third World.

- In what ways, according to Sinclair, does the success of media entrepreneurs in Latin America undermine the cultural imperialism argument?

- Sinclair is careful to qualify his critique in an important way. Try to say why and how he does this.

As Sinclair stresses, the examples he gives of the rise of dynamic centres of media production in Latin America do not suggest that the US audio-visual industries are 'a spent force' in the global market, much less that these new developments represent a 'reverse cultural imperialism'. Nor, it should be added, does the output of these companies necessarily represent the expression of the cultural autonomy or 'authenticity' of the countries they emerge from – they are after all capitalist institutions driven by similar commercial interests to those in the West. The point, rather, is that we have to take a more nuanced view of the globalized market in communications and media, recognizing the pluralization of cultural production centres around the world and the significance of, for example, the geo-linguistic factors Sinclair mentions in influencing market share. These are both points that the rhetoric of cultural imperialism tends to ignore and, as Sinclair suggests, this is in part due to the rigidities imposed by the core–periphery model. The 'decentring' of cultural imperialism in the context of globalization, then, is not an argument for the smoothing out of global power relations, but for a recognition of the increasingly complex configurations of power that globalization brings.

But should such indications of changes in the global balance of power surprise us? Well, not if we take seriously the much-used term *global* capitalism: for there is no reason to think of the capitalist system as having 'loyalty' to its birthplace in the West, and so there are no guarantees that the geographical patterns of dominance established in early modernity will continue. The long-term implications of capitalist globalization seem likely to include an eventual dismantling of the elective affinity between the interests of capitalism and of the West. We can see signs of this, for example, in the increasingly uneasy relation between the capitalist money markets and the governments and financial institutions of western nation-states. Perhaps the most spectacular recent illustration of this instability was the bankrupting of the British merchant bank Barings in 1995. This episode is very suggestive of the decentring implications of the globalization of capital: 'old European capitalism' in the shape of Baring Brothers – Britain's oldest merchant bank founded in 1762, Bankers to the Queen and so on – destroyed within a few days' trading by high-risk/high-speed electronically mediated dealings in the most refined, abstract example of market trading – derivatives – on the youngest of markets – that of Southeast Asia. It is difficult to resist taking this as a metaphor for the old, confident world of global imperial control being overtaken by the new decentred world of globalized capitalism – in which effects can be instantaneous, catastrophic and completely without regard to established traditions of influence.

To summarize then: recognizing globalization as a 'decentred' process obviously does not imply the imminent equalization of global economic or cultural power, and clearly those countries that have enjoyed dominance in the past will strive, with all the considerable resources at their disposal, to hang on to it. But, on the other hand, we have to recognize that there is nothing in the 'logic of capitalism' that ensures the maintenance of the present advantages of the West. And, as we have seen, the complexities of globalized networks and their unpredictable consequences may well in the long term shift the advantage away from the West.

In the final set of arguments, we will consider the relationship between the globalization process and the broader trajectory of western culture in a little more detail.

3.5 Globalization is a western project

Perhaps the most fundamental intuition in the cultural imperialism perspective is that globalization is, inevitably, a 'western project'. This implies something beyond the simple claims about the spread of western cultural goods, or even of the western provenance of capitalist institutions. It implies that globalization is the continuation of a long historical process of western 'imperialist' expansion – embracing the colonial expansions of the sixteenth to the nineteenth centuries – and representing an historical pattern of increasing global cultural hegemony.

The cultural imperialist approach takes this historical pattern as its major premise and argues – plausibly – that it would seem perverse not to locate contemporary globalization within it. The argument then is that what are being 'globalized' are cultural patterns at a much more profound level than tastes for film genres, jeans or soft drinks. Globalization involves the installation worldwide of western versions of basic social-cultural reality: the West's epistemological and ontological theories, its values, ethical systems, approaches to rationality, technical-scientific worldview, political culture and so on.

This argument is a particularly charged one because it relates to a question of cultural-political commitment amongst intellectuals. If we recognize the discursive struggle which established the critical terms – neo-imperialism, dependency theory, world-system theory, post-colonialism and so on – through which the history of the making of the Third World has become disclosed, then any theory which fails to engage with this context – to take it as a firm, hard-won, and enduring point of reference – is liable to some suspicion. The suspicion must be that globalization theory is just another theory through which the West formulates world history in terms of its own experience – a further example of 'a predominantly white/First World take on things' (Massey, 1994, p. 165). Given the long history of western-dominated global discourse, then, is it not reasonable to suspect globalization theory if it fails to place the history of western imperialism squarely at the centre of its analysis?

This argument, it should be noted, is rather different from the one that stresses the *uneven* nature of the globalization process and the implications of this for the Third World. What is at stake in the unevenness argument is what Doreen Massey calls the 'power geometry' of globalization: the fact that 'some people are more in charge of it than others; some initiate flows and movements, others don't; some are more on the receiving end of it than others ...'. The privileged players in the globalization process for Massey are 'the jet-setters, the ones sending and receiving the faxes and the e-mails, holding the international conference calls ...' (ibid., p. 149). But against this elite, largely First World group, Massey contrasts all those vast numbers who are affected by globalization but not in control of the process – including most obviously the labour migrants and *favela* dwellers in the Third World. The unevenness argument is therefore one focused largely on the exclusion and marginalization of large sections of Third World populations from the benefits of globalization. As we saw in the previous section, even allowing for the gradual decentring of capitalism from the West, this argument retains considerable force.

However, rather than marginalization and exclusion, the 'western project' argument implies an *absorption* of non-western cultures into an homogenized global culture dominated by the West. The long-term cultural implications of this view of globalization – what Ulf Hannerz (1991, p. 108) has dubbed the 'global homogenization scenario' – are actually rather more dramatic. It implies, for the world generally, a culture in which there will be only one way of understanding how life may be lived and, specifically for the Third World, the obliteration of a whole range of diverse, unique cultures which have sustained local communities.

3.6 Globalization is a global project!

Whilst recognizing the genuine concerns that inform the 'westernization/ homogenization' thesis, there are a number of ways in which it might be seen as unduly pessimistic.

First, and most broadly, it can be argued that, though the globalization process undoubtedly has its roots in the experience of the West, it now, as it were, 'belongs' to the world as a whole and will inevitably draw on and be influenced by non-western cultural traditions. This is essentially the argument of Anthony Giddens:

> [Globalization] is more than a diffusion of western institutions across the world in which other cultures are crushed. ... We are speaking here of emergent forms of world interdependence and planetary consciousness [and] the way in which these issues are approached and coped with ... will inevitably involve conceptions and strategies derived from non-western settings.

> (Giddens, 1990, p. 173)

In a later discussion Giddens goes further, suggesting that we can no longer think of globalization as 'only a matter of one-way imperialism' because 'increasingly there is no obvious direction to globalization at all and its ramifications are more or less ever-present' (1994, p. 96). Whatever its provenance then, globalization is now a *global* process. And, in fact, Giddens concludes from this that globalization actually involves 'the declining grip of the West over the rest of the world' (1990, p. 52) as the institutions of modernity that first arose there now become ubiquitous.

Now we *could* read Giddens here as simply proposing an ironical 'winner loses' situation: the very success of the West resulting in its loss of its socio-cultural advantage. However, we can put a little more flesh on the argument by asking whether the West might in some ways be *substantially* losing its cultural grip.

The first way in which this might be true is in relation to the tendency towards cultural hybridization that we mentioned in section 3.2. There we stressed the way in which the processes of 'indigenization' transform the reception of western cultural goods in the Third World. But there is, of course, another side to this and a case could be made for the increasing hybridization of cultural experience in the West as it becomes more and more connected with non-western societies. Examples can readily be found at the level of everyday cultural experience: the globalization of western food tastes, the influence of non-western forms in popular music and so on. But other examples can be found in practices which, perhaps, penetrate further into the 'deep structures' of western culture: the increasing numbers of westerners adopting non-western religions such as Islam or Buddhism, or the way in which western politicians and economists have recently begun to look at the political-economic culture of some Asian societies (the stress on self-reliance, communal and family values of the so-called 'Asian Model') in an attempt to learn from the rapid economic development of these societies. Such examples do not, of course, suggest that non-western cultures are displacing western ones, but they do indicate certain ways in which cultural interpenetration might be weakening the West's cultural hegemony – or at least that sense of cultural confidence that is associated with the idea of a cultural 'project'.

Another way of approaching this is to consider one of the very practical consequences of the globalization of capital: its displacement of huge numbers of people from their homes in Asia, Africa or Latin America to the West as either refugees or labour migrants. As Stuart Hall puts this:

> Driven by poverty, drought, famine, economic undevelopment and crop failure, civil war and political unrest, regional conflict and arbitrary changes of political regime, the accumulating foreign indebtedness of their governments to western banks, very large numbers of the poorer peoples of the globe have taken the 'message' of global consumerism at face value, and moved towards the places where 'the goodies' come from and where the chances of survival are higher. In the era of global communications, the West is only a one-way airline charter ticket away.
>
> (Hall, 1992, pp. 306–7)

The political-economic impact of such migrations is ambiguous for western nation-states, simultaneously offering cheap exploitable labour and representing a threat of demographic 'invasion'. The growing anxiety in the developed world over these population movements can be seen, for example, in the notoriously heavy policing of the US–Mexican border, and in the current debate about 'Fortress Europe'. However, the cultural implications of this sort of literal **deterritorialization** (Appadurai, 1990; Garcia Canclini, 1992, 1995) are likely to be more complex and, eventually, perhaps more significant.

deterritorialization

The anthropologist Renato Rosaldo, discussing the cultural implications of migration from Mexico to the USA writes that: '[T]he notion of an authentic culture as an autonomous internally coherent universe no longer seems tenable ... Rapidly increasing global interdependence has made it more and more clear that neither ''we'' nor ''they'' are as neatly bounded and homogeneous as once seemed to be the case' (Rosaldo, 1993, p. 217).

This claim raises some rather crucial issues of cultural identity: in the first place, of course, for the migrants themselves. There is a sense in which migrants inevitably live their identities in the interstices between their culture of origin and their 'host' culture. Where this migration becomes permanent – as in the post-colonial diasporas of Asian, African and Caribbean people – the question of cultural identity attaching to an authentic 'homeland' becomes entirely problematic and such people 'have had to renounce the dream or ambition of recovering any kind of ''lost'' cultural purity, or ethnic absolutism' (Hall, 1992, p. 310). One then has to ask how the discourse of cultural imperialism works for these diasporic cultures – and the answer is probably not very well. For it is difficult to see how its generalized rhetoric of 'cultural authenticity under attack' can possibly account for the lived experience of **hybridity** – of precisely *not* belonging to one culture.

hybridity

But the main question we can pose here is of the implications of migration for the maintenance of cultural identity in the countries of the West themselves. And here we can connect Rosaldo's observations with those of Kevin Robins, who argues that the post-colonial diaspora represents a sense in which the 'Other has installed itself within the very heart of the western metropolis; [t]hrough a kind of reverse invasion, the periphery has now infiltrated the colonial core' (Robins, 1991, p. 32). Robins draws an inference which is, I think, consistent with Giddens's ideas, that the self-confident, stable cultural identity of the West is becoming threatened: 'Through this irruption of empire, the certain and centred perspective of the old colonial order is confronted and confused' (ibid., p. 33).

What is at stake here is a shift in the cultural relations between the West and its post-colonial Others, a shift in the balance of what might be called 'cultural power', as distinct from political-economic power. The 'certain and centred perspective of the old colonial order' was established in some ways on the basis of unquestioned cultural assumptions and self-images which could only be maintained in binary oppositions preserved by the insulating power of distance. So long as the colonized Others stayed firmly in their place – both literally and metaphorically – the imaginary geographies generated in the West could, by mapping cultural and racial stereotypes on to place, maintain a sense of confidence in a universal order which both justified the colonial project, and fed back into confirmation of western self-images. But as global communications collapse physical distance – in this context bringing the subordinate cultures into direct proximity with the dominant one – so collapses the cultural distance necessary to sustain the myths of identity. It is as though the cultural pluralism which western modernity exported to the rest of the world – and which destroyed the certainties of tradition – now returns to undermine its own certainties.

Two general points emerge from this discussion. First, the globalization process is far too complex to be grasped in the rather simple, if dramatic, predictions of the 'global homogenization scenario'. Second, within this complexity of movements, flows and interpenetrations, the 'western cultural project' is unlikely to proceed unchecked; indeed, there are indications that western cultural power and (perhaps more importantly) *confidence* is in certain ways weakening. Given these considerations, one of the central informing images of the continuing long history of western cultural expansion must be cast in doubt.

4   Conclusion

I began this chapter by suggesting that you keep in mind the opposition between ideas of cultural regulation and de-regulation while you read it. As I hope you will have seen, these ideas, though they don't grasp everything of importance about the cultural imperialism debate, do help to unpack some of its contradictions and ambiguities. And we can conclude by returning to this theme.

We have seen that, contrary to the claims of the cultural imperialism thesis, globalization is unlikely to produce an entirely regulated, homogenized global culture. This is not to deny the drive of global capitalism to distribute its goods and its disposition towards cultural commodification and consumerism as widely as possible. But it is to argue that cultural practices and experiences are far more recalcitrant and unruly than this sort of scenario envisages. In a sense, cultures simply refuse to be regulated in this way. Indeed, rather than seeing cultural globalization as increasing regulation, it makes more sense to see it as predominantly de-regulating. But this is not only in the sense of an expanding unfettered capitalist market in cultural goods, but in a much broader sense of the increasing general mobility and mutability of cultural practices that we referred to as 'deterritorialization'. This undoubtedly poses problems for cultural identity and so it is not surprising that we should see a simultaneous movement towards various sorts of 're-regulation' and re-territorialization of culture – whether in the positive sense of people at local levels trying to take more control of their cultural experiences, or in the more negative form of the rise in cultural chauvinisms and the nationalist and ethnic cultural conflicts that are so much a feature of our time. But we also have to recognize that all these unforeseen consequences of globalization also pose problems for the smooth, homogenizing advance of global capitalism as it is envisioned in the cultural imperialism thesis – particularly as it posits a congruence between the dominance of capitalism and the 'project of the West'.

The balance of the argument in this chapter has clearly been against the cultural imperialism thesis as a general critical perspective on cultural globalization. However, the intellectual *debate* generated around the idea of cultural imperialism has thrown up a number of very significant issues:

- how we think about the specific nature of cultural as distinct from economic power and domination;
- the conditions for cultural autonomy;
- the relationship between cultural identity, place, space and time;
- the possibilities and justification for cultural regulation – 'protection' – by the state.

These debates not only help us to understand the political complexities we have to confront in a globalized world; they may also help to clarify our thinking about what 'culture' actually is, to whom it 'belongs' and how and whether it can/should be regulated, protected and so forth.

Now these are all large and difficult issues which are not likely easily or quickly to be resolved. And indeed the increasing impact of globalizing processes and technologies, in the short term at least, seems liable to compound these difficulties. As we have stressed throughout, the globalization process is not going to smooth out global inequalities in any sphere – cultural, political, or economic. There will surely be winners and losers in the coming phase of cultural globalization just as there were in earlier historical phases, and the USA, the West and western capitalism are not going to be removed overnight from the positions of dominance they have established over centuries. Given this, it seems likely that the general idea of cultural imperialism, despite all its theoretical shortcomings, will continue to be a tempting 're-regulating' critical standpoint, particularly as a focus for policy debates about national cultures.

However, what has also been argued throughout is that, in the longer term, globalization is unlikely to reproduce *exactly* the same patterns of domination that we have experienced in the past. In order to be able to understand and respond to these new patterns, what is needed is a far more nuanced, flexible and dialectical critical perspective than that provided by the cultural imperialism approach. Such a perspective should not attempt to 'totalize' in the manner of the cultural imperialism thesis, but to respond to the very different configurations of power and resistance – the various local– global dialectics – that we are increasingly likely to be confronted with.

References

ANDREWS, J. (1995) 'Culture Wars', *Wired*, No. 101, pp. 73–8.

ANG, I. (1985) *Watching Dallas*, London, Methuen.

APPADURAI, A. (1990) 'Disjuncture and difference in the global cultural economy' in Featherstone, M. (ed.) *Global Culture*, London, Sage, pp. 295–310.

ARDAGH, J. (1995) *France Today*, London, Penguin.

BARKER, M. (1989) *Comics: ideology, power and the critics*, Manchester, Manchester University Press.

BBC MONITORING (1995) *World Broadcasting Information*, Nos. WBI/0024 and WBI/0026, Caversham Park, BBC.

BOYD-BARRETT, O. (1982) 'Cultural dependency and the mass media' in Gurevitch, M. et al. (eds) *Culture, Society and the Media*, London, Methuen, pp. 174–95.

BURNS, C. (1996) 'France airs its distaste for foreign music', *The Guardian*, 1 January, p. 8.

COLLINS, R. (1990) *Culture, Communication and National Identity: the case of Canadian television*, Toronto, University of Toronto Press.

DORFMAN, A. and MATTELART, A. (1975) *How to Read Donald Duck: imperialist ideology in the Disney comic*, New York, International General Editions.

DZIADUL, C. (1993) 'Ready for primetime', *Television Business International*, May, pp. 52–61.

FEJES, F. (1981) 'Media imperialism: an assessment', *Media, Culture and Society*, Vol. 3, No. 3, pp. 281–9.

FOUCAULT, M. (1981) 'The order of discourse' in Young, R. (ed.) *Untying the Text*, London, Routledge and Kegan Paul.

FRIEDMAN, J. (1994) *Cultural Identity and Global Process*, London, Sage.

GARCIA CANCLINI, N. (1992) 'Cultural reconversion' in Yudice, G. et al. (eds) *On Edge: the crisis of contemporary Latin American culture*, Minneapolis, University of Minnesota Press, pp. 29–44.

GARCIA CANCLINI, N. (1995) *Hybrid Cultures*, Minneapolis, University of Minnesota Press.

GERAGHTY, C. (1991) *Women and Soap Opera*, Cambridge, Polity.

GIDDENS, A. (1990) *The Consequences of Modernity*, Cambridge, Polity.

GIDDENS, A. (1994) *Beyond Left and Right*, Cambridge, Polity.

GILROY, P. (1993) *The Black Atlantic*, London, Verso.

GODARD, F. (1993) 'Gatt real', *Television Business International*, Nov–Dec, pp. 14 –17.

HAERI, S. (1994) 'A fate worse than Saudi', *Index on Censorship*, Vol. 23, Nos 4–5, pp. 49–51.

HALL, S. (1991) 'The local and the global: globalization and ethnicities' in King, A. D. (ed.) *Culture, Globalization and the World Ssytem*, London, Macmillan, pp. 19–30.

HALL, S. (1992) 'The question of cultural identity' in Hall, S., Held, D. and McGrew, T. (eds) *Modernity and its Futures*, Cambridge, Polity/The Open University.

HAMELINK, C. J. (1994) *The Politics of World Communication*, London, Sage.

HANNERZ, U. (1991) 'Scenarios for peripheral cultures' in King, A.D. (ed.) *Culture, Globalization and the World System*, London, Macmillan.

HEBDIGE, D. (1988) *Hiding in the Light*, London, Routledge/Comedia.

HOSKINS, C. and MIRUS, R. (1988) 'Reasons for the US Dominance of the International Trade in Television Programmes', *Media Culture and Society*, Vol. 10, No. 4, pp. 499–515.

INSTITUTO DE LA MUJER (1986) *Mujer y Sociedad en Espana 1700–1975*, Madrid, Ministeria de Cultura.

LASH, S. and URRY, J. (1994) *Economies of Signs and Space*, London, Sage.

LIEBES, T. and KATZ, E. (1993) *The Export of Meaning: cross-cultural readings of Dallas*, Cambridge, Polity.

LULL, J. (1995) *Media, Communication, Culture: a global approach*, Cambridge, Polity.

MARTIN-BARBERO, J. (1993) *Communication, Culture and Hegemony*, London, Sage.

MASSEY, D. (1994) *Space, Place and Gender*, Cambridge, Polity.

McGREW, T. (1992) 'A global society?' in Hall, S., Held, D. and McGrew, T. (eds) *Modernity and its Futures*, Cambridge, Polity/The Open University.

McGUIGAN, J. (1992) *Cultural Populism*, London, Routledge.

McPHAIL, T. L. (1987) *Electronic Colonialism: the future of international broadcasting and communication*, Beverly Hills, Sage.

MOORES, S. (1997) 'Broadcasting and its audiences' in Mackay, H. (ed.) *Consumption and Everyday Life*, London, Sage/The Open University (Book 5 in this series).

MORLEY, D. and ROBINS, K. (1989) 'Spaces of identity: communications, technologies and the reconfiguration of Europe', *Screen*, Vol. 30, No. 4, pp. 10–34.

NEGUS, K. (1997) 'The production of culture' in du Gay, P. (ed.) *Production of Culture/Cultures of Production*, London, Sage/The Open University (Book 4 in this series).

POOL, I. DE SOLA (1979) 'Direct broadcast satellites and the integrity of national cultures' in Nordenstreng, K. and Schiller, H. (eds) *National Sovereignty and International Communications*, Norwood, NJ, Ablex.

ROBERTSON, R. (1995) 'Globalization: time–space and homogeneity–heterogeneity' in Featherstone, M., Lash, S. and Robertson, R. (eds) *Global Modernities*, London, Sage, pp. 23–44.

ROBINS, K. (1991) 'Tradition and translation: national culture in its global context' in Corner, J. and Harvey, S. (eds) *Enterprise and Heritage*, London, Routledge, pp. 21–44.

ROBINS, K. (1997) 'What in the world's going on?' in du Gay, P. (ed.) *Production of Culture/Cultures of Production*, London, Sage/The Open University (Book 4 in this series).

ROSALDO, R. (1993) *Culture and Truth: the remaking of social analysis*, London, Routledge.

SAID, E. W. (1979) *Culture and Imperialism*, London, Chatto and Windus.

SCHILLER, H. I. (1979) 'Transnational media and national development' in Nordenstreng, K. and Schiller, H.I. (eds) *National Sovereignty and International Communication*, Norwood, NJ, Ablex.

SCHILLER, H. I. (1985) 'Electronic information flows: new basis for global domination' in Drummond, P. and Paterson, R. (eds) *Television in Transition*, London, BFI Publishing, pp. 11–20.

SCHLESINGER, P. (1991) *Media, State and Nation*, London, Sage.

SCHOU, S. (1992) 'Postwar Americanization and the revitalization of European culture' in Skovmand, M. and Schrøder, K. (eds) *Media Cultures*, London, Routledge, pp. 142–160.

SINCLAIR, J. (1992) 'The decentering of cultural imperialism: Televisa-tion and Globo-ization in the Latin world' in Jacka, E. (ed.) *Continental Shift: globalization and culture*, Double Bay, NSW, Local Consumption Publications, pp. 99–116.

SKLAIR, L. (1991) *Sociology of the Global System*, Hemel Hempstead, Harvester-Wheatsheaf.

SREBERNY-MOHAMMADI, A. and MOHAMMADI, A. (1994) *Small Media, Big Revolution*, Minneapolis, University of Minnesota Press.

THOMPSON, J. B. (1995) *The Media and Modernity*, Cambridge, Polity.

TOMLINSON, J. (1991) *Cultural Imperialism: a critical introduction*, London, Pinter.

TORNABUONI, L. (1995) 'European cinema is dying ...', *The Guardian*, 2 March, p. 6.

TRACEY, M. (1985) 'The poisoned chalice? International television and the idea of dominance', *Daedalus*, Vol. 114, No. 4, pp. 17–56.

TUNSTALL, J. (1977) *The Media are American*, London, Constable.

VAN HEMEL, A. (1994) 'European culture versus GATT trade' in van Hemel, A. (ed.) *GATT, The Arts and Cultural Exchange between the United States and Europe*, Amsterdam/Tilburg, Boekman Foundation/Tilburg University, pp. 39–43.

VAN HEMEL, A., MOMMAAS, H. and SMITHHUIJSEN, C. (eds) (1996) *Trading Culture: GATT, European cultural policies and the transatlantic market*, Amsterdam, Boekman Foundation.

WEBSTER, D. (1988) *Looka Yonda: the imaginary America of populist culture*, London, Routledge/Comedia.

WOOLLACOTT, M. (1995) 'The mouse that soared', *The Guardian*, 19 August, p. 12.

READING A:

Herbert I. Schiller, 'Transnational media and national development'

How national is the national development that (sometimes) occurs in the poorer parts of the world? Domestic and international economic activities today, outside the state-planned societies, are organized according to the explicit and implicit rules of what Wallerstein (1974) calls the 'modern world-system'. What this amounts to, in fact, is a global market economy, presiding with varying flexibility over the allocation of resources, human and natural. Within this near-world orbit, each nation-state seeks, as a minimum, to provide its governing stratum protection and support in the system's overall operation. At the same time, the international division of labor and the allocation of resources are largely influenced, if not determined, by, and in, the advanced, industrialized centers of the global structure.

Consequently, it is somewhat fanciful to term the development of unindustrialized states, attached to the system, if and when it occurs, *national*. The decisions affecting their economies are made by forces largely outside national boundaries. In this process, transnational media occupy an important position. Though profitability is their main concern, they comprise, at the same time, the ideologically supportive informational infrastructure of the modern world system's core – the multinational corporations (MNCs).

[...]

Transnational media are engaged directly in the generation and transmission of messages inside and across state boundaries. They are film companies, publishing firms, TV producing businesses, and many other image-producing activities [...]. The powerful media corporations that finance and control the varied enterprises of message-making are still only a subset of the international informational system. At the system's center are the multinational corporations (some of which are themselves transnational media companies), engaged in manufacturing, industrial, financial, and administrative operations. The MNC, as Mowlana (1975) observes, 'has become one of the

chief organizers and manufacturers of the international flow of communications' (pp. 89–90).

[...]

The objectives of this diverse and multifaceted media mix, besides the immediate one of profitability, are the promotion, protection, and extension of the modern world system and its leading component, the MNC, in particular.

[...]

The internationalization of capital and the export of consumerism

The generative force behind the consumer culture has been the worldwide expansion of American corporate enterprise through the vehicle of what has come to be called the multinational corporation. [...]

Accordingly, in the modern world system, as it has evolved in recent years under American pressure, commercialization of the mass media is an almost universally observed tendency. Even in the most advanced capitalist countries, longstanding public (State) administration of communications facilities (postal systems, telegraph, and broadcasting) is being eroded. In Europe today, with the exception (temporary?) of Belgium, Denmark, Norway, and Sweden, television is relying heavily on advertising revenue. And the pressure for increased commercialization intensifies as the multinationals extend their economic activity. Locally, this is sometimes expressed as 'decentralization', with its implication of extending audience choice. Actually, it provides the means for the extension of advertising and commercialism.

Europe, with four hundred years of commercial and industrial development behind it, increasingly is unable to maintain autonomous national communications systems. Less developed and newly independent nations are even less capable of resisting the pressure of the modern world system.

[...]

Conclusions

The transnational media are inseparable elements in a worldwide system of resource allocation generally regarded as capitalist. They function as private profit-making enterprises seeking markets, which they term 'audiences'. They provide in their imagery and messagery the beliefs and perspectives that create and reinforce their audiences' attachment to the way things are in the system overall.

It is pointless, therefore, to attempt to measure the impact of any individual medium or message. Each is a contributor in its own way to a systematic process. All are mutually reinforcing and capable as well of absorbing occasional discordant messages and influences.

The consequences of the transnational media's heavy outputs are not measurable either. They are observable as typifying a way of life. For example, a minority report of a Brazilian governmental inquiry on the impact of the multinational corporation in Brazil, found that 'the multinationals have concentrated on producing expensive goods, such as automobiles and color television sets, that demand a concentration of income ... so more debts have been built up to finance the consumption of luxury goods instead of satisfying the minimum necessities of nutrition, health, housing, and employment' (Greenwood, 1975).

This describes a developmental path. It is a familiar one. It is what has come to be recognized, with apologies to the Chinese, as the capitalist road to development. In this process, the media, now many times more powerful and penetrative than in an earlier time, are the means that entice and instruct their audiences along this path, while at the same time concealing the deeper reality and the long-term consequences that the course produces. [...]

References

GREENWOOD, L. (1975) 'Multinationals drain Brazil, report says', *Los Angeles Times*, 1 December, p. 11.

MOWLANA, H. (1975) 'The multinational corporation and the diffusion of technology' in Said, A.A. and Simmons, L.R. (eds.) *The New Sovereigns: multinational corporations as world powers*, Englewood Cliffs, NJ, Prentice Hall, pp. 77–99.

WALLERSTEIN, I. (1974) *The Modern World System, Capitalist Agriculture and the Origins of the European World-Economy in the Sixteenth Century*, New York, Academic Press.

Source: Schiller, 1979, pp. 21–5, 30–1.

READING B:
Cees J. Hamelink, 'The politics of world communication'

[...] Concerns with regard to the world market in media services have been recently expressed in connection with the current Uruguay Round of multilateral trade negotiations. The special focus of these concerns is TV programmes and films and the existing and/or potential constraints to trading them across the world. The concerns focus on forms of national regulation that restrict imports of media services or national policies that protect national media industries. There are however also concerns about trade constraints that address the structure of the international media market, particularly with reference to the large share of market control by only a few transnational operators.

The world's largest exporter of films, the USA, has confronted protectionist measures in its largest export markets since its early beginnings. In Europe, for instance, the massive invasion of American films in the early 1920s caused restrictive measures, first by Germany, later by France and the UK. After the Second World War, with massive imports of US-made films, worries rose in European countries about the protection of national film production and about their balance of payments. These worries motivated measures of import control that largely worked along two lines. The number of imported films was limited (so-called number quotas) and screen time was shared between foreign and domestic films (so-called screen quotas). These protectionist policies changed in the 1960s when US exports declined, the European film industry became stronger, a strong trend towards trade liberalization emerged in Europe, and several co-production and co-investment schemes for film production developed between European markets and the US film industry.

The most active player in the search for solutions to the concern about trade constraints has been the US Motion Picture Export Association. The MPEA has sought unilateral US trade sanctions against countries that raised trade barriers to US produced films, television programmes and home videos. In

1989 the MPEA filed complaints to the US Trade Representative quoting Section 301 of the US Trade Act. It has targeted for retaliatory trade restrictions such countries as Brazil, Colombia, India, Indonesia, the Republic of Korea and Taiwan. Among the retaliatory actions proposed by the MPEA were restrictions on imports of textiles and electronics. The MPEA has identified various non-tariff trade barriers and has considered a lack of adequate intellectual property protection the most serious barrier to free world trade.

In September 1993 the French audiovisual industry took the initiative to protest against the inclusion of audiovisual products in the final text of the GATT Uruguay Round multilateral trade talks. In these negotiations, the USA demanded that the world trade in AV products follow the principles of free trade policy. This would imply that a variety of protectionist measures (such as national import quotas and state subsidies) which are common in European countries would have to be abandoned. Representatives of the French entertainment sector (with the support of the EU ministers of culture) claimed that only removing AV products from GATT rules could save the European film and entertainment industry. An appeal signed by over 4000 professionals in the industry accused the USA of 'cultural dumping'. In the European protest against GATT rules for audiovisual services, important economic interests were at stake. Some 80 per cent of the European AV market is controlled by US producers. The sales of US TV programmes in Europe have increased from US$330 million in 1984 to US$3.6 billion in 1992. In 1991 some 77 per cent of US AV exports went to the European market and this market grows at an annual 6 per cent. It can be expected that the introduction of more advanced AV technology will only lead to more channel capacity and thus more demand. A strong lobby against what was perceived as European protectionism was represented by the Motion Picture Association President Jack Valenti and film producer Steven Spielberg. Part of the disagreement was about the wish of the European Union to use a proportion of box office income to subsidize European films and the rule that at least 51 per cent of TV programmes in Europe should be of European origin. The European industry expressed as its position that the application of free trade rules would promote the global spread of Hollywood materials and would effectively annihilate European culture.

The positions

Perspectives on the issue of traded media services diverge. Some players claim that this trade should be unhindered and that foreign markets should be freely accessed. Others are concerned that without restrictions on media imports, local cultural industries cannot survive and local cultural heritage gives way to McDonaldization. The leading media production companies, their associations such as the MPEA, and the governments of exporting countries (especially the USA) have been very concerned about barriers to media trade. The concern about the lack of controls is largely articulated by small producers and by governments of importing countries (Third World countries, West European countries, Canada). Their preference for import restrictions is largely motivated by the desire to economically and culturally protect their own media industries. This is reinforced by the fear that transnational control over local distribution and exhibition mechanisms will exert a decisive influence on what cultural product is locally available.

The contending positions are liberal-permissive claims versus protectionist-restrictive claims. The liberal position prefers an arrangement that permits total liberalization of market access for media services. The more protectionist position favours levels of protection from media imports as instruments to support local media industries or protect local culture.

One of the complexities of addressing media services in a trade context is that not all of them have commercial purposes. A part of mass media production is typically oriented towards non-commercial, educational, artistic or socio-cultural goals. Although this is recognized in Article IV of the GATT, the big media exporters define their product in terms of a commercial commodity only. This implies the collision of the claim to the opportunity to increase markets for a profitable commodity with the claim to rightfully regulate media imports and protect national media markets for a variety of reasons.

For developing countries a problem with the liberalization claim is also that since media products are finished products, it is not likely that liberalization will increase labour or technology inputs for them. In contrast to tourism, for instance, media services do not bring employment or training. There is also the problem that market access is likely to be a one-way street. There is, given the economic realities of media production and distribution, little chance of exports from the Third World countries. [...]

The GATT accord that was concluded in mid December 1993 did not include the sector of audiovisual services. The most powerful players were divided among themselves and clashed on a free trade perspective promoted by the USA and a cultural policy perspective defended by the EU. The discord is only of marginal significance. There is no basic disagreement among the opponents about the commercial nature of culture and information as marketable commodities. European politics has already for some time established that broadcasting, for example, is a traded service and is subject to the rules on market competition of the EEC treaty. The European claim to exempt culture from international trade rules is not motivated by deep principles. In the bargaining at some point a deal will be made and a trade agreement will emerge. This will also be facilitated since protectionism is not a feasible proposition. The owners of satellite dishes cannot be stopped from receiving US audiovisual fare if they want to do so.

For the time being, the major players have agreed to disagree. However, in February 1994 both key US actors (such as the MPEA) and the European Commission indicated a desire to reconcile their divergent positions on the issue of traded media services. [...]

Source: Hamelink, 1994, pp.179-183

READING C:
John B. Thompson, 'The media and modernity' *

[...] Schiller argues that the American system of broadcasting – essentially a commercial system dominated by the large networks and funded primarily by advertising revenue – exemplifies the way in which some of the most important communication systems have been thoroughly permeated by commercial interests. Moreover, the American system of broadcasting has served as a model for the development of broadcasting systems elsewhere in the world, especially in Third World countries. The dependence on American communications technology and investment, coupled with the new demand for TV programmes and the sheer cost of domestic production, have created enormous pressures for the development of commercial broadcasting systems in many Third World countries and for the large-scale importation of foreign – mainly American – programmes. The result is an 'electronic invasion' which threatens to destroy local traditions and to submerge the cultural heritage of less developed countries beneath a flood of TV programmes and other media products emanating from a few power centres in the West. These programmes are infused with the values of consumerism, since they are geared above all to the needs of the manufacturers who sponsor television through advertising. Hence, when developing countries adopt a commercial system of broadcasting, they are also, argues Schiller, implicated in a process of cultural transformation and dependency in which the values of consumerism override traditional motivations and alternative patterns of value formation, and through which individuals are harnessed increasingly to a global system of communication and commodity production based largely in the US.

Schiller's argument [...] has the considerable merit of highlighting the global character of electronically based communication systems, of emphasizing their structured character and of underscoring the fact that communication systems are interwoven in fundamental ways with the exercise of economic, military and political power. Moreover, Schiller's argument brings sharply into focus the enormous financial constraints faced by Third World countries seeking to develop their own communication systems, constraints which make the importation of foreign-produced programmes very attractive. However, even if one sympathizes with Schiller's broad theoretical approach and this critical perspective, there are many respects in which his argument is deeply unsatisfactory. [...]

[One] problem with Schiller's argument concerns the ways in which imported media products are thought to affect their recipients in the Third World and elsewhere. Schiller argues, in essence, that TV programmes which are made for a commercial television system will unavoidably express consumerist values, both in the programmes themselves and in the advertising which constitutes the financial basis of the system; and that these representations will in turn create wants and foster consumerist motivations in their recipients, in such a way that these recipients become harnessed to a Western-based system of commodity production and exchange. No doubt this rather hasty argument, in its concern to highlight the connection between broadcasting media and a capitalist system of commodity production and exchange, has placed too much emphasis on the role of consumerist values and has neglected the enormous diversity of themes, images and representations which characterize the output of the media industries. But there is another weakness in this argument which is of particular relevance to the issues that concern us here: the argument presupposes a much too simplified account of what is involved in the reception and appropriation of media products. Like many arguments influenced by Marxism, Schiller's argument commits a version of what I have described elsewhere as the 'fallacy of internalism'. Schiller tries to infer, from an analysis of the social organization of the media industries, what the consequences of media messages are likely to be for the individuals who receive them. But inferences of this kind must be treated with scepticism. Not only are they very speculative but, more importantly, they disregard the complex, varied and contextually specific ways in which messages are

interpreted by individuals and incorporated into their day-to-day lives. In short, Schiller's argument ignores the hermeneutic process of appropriation which is an essential part of the circulation of symbolic forms (including media products).

In recent years, a number of researchers have shown – through ethnographic studies in contexts that are particularly suitable for assessing the plausibility of the cultural imperialism thesis – that the processes of reception, interpretation and appropriation of media messages are much more complicated than Schiller's argument assumes. Thus Liebes and Katz, in a well-known study (1993), examined the reception of *Dallas* among different ethnic groups in Israel, comparing their responses with groups in the United States and Japan. They show that different groups found different ways of making sense of the programme, different ways of 'negotiating' its symbolic content. The process of reception was not a one-way transmission of sense but rather a creative encounter between, on the one hand, a complex and structured symbolic form and, on the other, individuals who belong to particular groups and who bring certain resources and assumptions to bear on the activity of interpretation. So Liebes and Katz found, for instance, that there were systematic differences in the ways that groups recounted the programmes they had seen. The groups of Israeli Arabs and Moroccan Jews emphasized kinship relations, interpreting the motivation of characters primarily in terms of the hierarchical order of the family and the continuity of the dynasty. The groups of Russian émigrés, by contrast, paid relatively little attention to kinship relations and were more inclined to take a critical view, seeing the characters as manipulated by the writers and producers of the programme. The groups of kibbutz members and of Americans were also inclined to take a critical view but they interpreted the programme in more psychological terms, as an ongoing saga of interpersonal relations and intrigue.

Studies such as this have shown convincingly that the reception and appropriation of media products are complex social processes in which individuals – interacting with others as well as with the characters portrayed in the programme they receive – actively make sense of messages, adopt various attitudes towards them and use them in differing ways in the course of their day-to-day lives. It is simply not possible to infer the varied features of reception processes from the characteristics of media messages considered by themselves, or from the commercial constraints operating on the producers of TV programmes. In this respect, Schiller's argument involves a theoretical and methodological short-circuit. The electronic invasion of American films and TV programmes would serve to extend and consolidate a new imperial regime only if it could be reliably assumed that the recipients of these programmes would internalize the consumerist values allegedly expressed in them; but it is precisely this assumption that must be placed in doubt.

This line of criticism presses to the heart of the cultural imperialism thesis. It shows that this thesis is unsatisfactory not only because it is outdated and empirically doubtful, but also because it is based on a conception of cultural phenomena which is fundamentally flawed. It fails to take account of the fact that the reception and appropriation of cultural phenomena are fundamentally hermeneutical processes in which individuals draw on the material and symbolic resources available to them, as well as on the interpretative assistance offered by those with whom they interact in their day-to-day lives, in order to make sense of the messages they receive and to find some way of relating to them. For the cultural imperialism thesis, the process of reception is essentially a 'black box' into which media products infused with consumerist values are poured, and from which individuals oriented towards personal consumption supposedly emerge. But this clearly will not do.

[...]

Reference

LIEBES, T. AND KATZ, E. (1993) *The Export of Meaning*: *cross-cultural readings of Dallas*, Cambridge, Polity Press.

Source: Thompson, 1995, pp. 116, 170–3.

READING D:

John Sinclair, 'The decentring of cultural imperialism: Televisa-tion and Globo-ization in the Latin world'

[...] David Morley and Kevin Robins sum up the effects of language-based cultural discounts in the current European television market in these terms:

> Attempts to attract a European audience with English language programming, not unlike the attempt to create European advertising markets, do seem to have largely foundered in the face of linguistic and cultural divisions in play between the different sectors of the audience ... There is a growing realisation that the success of American-style commercial programming in Europe is context-dependent in a very specific sense. US imports only do well when domestic television is not producing comparable entertainment programming – and whenever viewers have the alternative of comparable entertainment programming in their own language, the American programmes tend to come off second best.
>
> (Morley and Robins, 1989, p. 28)

Some of the elements which have been identified [...] – indigenization, language difference, and domestic market strength – are at the heart of another phenomenon which can now be found in cultural imperialism's blindspot, and that is the rise of other, non-anglophone 'centres' of international media production and trade based on what might be called 'geolinguistic regions': Bombay for the Hindi film industry, Hong Kong for Chinese genre movies, Cairo for Arabic film and television, and Mexico City for film and television production in Spanish, particularly in the 'indigenized' *telenovela* genre, as well as for dubbing US programs into Spanish for re-export. These centres are not at all 'new', having already been in evidence when Jeremy Tunstall wrote *The Media Are American* in 1977 and predicted that their 'hybrid' genres, what we would now call 'indigenized' versions of the US musical, action movie and soap opera, would grow to form their own stratum in international exchange.

Armand Mattelart and his collaborators give attention to the geolinguistic factor in their investigation of the difficulties faced by the cultural industries of certain European and 'Third World' countries in the development of a 'Latin audiovisual space' within contemporary 'international image markets' (Mattelart et al., 1984). As Schlesinger reminds us, 'the "audiovisual" is both a symbolic arena and an economic one' (1987, p. 228). The work is tendentious in its origins, given that it was commissioned by the French Minister of Culture after a meeting in 1982 with his counterparts from Mexico and Brazil as well as Spain, Portugal and Italy, which agreed to promote 'co-operation between countries with a language of Latin origin' (cited in Mattelart et al., 1984, p. ix). *Et tu, Brute*? It should be said that the Mattelart group distance themselves from the inherent traps of this patronage and pursue their own diverse interests (1984, pp. 17–18). They strive to move beyond the determinism and functionalism which has characterized the cultural imperialism standpoint with which much of their own former work is identified, and towards an 'internationalist' or globalized perspective which reaffirms the more dialectical qualities of thought to be found in the Western Marxist tradition, and combines a 'sceptical empirical understanding of the media industries. They also are able to avoid the reflexive sloganized dogmatism of what Garnham has called 'Third Worldism' and 'cultural anti-Americanism' (1984, pp. 1–6).

As Anthony Smith observes, the spread of a *lingua franca* throughout such a 'culture area' provides the potential rather than the necessary conditions for the emergence of transterritorial communications (1990, p. 186). In this case, the potential lies in the linguistic and other cultural similarities which might be cultivated to create an intercontinental media market across all those countries which have Latin-based languages: Spanish, Portuguese, French and Italian; that is, the geolinguistic region of Latin America and Southwest Europe, itself a fusion of the cultural legacies of former empires.

The cultural imperialism approach and the Marxist theoretical tradition in general have had no more than a negative interest in the classical economists' concept of 'comparative advantage', and even Ricardo would never have thought to apply the

notion to language. However, in the context of the flow patterns of international trade in audiovisual products, and particularly when taken in relation to size and structure of the domestic market, language of origin emerges if not as a determinant, then at least as a factor of potential advantage in the international market. Richard Collins has drawn attention to English as 'the language of advantage' in the 'tradeable information sector' of the global economy, though also emphasizing its potential rather than necessary status:

> The size and wealth of the anglophone market provides producers of English language information with a considerable comparative advantage *vis-à-vis* producers in other languages. But it is important to recognize that this is a *potential* advantage which may or may not be realizable. Not all anglophone producers will succeed, and producers in other languages are not necessarily doomed to fail.
>
> (1990, p. 211)

Indeed, an examination of the geolinguistic dimension of global media flows, made with due regard to certain 'multinationals of the Third World' which have transformed themselves into 'international multimedia groups', demonstrates that a kind of Latin audiovisual space is in fact being created by these private corporate interests, in which the comparative advantage of language is a key factor (Mattelart et al., 1984, pp. 51–7). These private corporations are Televisa, which all but monopolizes the audiovisual industries of Mexico, and TV Globo, the dominant television network in Brazil.

In the case of Televisa, the domination it has long held over its home market in the world's largest Spanish-speaking nation has become a raft for its various international ventures. Spanish is the second most widely-spoken European language in the world after English, but like the other languages which have generated their own regional media industries, it has been only in the peripheral vision of the cultural imperialism perspective. TV Globo is different in so far as it has had to decode and dub its programs for several export markets, but it too first based its international push into Europe and Africa on [Brazil's] comparative advantage as the world's largest Portuguese-speaking country, Portuguese being the world's fourth most widely spoken European language (Hoffman, 1989, pp. 224–225). Once again, the critique reproduces its object, to the extent that critics of cultural imperialism, or indeed theorists of globalization who are born into English-speaking cultures, take for granted the pre-eminence of English as a global language, and hence their own position as beneficiaries of centuries of anglophone colonialism (Featherstone, 1990, pp. 11–12). It is thus difficult to appreciate that Televisa and TV Globo, based on the languages of an older era of colonialism, have become the biggest television networks in the world outside of the US. Even if their markets are not as lucrative as the English-speaking ones, and there is a heavy cultural discount applied to foreign language programs in the anglophone world, a different set of relativities applies when the world is viewed from Mexico City or Rio. To take a notable example, the 'Hispanic' population of the US, although less than 10% of the total population and relatively deprived as a group, is none the less the sixth largest Spanish-speaking population in the world, and also the most affluent: on the face of it, a natural constituency for Televisa (Strategy Research Corporation, 1987, p. 38).

Since comparative advantage is potential rather than actual, there are other factors to be taken into account in the expansion of these networks, but even these factors have not been within the range of vision of the cultural imperialism perspective. Because that view emphasized the technological and political strengths of the West, and especially the US, it was included to see the adoption of new forms of the mass media as a process in which the US imposed its new media technologies, television in particular, on weaker, 'less developed' nations. This was seen to achieve a new market for US transmission and reception technologies, that is, both producer and consumer goods, as well as for US programs, not to mention access to audiences for US-based advertisers and general control of the medium's ideological ethos. Because of this assumption of Western commercio-technological domination, and its theoretical commitment to objective structural forces as the prime movers of historical change, what the cultural imperialism perspective did not take account of was the degree to which individual entrepreneurs in the subordinate countries might have sought to attract and give active encouragement to this process, and so secure for themselves a place in the consequent structure of 'dependent development'.

[...]

The cultural imperialism perspective also underestimated the degree to which the media entrepreneurs in the subject countries would use and adapt new technologies for their own innovation. In the Mexican case again, the advent of videotape was seized upon to build up program export activities, while at a later stage, satellite technology was used to interconnect the various Spanish-language television stations which Televisa for many years controlled throughout the US itself (as mentioned, the sixth largest Spanish-speaking nation in the world, and the richest), thus establishing a national network for Mexican-originated programs and creating a national audience of 'Hispanics'. The international expansion of Televisa and its corporate ancestors has always been production-driven, based on an economics similar to the export of domestic product upon which the US cultural industries have built themselves. As early as 1954, Azcarraga (Senior) had attempted to sell his programs to US networks, and when they were rejected as only fit for 'ghetto time', began establishing his own stations throughout the US, and a network to distribute programs and sell advertising for them. In these enterprises, his *prestanombre*, or 'front-man', was Rene Anselmo, a US citizen. By 1986, a national network of broadcast stations, low power repeater stations and arrangements with cable stations, all interconnected by satellite, was reaching a claimed eighty-two per cent of Hispanic households, or fifteen million viewers (bigger than NBC, it was said), supplying them with programs largely beamed up from Mexico City (Sinclair, 1990).

[...]

The unforeseen development of such intercontinental media markets based on the comparative advantage of geolinguistic region, domestic market size and technological adaptation does not repudiate the rationale of the cultural imperialism critique as it developed in the 1970s, insofar as it sought to comprehend the cultural dimension of unequal relations between nations. Of course basic structural inequalities still remain.

The suggestion sometimes made that Televisa's incursion into the US market or TV Globo's exports to Portugal and Italy are forms of 'reverse cultural imperialism' is a canard, based on cynicism at worst or ignorance at best. Indeed, the energetic pursuit of overseas markets by Televisa and TV Globo can be explained also in terms of the constrictions which inflation, economic crisis and the imposition of debt discipline have placed upon their growth in their respective domestic markets, still in a condition of 'dependent development'.

[...]

[However, what] can be said is that the cultural imperialism perspective was limited by its undialectical centre-periphery model of structural relations between nations, its assumption of credulous, homogenized consumers of cultural products and of a supine *comprador* bourgeoisie in the subordinate countries, and its disregard for the specificities and complexities to be found amongst the various nations of the erstwhile Third World. The processes of national disaggregation and interpenetration between new international entities in the era of globalization calls for less abstract and dogmatic, more particular and empirical ways in which to apprehend the world.

References

COLLINS, R. (1990) *Culture, Communication and National Identity: the case of Canadian television*, Toronto, University of Toronto Press.

FEATHERSTONE, M. (1990) 'Introduction' to Featherstone, M. (ed.) *Global Culture: nationalism, globalization and modernity*, London, Sage (Special issue of *Theory, Culture and Society*, Vol. 7, No. 2–3), pp. 1–14.

GARNHAM, N. (1984) 'Introduction' to Mattelart et al., pp. 1–6.

HOFFMAN, M. (ed.) (1989) *World Almanac*, New York, Pharos Books.

MATTELART, A., DELCOURT, X. and MATTELART, M. (1994) *International Image Markets: in search of an alternative perspective*, London, Comedia.

MORLEY, D. and ROBINS, K. (1989) 'Spaces of identity: communications, technologies and the reconfiguration of Europe', *Screen*, Vol. 30, No. 4, pp. 10–34.

SCHLESINGER, P. (1987) 'On national identity: some conceptions and misconceptions criticised', *Social Science Information*, Vol. 26, No. 2, pp. 219–64.

SINCLAIR, J. (1990) 'Spanish-language television in the United States: Televisa surrenders its domain', *Studies in Latin American Popular Culture*, Vol. 9, pp. 39–63.

STRATEGY RESEARCH CORPORATION (1987) *1987 US Hispanic Market Study*, Miami, Strategy Research Corporation.

TUNSTALL, J. (1977) *The Media Are American*, London, Constable.

Source: Sinclair, 1992, pp. 99–116.

NATIONAL CULTURE AND MULTICULTURALISM

Bhikhu Parekh

CHAPTER FOUR

Contents

1   Introduction

The past three decades have witnessed the emergence of a cluster of new social movements led by such diverse groups as the indigenous peoples, old and especially new immigrants, women, national minorities, and gay men and lesbians. These movements, generally subsumed under the capacious term *multiculturalism*, attack the dominant culture for taking a demeaning view of and discriminating against the groups involved, and demand regulatory policies to ensure equal public recognition and legitimacy for their distinct cultural perspectives or ways of life. Agitations of the indigenous peoples in Canada, Australia, New Zealand, the USA, Latin-America and India, of the ethno-nationalist groups in such places as Quebec, Kashmir and Catalonia, the protests by Muslims against Salman Rushdie's novel *The Satanic Verses* in Britain, the controversy in France about Muslim girls wearing headscarves in school, and so on, are all examples of this.

Multiculturalism, and regulatory policies to promote it, have provoked varying degrees of resistance. In the eyes of its critics it rests on what might be called **cultural relativism** – the belief that all cultures are equally good, that there are no intercultural or universal standards of moral judgement, and that no cultural practice may be criticized, however offensive it might seem to outsiders. For the critics this involves an abdication of all moral judgement, a dangerous moral *laissez-faire*, and is not only false but an enemy of all that western civilization stands for. They also argue that since no stable social life is possible without a shared national culture, multiculturalism is a recipe for social chaos and political disintegration. It breaks up society into neatly insulated cultural units, each claiming sovereignty over its internal life and immunity from external criticism and all sharing nothing in common. The critics argue that no civilized and stable social life is possible on such a basis.

cultural relativism

In this chapter we shall discuss what multiculturalism stands for and whether the criticisms of it are fair. Since the term multiculturalism is of relatively recent origin and has been promiscuously used to include a wide variety of otherwise unrelated movements, we shall begin with a brief discussion of what it means. In section 3 we shall then look at multicultural movements in three countries, exploring why they occurred there and in what forms. We shall end the chapter by discussing the kind of case that can be made for multiculturalism and how a society can be both plural and cohesive.

The approach taken in this chapter differs from that of some other authors who have focused on the shifting nature of cultural identities (for example, **Gilroy**'s (1997) discussion of diaspora identities). Here I will be concentrating on the politics of multiculturalism – the relations between groups and cultures – within a pluralistic, or 'liberal', society, which involves struggles for equal recognition on behalf of minority cultures.

2   What is multiculturalism?

multiculturalism

The term **multiculturalism** has three components. First, it has something to do with culture. Second, it points to a plurality of cultures. And, third, it refers to a specific manner of responding to that plurality, hence the suffix 'ism' which here, as elsewhere, signifies a normative doctrine. Let us take each in turn.

2.1   Culture

culture

The term **culture** is one of the most slippery and elusive terms in the vocabulary of social and political theory (see the discussion in **du Gay, Hall et al.**, 1997, section 1). People may talk of culture in an unspecified way, as well as of high or popular culture, literary culture, organizational culture, drug culture, primitive or advanced culture, and so forth. One broad meaning of the term culture refers to the body of beliefs and practices governing the conduct of the relevant area, be it a specific activity, an aspect of human experience, an organization or human life as a whole. When it is used in an unqualified way it may refer to beliefs and practices regulating all or major areas of human life, and have broadly the same meaning as the older term 'a way of life'. When it is adjectivized and qualified, the adjective expresses a judgement on it, or points to its bearer, or highlights a specific area of life. Thus the term 'primitive culture' refers to a way of life judged to be backward and insufficiently advanced; 'advanced culture' has the opposite meaning. 'Moral' or 'political' culture refers to a set of beliefs and practices governing the conduct respectively of moral and political life; and 'drug culture' refers to beliefs and practices legitimizing and governing the use of drugs.

In this chapter I am going to adopt a broad definition of culture, traditionally favoured in anthropology and moral and political theory, which refers to a way of life, that is, to a way of understanding, structuring, conducting and talking about human life, and encompassing all that is necessary for that purpose. Although different cultures define and relate them differently, every culture or way of life might be thought of as having the following components. First, it includes a body of beliefs including ideas, images, myths, maxims, and proverbs pithily expressing its collective wisdom, in terms of which its members understand themselves and the world and assign meaning and significance to their lives, social relations, actions and utterances. Second, it includes values, ideals of excellence, norms of behaviour and a specific conception of the good life, which regulate social relations, food, dress, modes of greeting, and such important events in life as birth, marriage and death. Fourth, cultures tend to possess rituals, traditions of music and arts, written or unwritten literature, stories and so on, through which they express collective emotions, experiences and self-understanding. Fifth, members of a cultural group have some conception of how it began and developed, how it differs from other cultures, what it stands for, who its heroes and villains or friends or foes are, and a more or less coherent narrative of its origins, struggles, achievements, failures and aspirations. Finally, since a culture involves a special mode of behaviour and a specific understanding of life, it can encourage specific traits of temperament, capacities, psychological and moral dispositions, motivational structures, a specific range of emotions and modes of expressing them, and so forth. In other words, every culture tends to presuppose and cultivate what may loosely be called a common social character among its members (what elsewhere may be called 'subjectivities'). As a result, to varying degrees they may internalize and feel attached to the culture, regard it as 'their' culture, feel at home in it, and see it as an expression of themselves, of their identities. In modern society individuals lead different ways of life, take pride in developing different personal identities, and acquire different qualities of temperament and character. Although their social character therefore contains great internal variations, it might be argued that they cannot share a common way of life and sustain constant and close interactions without acquiring a family of broad characteristics in common.

The six components of culture are interrelated and derive their meaning and significance from their relations with each other. Two cultures might and often do share common practices, but the ways in which they justify them and the meaning and importance they assign to them could be, and are generally, quite different. Both secular humanists and devout Catholics cherish the practice of monogamy, but it has very different meanings for them. Two cultures, again, might share some common beliefs, but they might define them differently and derive very different practices from them. All cultures, for example, value human life, but disagree about when it begins and ends and what obligations and rights it entails. The individuality of a culture lies not only in its beliefs and practices but also in the way in which they are interrelated and form an intelligible whole.

The relationship among and between beliefs and practices is neither deductive nor contingent and accidental but one of mutual entailment and support. Since a culture evolves over time, is a precipitate of diverse influences, and has no co-ordinating authority, it is never entirely coherent. However, it can be argued that no culture is an eclectic and chaotic collection of beliefs and practices, both because human beings reflect upon and seek coherence in their lives and because their mutually regulating beliefs and practices generate some degree of internal consistency. The fact that cultures overlap and cannot be neatly individuated or clearly marked off from each other does not mean that they are indistinguishable or lack individuality. After all, languages and religions, too, overlap and cannot be neatly separated, but that does not deny their individuality. Cultures, societies, human beings etc. are not like material objects, and hence the criteria used to define and distinguish the latter are inapplicable to them.

cultural community

In so far as a group of people is united in terms of their allegiance to a common culture, they might be said to constitute a **cultural community**. Every organization that has gone on long enough, such as a university or a business corporation, develops elements of shared culture (as discussed in **du Gay**, 1997, and **Salaman**, 1997). Du Gay and Salaman do indeed argue that corporate businesses increasingly are being theorized as – and regard themselves as – 'cultures'. However, I would argue that they are not cultural communities in the sense described above, because they are created to achieve specific substantive goals, of which the common culture is an incidental and largely instrumental aspect. I would also argue that, although political communities are often called cultural communities, in terms of the definition I am using here, they are not. Their principle of unity is political not cultural, and at best they share common beliefs and practices about political life but not about the world, the meaning of life, moral ideals, or the best way to live one's life.

Sharing a culture is a matter of degree. As we have seen, a culture is articulated at various levels and has several components. One might subscribe to some parts of it but not others: for example, to its system of meanings and view of the world but not to its customs and practices, or to the latter but not to some of its values. Gay men and lesbians generally share a common culture with heterosexuals, but differ from them in their sexual beliefs and practices and in the subculture they develop around these. This is also the case with couples following different forms of living together or family structures. Jewish people who reject their religion or dietary taboos but not the rest of their culture provide another example of differential relation to one's culture. With the exception of the most conservative societies insisting on total allegiance to all its beliefs and practices, all societies allow such departures, and some might depend on them for their self-renewal. There is often a dispute, sometimes fierce, as to whether and when these departures amount to a rejection of the culture itself, and each culture either resolves it in its own way or faces a split. Most cultures contain a variety of cultural practices and such subcultures as these might throw up, and provide ways of coping with the internal heterogeneity.

2.2   Multiculture

Just as a society with several religions or languages is multireligious or multilingual, a society containing several cultures is multicultural. We have already seen what a culture is, and we have also seen that, although cultures cannot be neatly separated, they do have an individuality. A multicultural society, then, is one that includes several cultural communities with their overlapping but none the less distinct conceptions of the world, systems of meaning, values, forms of social organization, histories, customs and practices.

Not all multicultural societies are identically multicultural, for they vary both in the range and the depth of their **multiculturality**. Some might include a larger number of cultural communities than others. The USA has more cultural communities than Great Britain, and its *range* of multiculturality is thus wider. Again, differences between cultural communities in one society might be deeper than those in another, and then we might say that the *depth* of multiculturality in the former is greater. Thus whites and Aborigines in Australia differ far more from each other than do the Tamils and the Sinhalese in Sri Lanka, the Serbs and the Muslims in Bosnia, or the English and the Scots in Britain.

multiculturality

We have suggested that a multicultural society is one with several distinct and well-developed cultural communities. What about societies sharing a common culture but containing several subcultures or a wide variety of diverse cultural practices? As we saw, gays and heterosexuals, or those preferring conventional and unconventional lifestyles, generally share the common culture of the wider society including a common system of meanings, history and a view of the world, but they differ in their sexual practices or lifestyles and the subcultures that develop around these. How should we describe such a society? Since it does not have distinct and autonomous cultural communities, it is not exactly multicultural. However, it does contain considerable diversity and is not monocultural in a way that a thoroughly homogeneous society is. Just as there are degrees of multiculturality, there are degrees of **monoculturality**, and not all monocultural societies are equally and identically monocultural.

monoculturality

Since both monoculturality and multiculturality are matters of degrees, there is an inescapable element of arbitrariness as to where we draw the line and what societies we call mono- or multicultural. We might say that only a society with several distinct and relatively self-contained cultural communities is multicultural. Or we might say that an otherwise monocultural society that exhibits some or at least a significant degree of cultural diversity should also be called multicultural. If we took the former view, we would have to say that the feminist and gay liberation movements do not form part of multiculturalism. Although they challenge many a belief and practice of the prevailing culture, they share much in common with it and do not form distinct and autonomous cultural communities. If we took the second wider view, we would arrive at the opposite conclusion.

Although both views have much to be said in their favour, in my view, the narrower interpretation is marginally preferable for three reasons. First, since almost all societies permit some cultural diversity, the wider view requires us to call them all multicultural, thereby rendering the term too vague to be analytically useful. Second, unlike the wider view which encompasses all kinds of differences and degenerates into an amorphous discussion of difference *per se*, the narrower view concentrates on a specific kind of difference and has a clear focus. Third, differences between cultures raise problems that are quite different in nature from those that are indigenous to them. They require different modes of argumentation and are also far more intractable. As such they deserve to be distinguished and highlighted.

2.3   Multiculturalism

multicultural society

When confronted with a **multicultural society**, that is, a society consisting of several identifiable cultural communities, we need to decide how to respond to the fact of *cultural plurality*. This is where the questions about cultural regulation arise in relation to this topic. We could take one of two views, each in turn capable of taking several different forms. First, we could say that cultures *qua* cultures deserve no respect. We should judge and grade them and assimilate the inferior ones into one judged to be the best. If we feel that such an objective judgement is impossible, we might argue that every society has its own long-established and distinct culture which, although not objectively the best, is best *for it*. The culture has stood the society in good stead, is woven into its way of life, and is uniquely its own. As such the society has a right and a duty to preserve it, and to assimilate its minorities into it. We might think that such assimilation is likely to provoke resistance or to involve an unacceptable degree of coercion, and decide reluctantly to tolerate minority cultures in the hope that over time they will either merge into the mainstream national culture or unobtrusively survive on its margins. In this view there is only one way of leading the good life, either in general or for the society in question, and minorities have nothing to contribute to its enrichment. We may call this view **monoculturalism**. It is commonly associated with **assimilationist** policies.

monoculturalism
assimilationist

Secondly, we could argue that all cultures deserve respect and should enjoy the freedom and the opportunity to preserve and reproduce themselves. We might defend such a view on a number of grounds, some more coherent than others. We might argue that the good life can be led in several different ways, that no cultural community has the monopoly of it, and that each benefits from a sympathetic dialogue with others. Or we might argue that a stable cultural community is vital to human well-being, and that to assimilate or discourage minority cultures is to cause their members grave harm. Or we might argue that since the majority community claims the right to retain its culture, consistency demands that it should concede the same right to its minority cultural communities as well. However we defend our view, we might insist that society should welcome and cherish cultural diversity. We may call such a view *multiculturalism*. It is a normative doctrine advancing a specific view on how we should respond to cultural diversity, and entailing significant regulatory policy recommendations.

ACTIVITY 1

Consider the distinction between multiculturality as a fact and multiculturalism as a doctrine or policy. Can you think of some examples of regulatory policies that promote multiculturalism?

3   Emergence of multicultural movements

3.1   United States of America

Multicultural movements emerged in the 1960s, first in the United States and then elsewhere. They shared much in common. However, since they were led by different groups and occurred in different societies with different traditions and histories, they also differed in significant respects. A brief discussion of the United States, Britain and Canada will illustrate the point.

In the USA the 1950s witnessed the rise of the civil rights movement. Since the main concern of most black Americans was to assimilate into the mainstream white society and to share in the opportunities it offered, they demanded equal rights and positive state help, including **affirmative action**. Their goals were primarily political and economic. They had no quarrel with the dominant US culture, which in their view cherished the ideals of human dignity and equality and provided the basis on which to attack the racism of US society.

affirmative action

Within a few years the black struggle took a cultural turn, stressing the importance of black culture and attacking the dominant Euro-American 'wasp' culture (White Anglo-Saxon Protestant). Many factors were responsible for this, of which three are relevant to our discussion. They all relate to the changing self-understanding of the significant body of African-Americans. First, thanks to the decades of slavery and the black internalization of the heavily negative white representation of them, blacks lacked self-confidence and self-esteem and were poorly motivated. Black leaders argued that since they could not therefore compete as equals, formal equality of rights and even a limited programme of affirmative action were of only limited help. Many of them pointed to the educational underachievement of black children and blamed it on their low self-esteem. They thought that the way to build up their self-esteem was twofold: to restore their pride in their own history and culture and to challenge the dominant culture's view of them and itself. The two were closely connected.

Secondly, the law had its limits for it could do little about racist attitudes, jokes, remarks, and countless daily acts of subtle discrimination. These sprang from the pervasive racist culture which had to be fought at all levels. Black leaders thought that, so long as that culture was dominant, their future prospects were extremely dim, and that a cultural struggle had to underpin and accompany the political.

Thirdly, many African-Americans began to challenge the assimilationist goal of the civil rights leaders, and wondered if they should have no other ambition than to become like whites. They had their own culture, musical and spiritual traditions, forms of religious expression, humour, ways of relating to one another, and so forth. It seemed wrong, demeaning and even sacrilegious to barter away all this in return for the assimilationist equality. Indeed to seek such assimilation was to admit that their ancestors had no worthwhile achievements to their credit, and thus to concede their racial inferiority. They therefore felt that they needed to articulate their own distinct vision of life which both suited their traditions and temperament and established their cultural equality with white America. Since there was a distinct ethnic revival in the country in the 1960s leading to public self-assertions by different ethnic groups, the emphasis on a distinct black culture was particularly appealing.

As the black struggle took a cultural turn, it ceased being exclusive and was joined by other groups who shared its cultural concern. They included Puerto Ricans, Mexican Americans, Jews, some groups of new, mainly Asian, immigrants, and women. They were all concerned in their own different ways to assert the integrity of their cultures and to challenge the hegemony of the dominant white culture. Since education is the main vehicle for defining, consolidating and transmitting culture, their demands took an educational turn, including both schools and universities. Not surprisingly, education became the central site of cultural struggle, so much so that multiculturalism in the United States came to be equated with multicultural education. Since the groups spearheading the demand for multicultural education had different backgrounds, interests and expectations, they defined and defended it differently.

Some, mainly the Asians, had limited interest in a radical critique of the dominant culture. As culturally self-confident immigrants they were anxious to get on in US society, and did not mind partial assimilation into its culture so long as they were able to retain much of their traditional culture and social cohesion. By and large they welcomed the mainstream education and only demanded that it be broadened to include their histories, cultures and languages. African-Americans and feminists were far more radical. They were concerned, for their own different reasons, about the damaging effects of the way in which the dominant culture represented them, and demanded its radical reappraisal including a thoroughgoing revision of text-books and secondary literature. They also demanded equal or at least adequate curricular representation of black and feminist writings, and at the university level separate courses devoted to their histories and struggles. They stressed the importance of role models and sympathetic teaching, and demanded their fair share of positions at all levels of academic and administrative hierarchy. This sometimes led to a call for positive or affirmative action, but by and large it was a plea to end the conscious and unconscious discrimination practised against them out of inertia, prejudice, misplaced fears and anxieties, or a racist and sexist institutional culture.

As we saw, African-Americans were deeply worried about the educational underachievement of their children. They blamed it on black low self-esteem, and thought that it could only be countered by restoring the integrity of their culture and deflating the pretensions of the dominant Euro-American culture. However, they were deeply divided on how these two objectives were to be achieved. Some thought that the answer lay in teaching *all* pupils a critically reinterpreted and broadly based multicultural curriculum with additional provisions for African-Americans to concentrate on their own history and culture. Others strongly disagreed and demanded separate black schools or classes devoted to black history and culture taught by sympathetic African-American teachers. In their view black pupils needed such temporary separation or isolation to escape the subtle and relentless white indoctrination, to reappropriate their past in their own way, and to build up their fractured solidarity. As for deflating the claims of the dominant Euro-American culture, they relied on such scholarship as was available at the time to show that this culture had its roots in non-western, especially African cultures, and that it was not as original and autonomous an achievement of the European people as the dominant Eurocentric view asserted.

It was in this context that the term **Afrocentrism** was introduced. It was used in two related senses. First, it referred to the demand that African-Americans should be primarily taught or should focus on their own history and culture. Secondly, and more importantly, it referred to the view that the Euro-American culture should be traced beyond the conventional Graeco-Roman to its real and long-neglected African roots. Some of the advocates of Afrocentrism appreciated that this kind of education was no more multicultural than its Eurocentric rival. They rightly refused to call it multicultural education, which some of them dismissed as a liberal trap.

Afrocentrism

Multicultural education in the USA thus covered a wide spectrum. At one end it meant little more than teaching minority languages, history, cultures and so on within the mainstream education. At the other extreme, it involved Afrocentric education. Between these two lay varieties of proposals which, although differing greatly in their degree of radicalism, shared three basic beliefs in common, namely that multicultural education was meant for all pupils, that it should include and offer sympathetic though not uncritical accounts of non-western cultures, and that it should take a critical view of the Eurocentric assumptions of the dominant culture.

Of the three major forms of multicultural education, the first enjoyed widespread support, whereas the second was widely attacked as misguided and not really education at all. As for the third, some varieties of it enjoyed support whereas others were attacked. There was much sympathy for the view that the curriculum should include the histories and literatures of great non-western civilizations, but little for the demands that the US culture and history be critically examined from African-American (or feminist) perspectives, and that the traditional teaching of English literature be widened to include African-American and feminist writings. There were several reasons why history and English literature became subjects of an acrimonious debate.

The history of a country can be told in several different ways, some more plausible than others but none objectively true. *Prima facie* it would therefore seem educationally desirable that pupils should be exposed to a variety of them and equipped to assess their relative validity. Things, however, are not so simple. To read the past in a certain way is to remember or cherish some historical events and not others, to define the relative place of different social groups in a specific way, to understand the identity and development of the national community in a certain manner, to cherish one set of moral and political values in preference to another, and so forth, and all this necessarily shapes the mutual expectations and self-images of different sections of society. Being a central site of struggle for collective memory, cultural representation, political legitimacy, morality of mutual claims, and ownership of the national identity, history can never be a politically neutral form of inquiry.

Every country therefore aims so to control the teaching of its history that it legitimizes the prevailing structure of power and mobilizes its future citizens around a specific view of its identity and central values. In the United States, which has had to build a cohesive nation out of waves of new immigrants, history teaching has long been viewed as one of the major means of forging national unity and has acquired a quasi-theological significance. The standard narrative of the birth and growth of the US republic could not altogether ignore dark historical passages related to its treatment of the indigenous peoples and slaves. But it was expected to stay within certain clearly stated parameters. It was to present the dark passages as at best regrettable aberrations, to show that the constitutionally enshrined values of the republic were objectively the best – or at least for the American people, to depict national heroes in a favourable light, to present Americans as 'one and united people', and so forth. Critics of multicultural education, especially its radical strand, therefore dismissed its view of US history as anti-national, politically motivated, a recipe for national disintegration.

The multiculturalist response to these criticisms was along predictable lines. It accused the critics of self-contradiction. On the one hand they swore by the values of truth and objectivity; on the other hand they took a highly political view of history with all its inevitable distortions, misrepresentations and even falsehoods. The critics of multiculturalism could not maintain both that history teaching should be objective and free of ideological and political biases and also that it should stress a specific view of national identity and do nothing to weaken national unity. The multiculturalists also argued that, since the standard narrative aimed to transmit a specific view of national identity, consistency demanded that those taking a different view of the latter should be equally free to press for an alternative narrative. They also thought that national unity could be achieved in several different ways, and that it was more likely to be secure if it was embedded not in the suppression but an open acknowledgement of differences of historical experiences and perspectives.

Like history, English literature became an arena of struggle. Critics of multiculturalism could not see the point of giving equal, adequate or even any curricular place to African-American and feminist writings. The purpose of teaching literature was to get the pupils to appreciate and grapple with the classics or the greatest works written in the English language as judged by generations of scholars. To include works that were politically correct but of inferior quality was to defeat the very purpose of teaching literature and to short-change pupils. It was regrettably true, they argued, that all great writers were male and white, but that was just a historical accident that in no way diminished the value of their works. Indeed they were great precisely because they transcended the particularities of 'race' and gender, dealt with the universally common human experiences, and had something important to say to all human beings. Would we think differently or take a lower or higher view of Milton or Shakespeare if we discovered that their works were really written by their wives or their black servants?

Advocates of multicultural education were unconvinced by these arguments. They said they were not concerned to reject the classics, only to make room for other writings. Furthermore, they argued, the classics reflected the personal prejudices and social backgrounds of their authors, and either drew upon a limited range of human experiences and emotions or explored universally common human experiences from narrow perspectives. As such, they not only had a limited value but also unconsciously served the political purpose of denigrating or delegitimizing certain sorts of experiences and emotions and their social bearers. There was therefore a strong educational and moral case for including works dealing with neglected or distorted experiences. These works might lack the imaginative power and technical virtuosity of the classics, but they had compensating advantages. Furthermore it was only by including them in the curriculum, and thereby both encouraging and subjecting them to literary criticism, that one was likely to create a climate in which they might one day throw up great works.

READING A

Now read the piece from Dinesh D'Souza's *Illiberal Education* reprinted as Reading A. It provides one way of defending multicultural education and criticizing the emphasis on classics. Do you find Carson's arguments convincing? In what sense do black students feel alienated from classics? Are they right to do so?

3.2 Britain

In Britain the multicultural movement took a somewhat different form. When the Afro-Caribbean and Asian immigrants began to arrive in the 1950s, there was a widespread view that they should – and would indeed want to – assimilate into British culture. Their languages were not taught in schools; they were discouraged from speaking them on school premises; and if their number exceeded a certain percentage, they were bussed to schools where there were fewer of them. Sikhs refusing to wear helmets were not allowed to ride motor-cycles, and the courts of law often refused to take account of cultural differences. Several surveys and the 1958 riots in Nottingham and Notting Hill showed that black and Asian assimilation was rendered difficult by two factors: widespread discrimination against them in such areas as employment and housing, and white anxiety about the presence of too many immigrants. Successive governments therefore settled upon the dual strategy of anti-discrimination legislation and restricted immigration as ways of facilitating minority assimilation.

From the 1960s onwards, as in the US, the debate took a cultural turn. As the second generation of Asians began to go to school, their dietary habits, dress, reluctance to attend religious assemblies and to take part in certain sports and so on, attracted attention. Like their US counterparts, their parents feared for the stability of their family and communal structures, and began to demand greater respect and some institutional provision for the teaching of their languages and cultures. The prolonged Sikh agitation for the right to wear turbans when riding motor-cycles or working on building sites, the Asian women employees' refusal to wear required uniforms in preference to their traditional dress, and the general Asian reluctance to give up some of their cultural beliefs and practices, forced the country to start taking account of Asian cultural needs. The fact that this was a period when liberal thinking was quite strong in Britain also helped.

So far as the Afro-Caribbeans were concerned, it was initially believed that they were culturally British. They spoke the same language, shared the same religion, dressed similarly, regarded Britain as their mother country, knew and generally identified with its history, played cricket, loved sports, shared British popular culture, and so on. Gradually this view began to change. Creole was acknowledged to be not corrupt English but a distinct dialect; Afro-Caribbean Christianity had a distinct character and content; their family structures, lifestyles and patterns of social relation were different; and so forth. Due also to the racism they were experiencing in British society, many Afro-Caribbeans felt alienated from it and sought to redefine their identity in non-British and largely cultural terms.

The continuing underachievement of Afro-Caribbean children, which aroused considerable concern in the 1960s, also reinforced the growing salience of culture. The range of explanations was wider than in the USA, however. Some blamed their family structure including the lack of parental encouragement and support. Some blamed their low self-esteem and their alienation from the exclusively white curriculum. Others blamed teacher racism including low teacher expectations, and the racism of the society at large which conveyed demeaning views of Afro-Caribbeans, and whose discriminating practices stifled their ambition and drive. All these in their own different ways emphasized the role of culture.

Thanks to all this, Britain began to realize that its immigrants were not just 'black' or 'coloured' but distinct communities with their own cultural identities, and that it was now a culturally diverse or plural society. Increasingly it came to be described, especially in liberal circles, as multiracial, multi-ethnic, multicultural and, in the aftermath of the Rushdie affair, as multi-faith. Although the terms were rarely defined and distinguished, the contemporary usage indicated that the first term was preferred when the Afro-Caribbeans were in mind, the second when both they and the Asians were intended, the third when both of them and white subcultures were in mind, and the fourth when the reference was to religious groups. Since the term 'race' was increasingly seen to be problematic, and since the term culture was too wide, the term multi-ethnic became most popular. It is striking that blacks and Asians were described as ethnic *minorities* rather than as ethnic *groups,* a term widely preferred in the USA and Canada, and sometimes as minority *communities,* a term rarely used in any other western country.

Some of the more conservative and nationalist politicians in Britain, knowing the power of words, felt concerned that the emerging vocabulary foisted an identity on the country that they did not like. To call Britain multicultural or multi-ethnic was to imply that whites were *just* one group among many, that they did not enjoy a historically or politically *privileged* status, that the ethnic minorities were *central* to British identity, that the country was not only multicultural as a matter of historical fact but *should* remain and even relish being one, and that its minorities were not just collections of individuals sharing certain features in common but organized *communities* that required to be treated as such. Not surprisingly, conservative and nationalist spokespeople rarely used such terms as multicultural, multi-ethnic or ethnic minority communities. They were convinced that Britain's multiculturality posed a deep threat to its stability and identity, and that it must be drastically reduced either by vigorous assimilation or repatriation. Enoch Powell's infamous 'rivers of blood' speech in April 1968 reflected this view well.

Despite conservative resistance, the bulk of influential opinion increasingly defined Britain as a 'multicultural' society consisting of 'ethnic minorities'. This was a great symbolic achievement with important policy implications for all areas of life. Since Britain now had a new identity, it could not consistently pursue the earlier assimilationist project, and needed to explore a pluralist alternative. Roy Jenkins, a former Home Secretary, articulated the change well in his influential statement:

> Integration is perhaps a loose word. I do not regard it as meaning the loss, by immigrants, of their own characteristics and culture. I do not think that we need in this country a 'melting pot', which will turn everybody out in a common mould, as one of a series of carbon copies of someone's misplaced vision of the stereotyped Englishman. I define integration, therefore, not as a flattening process of assimilation but as equal opportunity, accompanied by cultural diversity, in an atmosphere of mutual tolerance.

(Jenkins, 1966, quoted in Solomos, 1994, p. 65)

integration

Although the term **integration**, as Jenkins himself admitted, did not adequately convey his liberal vision of Britain, it soon gained currency and provided the guiding principle in all areas of life. Private employers, health authorities and others were more accommodative of minority cultural requirements than before, and so were local authorities in the formulation and implementation of their employment and housing policies. The courts of law began to show greater respect for minority cultures in deciding relevant cases. Such public bodies as the Arts Council showed more interest in and increased their funding for minority arts. The government ministers began to speak more positively about the contributions of ethnic minorities, and Prince Charles – going further than most – supported minority associations and festivals. The fact that minority cultures were respected and publicly funded, and their needs taken into account in deciding public policies, gave them public legitimacy in their own and especially the majority community's eyes. Contrary to the assimilationist argument, respect for cultural diversity brought the two communities together and seemed to promote integration.

The new spirit of multiculturalism led to a demand for multicultural education, of which liberals were the greatest champions. First, they were worried about the Afro-Caribbean educational underachievement. And since they blamed it on low teacher expectations, low black self-esteem and black alienation from the monocultural curriculum, they thought that multicultural education in schools and teacher-training colleges provided the answer. Secondly, liberals genuinely valued cultural diversity and thought that the traditional British curriculum was narrowly Eurocentric. And, thirdly, they were concerned to combat white racism, which they attributed largely to prejudice and ignorance and which in their view was best countered by a greater knowledge and understanding of minority cultures. The Swann Report, suggestively entitled *Education For All* and published in 1984, offered a coherent and influential statement of the liberal philosophy of multicultural education.

There are four striking features of British multicultural education that distinguish it from its US counterpart. First, from the very beginning it was meant for all and not just the minorities. Although some blacks and Asians advocated separate schools, the demand was extremely limited and made principally because the mainstream education had failed to live up to its multicultural ideal. Second, unlike the USA where religion is excluded from schools, multicultural education in Britain included minority religions. While this had the advantage of publicly affirming and valuing them, it also generated a controversy about how they were to be taught and by whom. Third, for reasons having to do with the British educational system and the place of universities in British public life, multicultural education in Britain was confined to schools and not extended to universities. Fourth, the purpose and content of multicultural education in Britain were defined in highly restricted terms. Although it was intended both to improve intercultural understanding and to enhance black performance, it had no clear understanding of how this was to be done. Not surprisingly, it included

FIGURE 4.1   A primary school in Bradford: despite the obvious cultural diversity that now exists, Britain has been reluctant to promote multicultural education.

little more than bits of minority history, culture and religion, which seemed to achieve neither objective and soon lost the support of blacks and Asians. Unlike in some parts of the USA, multicultural education in Britain neither challenged the Anglocentric orientation and the Eurocentric bias of the curriculum, nor showed any appreciation of the deeper structures of power that shape the ways in which cultures define and relate to each other. It therefore remained somewhat limited, lacked a critical and transformative power, and made no dent in the mainstream education. It was hardly surprising that multiculturalism and anti-racism, which were closely related in the USA, became separated in Britain to the detriment of both.

From the mid-1970s onwards, multiculturalism came under considerable criticism from the New Right, the rise of which was the result of a combination of factors. Since the mid-1960s British society had begun to undergo significant changes. Thanks to a less puritanical moral climate, the British people became much more open and uninhibited about their choices of lifestyles and sexual preferences, and demanded an end to the prevailing forms of legal and social discrimination. As a result of the decolonization of most of the empire, Britain's three centuries of imperial adventure came to an end, leading to a drastic shrinkage in its geographical expanse and political power. Thanks to the arrival of a large number of black and Asian immigrants from the erstwhile colonies and their concentration in the major cities, British society was becoming recognizably different. The British economy was in a state of decline. Its industrial productivity was low, its technology outdated, the quality of its industrial management poor, and its balance of payments unfavourable. British political institutions were widely perceived to be ineffective and commanded only a limited popular support. The pressure from influential quarters to join the European Community generated widespread fears about the loss of its distinct political identity. The emergence of Scottish, and to a lesser extent Welsh, nationalism also aroused fears about Britain's territorial and political integrity. In short, almost all the traditional sources of pride in terms of which Britain had for several centuries constructed its collective identity, namely the empire, social cohesion, stable democratic institutions, industrial leadership of the world, political leadership of the rest of Europe during the Second World War, political unity and so on, were proving problematic. The cumulative impact of these and related changes was considerable. Not surprisingly, they created a widespread feeling of decline and disorientation, and provoked a debate on the causes and the best ways of arresting them.

It was in this context that the New Right, which was finely tuned to the national mood, introduced its programme of national regeneration. In its view Britain was steadily declining because, among other things, its national identity was being increasingly eroded. Lacking a clear conception of what it stood for and a sense of national purpose, it was increasingly being seduced by the fashionable but highly dubious ideas and practices imported from abroad. It was also losing touch with its great past and becoming devoid of the qualities of character that had made that past possible. For the New Right the answer to Britain's predicament was obvious. It needed to return to its roots, to re-establish contacts with its past, and to revive its characteristic virtues. British national identity, a product of its long history, was already formed, and the British people only needed to know it. As the New Right defined it, British national identity largely consisted in a specific body of virtues and values and a specific form of historical self-understanding. This narrowly defined national identity was to be articulated and transmitted by educational institutions, the central agencies of the New Right project of cultural engineering. Accordingly, the government of Margaret Thatcher devoted considerable energy to educational reform. It centralized education, created a fairly rigid national curriculum, and paid particular attention to the teaching of history, English literature and religion – the three major sites of the construction of national identity and moral renewal.

Given the New Right emphasis on the consolidation of the national culture, predictably it dismissed multiculturalism as a false and subversive doctrine. It was false because every society including Britain needed a clearly defined national culture for its cohesion and stability, and that culture could only be one which it had historically evolved and which was inscribed in its institutions and practices. As a liberal society, Britain did have a duty to respect other cultures, but the respect could neither be equal nor at the cost of its own cultural integrity. Britain should not suppress them but it did not have to grant them public recognition and support, let alone accept them as part of its national identity. The New Right was particularly contemptuous of multicultural education which, in its view, subverted the British sense of national identity, diluted British history and culture by putting them on a par with others, failed to promote British cultural values and even destroyed them by relativizing them, and included material that pampered minorities but lacked educational value. Not surprisingly, it mocked and ridiculed both the Swann Report and the limited multicultural experiments it had encouraged. Even such a determined leader as Margaret Thatcher could neither dismantle the intellectual and institutional legacy of the earlier period nor overcome the resistance of those holding a different view. Although her views did not completely prevail, she did change the political climate and set in place institutions inhospitable to multiculturalism in all walks of life, especially the educational.

3.3   Canada

Unlike the USA and Britain, multiculturalism in Canada had a relatively easy birth with the government acting as an obliging midwife. Over the years the country had attracted large bodies of immigrants, some of whom retained their culture but many abandoned it in favour of assimilation into the mainstream Canadian society. In 1961 Canadians of British ancestry made up just under 40 per cent of the population, those of French ancestry just over 30 per cent, native peoples just over one per cent, and 'others' – a rapidly growing group of immigrants and a ready constituency for multiculturalism – just under 25 per cent. When Quebec demanded greater cultural and political autonomy and equal recognition in the country's self-definition, the federal government set up in 1963 the Royal Commission on Bilingualism and Biculturalism.

The Commission's terms of reference talked of 'an equal partnership between the two founding races' and, almost as an afterthought, referred to the 'contribution made by other ethnic groups to the cultural enrichment of Canada'. Since this appeared to the latter to imply two tiers of citizenship and to establish a kind of ethnic hierarchy with them occupying the bottom rung, the immigrants protested in the strongest terms. They argued that to declare Canada bicultural was to delegitimize or at least to marginalize them. Canada could not be declared bilingual either for, if English and French were to be recognized as national languages, the widely spoken minority languages should also be recognized as 'regional languages' in the relevant parts of the country. Although the Commission's final report was conciliatory and even included a fourth volume on the contribution of the ethnic minorities, its overall concentration on the two 'founding races' remained open to strong criticism.

Faced with these objections, the Trudeau government replaced **biculturalism** with multiculturalism and only insisted on bilingualism. The move was designed partly to assuage the protesters and partly, some think mainly, to undercut Quebec nationalism. To declare Canada bicultural would have come close to accepting that it consisted of two distinct territorially based

biculturalism

communities and that Quebec was the ethnic homeland of the
Francophones. Trudeau announced a policy of 'multiculturalism within a
bilingual framework' and officially committed the country to it in 1971. As
he put it:

> The policy of multiculturalism within a bilingual framework commends
> itself to the Government of Canada as the most suitable means of
> assuring the cultural freedom of Canadians. National unity, if it is to
> mean anything in the deeply personal sense, must be founded on
> confidence in one's own individual identity; out of this can grow respect
> for that of others and a willingness to share ideas, attitudes and
> assumptions. A vigorous policy of multiculturalism will help to create
> this initial confidence. It can form the base of a society which is based
> on 'fair play for all'.

(Trudeau, 1970, quoted in Webber, 1994, p. 68)

As Trudeau understood it, multiculturalism was intended to reconcile two
apparently conflicting objectives. It aimed to build up the self-confidence of
the cultural minorities and to reassure them that they were a valued part of
the national culture. It also aimed to draw them out of themselves, to foster
cross-cultural interaction, and to encourage them to help create a common
national culture in which they all felt affirmed. Trudeau thought that such
an approach both strengthened the national unity and sustained cultural
diversity, and gave the Canadian state deep roots in the moral and emotional
lives of its citizens.

Under the policy of multiculturalism the federal government appointed a
minister of Cabinet rank responsible for its oversight and implementation,
two advisory bodies, and a programme of grants to support minority
languages and cultures. Multiculturalism was also given a constitutional
status. Section 15 of the Charter of Rights and Freedoms guaranteed equality
to cultural minorities, and the interpretative principle in Section 27 required
that the Charter be interpreted in 'a manner consistent with the preservation
and enhancement of the multicultural heritage of Canadians'. Public funding
was provided, when necessary, for minority cultural events, festivals,
newspapers, languages and voluntary organizations. Schools were
encouraged not to ghettoize and 'exoticize' minority languages and cultures
but to integrate them into their mainstream curriculum and to present them
as an integral part of the national heritage. Their pupils' differences were to
be respected and explained; they were to be encouraged to share their
experiences, to talk about their food, clothes, festivals, languages, and in
general to learn to appreciate and take delight in differences. As one would
expect, not all parts of Canada showed equal enthusiasm for the policy,
implemented it with the required degree of sensitivity, or kept up the
momentum. However, the policy embodied a clearly stated national goal, and
provided both an inspirational model and a standard of measurement. In a

somewhat weakened form, it still remains in force and enjoys popular support.

While the old and new immigrants were reasonably happy with the policy of multiculturalism, two major groups were not. The Québecois, who demanded recognition as a distinct society with a unique French identity, felt reduced to the status of a cultural group with no special claims on the Canadian state. The native peoples felt similarly demoted at being treated no differently from the immigrants. Neither the Québecois nor the native peoples minded Canada's generous treatment of its ethnic minorities, but they were strongly opposed to a multiculturalism that failed to recognize their privileged historical status and distinct needs. Quebec welcomed multiculturalism provided that it was accommodated within a bicultural framework. This would recognize it as a distinct society and enable it to practise multiculturalism without compromising its own distinct French identity. The native peoples were happy with multiculturalism in the rest of Canada but not within their own borders.

Canada is interesting for several reasons. Unlike the USA and Britain, it has a generous and reasonably coherent policy of multiculturalism that shows how national unity can be reconciled with cultural diversity. It also highlights the fact that multiculturalism can take many forms, and that one preferred by some ethnic groups might be wholly unacceptable to others. Both Quebec and the rest of Canada welcome multiculturalism, but define it somewhat differently. Again, Canada shows that since different cultural communities in a multicultural society sometimes have different needs, a collectively acceptable form of multiculturalism must acknowledge and accommodate these differences. The multiculturalism favoured by Trudeau was intended to accommodate – and could only accommodate – those cultural minorities that defined themselves in exclusively cultural terms and only asked for conventional cultural rights, not those that were territorially concentrated and sought legal and political powers necessary to preserve and perpetuate their cultural identity. Not surprisingly, Trudeau's insistence on treating all cultural communities alike within a uniform model of multiculturalism left both the Québecois and the native peoples deeply dissatisfied.

We have so far discussed the different ways in which the USA, Britain and Canada have coped with multiculturalism. Others such as Australia, India and Trinidad are trying out yet other forms of it. Some have been more successful than others, but none is without its problems. Britain takes some account of minority cultural needs in its social, educational and public policies, but its response remains grudging, tentative, lacks national consensus and commitment, and is subject to the constant carping of the New Right nationalists. As a result, its minorities feel somewhat insecure and besieged, and remain prone to the kind of extremist mobilization we saw during the Rushdie affair. The United States encourages public expressions of ethnicity, cherishes hyphenated identities, provides limited public support for minority languages and cultures and so forth, but remains deeply divided on multicultural education. Canada has officially accepted multiculturalism as an important part of its national self-definition, but it still continues to provoke fierce resistance in some quarters as became evident when a nationwide campaign was launched to stop Sikh recruits to the Royal Canadian Mounted Police from replacing the traditional Stetson with the turban. Furthermore, as we saw, Canadian multiculturalism is centred on cultural minorities, especially the immigrants whose demands are limited in nature and easily met within the framework of the nation-state. It does not come to grips with cultural nations or national minorities, that is, with territorially concentrated minorities jealously seeking to protect their cultural identity within an autonomous legal space. As a result, it is unable to satisfy some of the legitimate aspirations of Quebec and has, only after considerable resistance, accommodated those of the native peoples. In all three countries, as in many others, minority cultures operate within the parameters set by the dominant culture. There is only a limited dialogue between the two, and very little critical self-examination by the dominant cultural community.

4   Forms of multiculturalism

If we analysed the multicultural movements in the three societies that we have discussed and many others, we would see that they differ greatly in their goals, aspirations and visions of the ideal multicultural society. Broadly speaking we can distinguish five kinds of multiculturalism, which for convenience we shall call *isolationist, accommodative, autonomist, critical* or *interactive,* and *cosmopolitan.* Obviously they overlap and are not mutually exclusive and, since other forms of multiculturalism are not unimaginable, neither are they collectively exhaustive.

isolationist multiculturalism

Isolationist multiculturalism refers to a vision of society in which different cultural groups lead autonomous lives and engage in minimum mutual interaction necessitated by their having to live together. The Millet system under the Ottoman Empire in which different religious communities led self-contained lives and ran their affairs themselves was this kind of society. In modern times such groups as the Amish in the USA and a small group of Black Muslims in the USA prefer a society that makes no or minimal demands on them and leaves them alone to pursue their ways of life.

accommodative multiculturalism

Accommodative multiculturalism refers to a society which rests on a dominant culture but makes appropriate adjustments and provisions for minority cultural needs. It interprets and applies its laws, and formulates and implements its policies, in a culturally sensitive manner, and gives its minorities the freedom and sometimes the resources to maintain their languages and cultures. Multiculturalism in Britain, France and several other European countries has taken this form. As we saw, it is also the form of multiculturalism generally preferred by the old and new, mainly non-Muslim, Asian immigrants to the USA, Europe and elsewhere. These groups do not challenge the dominant culture of the wider society either because they admire several aspects of it, or because they generally take an instrumental view of it, or because as immigrants they do not think it right to question the way in which the wider society is organized. They accept it as a fact of life, learn to negotiate their way around in it, and build their autonomous cultural lives within it.

Autonomist multiculturalism refers to a vision of society in which major cultural groups seek equality with the dominant culture and aim to lead autonomous lives within a collectively acceptable political framework. Their primary concern is to maintain their ways of life, which they think they have as much right to do as the dominant cultural group, and to enjoy the maximum possible degree of self-government. They challenge the hegemony of the dominant cultural group and seek to create a society in which they can all exist as equal partners leading their self-contained lives. This form of multiculturalism is favoured by the indigenous peoples all over the world – the Québecois, the Basques, the Bretons, and others. Although it is both possible and popular when the cultural minorities are territorially concentrated, it is also demanded by some groups of Muslim migrants in Europe. They would like to be governed by the *Sharia*, to educate their children in Muslim schools, to have their own self-governing national bodies, and so forth.

autonomist multiculturalism

Critical or interactive multiculturalism refers to a society in which cultural groups are concerned not so much to lead autonomous lives as to create a collective culture that reflects and affirms their distinct perspectives. Since the dominant culture is reluctant to do so, cultural minorities challenge it both intellectually and politically. It is also often the case that the dominant culture has long taken, and enforced by all means at its disposal, a demeaning view of the capacities, cultures and histories of the minorities, which the latter often internalize with obvious damage to their self-respect, self-confidence and capacity to compete as equals. Their view of themselves is closely bound up with the dominant culture's view of them, the latter in turn is but a converse of its view of itself, and that view both expresses and legitimizes the prevailing structure of power. Cultural minorities therefore have an additional reason to question the dominant culture's political and intellectual hegemony and to create a climate conducive to the co-operative creation of a new and genuinely egalitarian collective culture. As we saw, this form of multiculturalism is much favoured by black leaders and intellectuals of the left in the USA, Britain and elsewhere.

critical or interactive multiculturalism

Cosmopolitan multiculturalism seeks to break through the bounds of cultures altogether and to create a society in which individuals, now no longer committed to specific cultures, freely engage in intercultural experiments and evolve a cultural life of their own. According to its advocates, human beings, who are reflective and self-determining agents, are

cosmopolitan multiculturalism

neither determined or constituted by nor under an obligation to maintain and transmit their culture. They should therefore view all cultures including their own as a resource, as a range of options, and either freely choose or, better still, evolve one that appeals to them most. In its extreme form cosmopolitan multiculturalism sees cultures as articles in a global supermarket. In its more moderate form it loosens up cultures and encourages critical self-reflection and intercultural dialogue. Cosmopolitan multiculturalism is much favoured by diasporic intellectuals and some groups of liberals, and has a distinct post-modernist orientation.

ACTIVITY 2

Consider each of the five forms of multiculturalism and your reactions to them. What are the implications of each of them for regulation?

The five forms of multiculturalism are obviously concerned with different things and cannot be adequately conceptualized in terms of a single body of concepts. Isolationalist and accommodative multiculturalism are primarily concerned to secure certain cultural *rights* for minorities. Autonomist multiculturalism is primarily concerned to secure equal public *recognition* and esteem for minority cultures and the identities associated with them, and stresses rights only as an expression of and a means of giving reality to equal recognition. Critical multiculturalism has a very different orientation. Although it is interested in minority rights and recognition, its primary concern is twofold: to acquire cultural pride and self-confidence by challenging the dominant culture's representation of minorities, and to co-operatively reconstruct a new more democratic culture. Unlike the isolationist and accommodative multiculturalism, it is not interested in cultural rights as defined by and granted within the confines of the dominant culture; and unlike autonomist multiculturalism it has little interest in securing recognition from what it regards as a deeply biased and unjust dominant culture. Cosmopolitan multiculturalism is different from all others. It is interested neither in minority rights and recognition nor in reconstituting a new collective culture. Its primary concern is to reject the claims of all cultures and to leave individuals free to fashion their own.

Many writers on multiculturalism, including the most eminent among them, fail to appreciate this diversity within the mulitcultural movement, and end up conflating different forms of multiculturalism. Will Kymlicka (1995) takes multiculturalism to be about minority rights and subtitles his important book 'a liberal theory of minority rights'. Charles Taylor (1994) takes multiculturalism to be about the 'hunger for recognition'. Kymlicka is primarily interested in the immigrants and the indigenous peoples of Canada, and well captures their demands. Taylor is primarily interested in Quebec's national aspirations and brilliantly articulates the kind of multiculturalism it seeks. However, since both writers generalize from a limited subject matter, their theories of multiculturalism remain too monocultural and simplistic to capture the full range of multicultural movements.

5   Liberal society and multiculturalism

What problems do the different forms of multiculturalism pose for the type of society with which we are most familiar in the West, the so-called 'liberal society', which prides itself on respect for individual, civil and political rights?

We outlined above five different forms of multiculturalism and their visions of an ideal multicultural society. Since different cultural groups have different needs and relate to the wider society differently, they obviously press for a form of multiculturalism that best suits them. And so far as the wider society is concerned, its traditions, history and appreciation of the value of cultural diversity determine the kind of multiculturalism it welcomes or is willing to concede under pressure. The forms of multiculturalism preferred by the cultural minorities and the wider society do not always harmonize, and then there is a struggle, resulting in a stalemate, or a victory for either side, or – often – a compromise.

Although liberal society, based on principles such as tolerance and individual rights, is hospitable to cultural diversity, the kind and range of diversity it accommodates are considerably limited. This is so because it is committed to the individualist view of the good life. Broadly speaking, it takes the view that the good life should be self-chosen, autonomous, self-critical, based on continuing choices, self-conscious, orientated towards self-knowledge, active and energetic, averse to wasting natural and human resources including human talents, free of dogmas and superstitions, largely concerned with worldly though not necessarily material concerns, and based on equal respect for others' interests. Although some liberals are sympathetic to and even admire non-liberal ways of life, they think them worthy of respect only if they meet their test of 'reasonableness'. Not surprisingly, they take a dim view of ways of life that are traditional, communal, deeply religious, hierarchical, not given to self-knowledge, averse to constant self-criticism, or contemptuous of worldly interests and achievements.

ACTIVITY 3

Obviously a liberal society cannot tolerate all minority values and practices. How should it decide which ones to tolerate, which to discourage, and which to ban?

Liberal society's tolerance, then, is limited by its more basic commitment to a specific way of life, and it either refuses to tolerate non-liberal ways of life or does so grudgingly. As we saw in our discussions of Britain, Canada and the USA, it has offered varying degrees of resistance to almost all forms of multiculturalism. Although generally willing to respect the cultural autonomy of the Amish, the Black Muslims and others, liberals feel troubled if they believe that the children fail to develop their powers of autonomy and critical thinking and have highly restricted choices as to the life plans. Liberals feel the same way about accommodative multiculturalism. While showing the necessary sensitivity to minority cultures, they worry about the children's lack of personal autonomy and limited choices, and often rely on educational institutions to wean them away from their parents' way of life.

Liberals have difficulty with autonomist multiculturalism as well. They feel that autonomous cultural communities might not be hospitable to liberal values. And since different communities seek different forms of self-government, liberals feel that autonomist multiculturalism violates the principles of equality of rights, uniformity of treatment, and common citizenship. These were some of the grounds on which Trudeau and other Canadian liberals repeatedly rejected the demands of Quebec and the indigenous peoples for cultural and political autonomy. Although liberals prize critical thought and should be hospitable to critical multiculturalism, they have sometimes been hostile to it. They have claimed that liberal values represent the greatest human achievements and are best, if not for all humankind, at least for the societies that have grown up with them. As we saw in our discussion of US multiculturalism, and as the British liberal reaction to Muslims during the Rushdie affair showed, some liberals tend to dismiss challenges to their basic values as barbaric, anti-western and tribal. So far as cosmopolitan multiculturalism is concerned, liberals are generally most sympathetic to it, as it realizes their vision of a free and self-determining human agent.

It is possible to argue that liberal societies cannot accommodate some of the most significant and widely demanded forms of multiculturalism. Being committed to a specific vision of the individual and society, they may welcome multiculturalism only if it respects and remains within the confines of that vision. Not surprisingly, liberal societies sometimes disallow or discourage those minority cultures that either reject the individualist view of life or assign it a limited place. There is thus an underlying tension between liberalism and multiculturalism. Liberalism would seem to set clear limits to cultural diversity and to the acceptable forms of multiculturalism. For their part, some forms of multiculturalism see liberalism not as a self-evidently true account of the individual and society, as many liberals do, but as a historically specific body of ideas, as a culture with its own inherent biases and representing one among several possible ways of leading the good life. In so doing, such multiculturalism de-absolutizes liberalism and puts it in the philosophically uncomfortable position of having to defend and justify itself in a non-circular manner.

ACTIVITY 4

In the light of what you have read so far, do you think it is possible to reconcile liberalism and multiculturalism?

The answer to the question of whether liberalism and multiculturalism can be reconciled is not simple or obvious. This raises many difficult further questions, of which two deserve particular attention. First, should liberal society be more hospitable to cultural diversity than it has been so far? Why can't it say that it has a right and a duty to maintain its way of life and to require all minorities to adjust to it? Secondly, if liberal society does allow a greater range and depth of cultural diversity, how is it to hold itself together? Does it not need a common national culture in order that its diverse groups can communicate with one another and create a reasonably cohesive society? If it does, would that not severely limit its capacity to accommodate cultural diversity? We shall take the questions in turn.

Those who argue for a more welcoming attitude to cultural diversity usually do so for one or more of the following four reasons. First, cultural diversity would seem to be a fact of contemporary life. All modern societies are multicultural, and their minorities cherish their various cultural identities. If we try to suppress their identities and to assimilate them into the dominant culture, we are likely to provoke fierce resistance. The Jews have survived two millennia of periodic Christian oppression; the ethnic and cultural minorities in the ex-Soviet Union and Eastern Europe have outlived the most brutal repression; and not all the assimilationist economic and cultural pressures of the United States have succeeded in creating a melting-pot.

Assimilationist projects fail for a variety of reasons. Cultures are too deeply woven into the fabric of social groups for their members to be fully conscious of their influences, let alone to jettison them in favour of some other. Besides, most cultures are deeply embedded in or at least intertwined with religions, and outsiders cannot assimilate into them without changing their religion, which they are often most reluctant to do. Cultures are also extremely complex structures whose nuances, unspoken assumptions and deepest sensibilities cannot be acquired unless one is born into them. Total cultural assimilation requires biological assimilation, and that is not a price most outsiders are willing to pay. Again, assimilation is rarely able to redeem its promise of full and unqualified acceptance. Although one might, after a strenuous effort, assimilate into the dominant culture, there is always the danger that one's slightest difference or past background might be made the basis of discrimination by the whole or a section of the dominant cultural community. Since cultural diversity is a stubborn and seemingly inevitable feature of modern life, both prudence and democratic decency suggest that societies should gracefully accept and suitably adopt their institutions to its demands.

While the first argument is based on prudence and political realism, the other three are normative in nature. The second argument in favour of a greater tolerance of cultural diversity stresses the value of culture. According to this view human beings are culturally embedded. Their culture helps them to make sense of the world, gives their lives a sense of meaning, continuity and identity, offers them a cognitive and moral compass, structures their personality, provides them with values and ideals, and so on. It also integrates them into an on-going community, provides them with a rich network of social relations, and ensures intergenerational continuity. For these and related reasons culture matters a great deal to individuals, and is a vital source of their well-being. To denigrate, suppress or deny its legitimate demands can cause them grave moral harm. The long-term damage that slavery did to the personal and social lives of the blacks, and colonialism to the indigenous populations, testifies to this.

Thirdly, liberal society is committed to equal respect for persons. Since human beings are culturally embedded, respect for them requires respect for their cultures. To respect them but not their cultures is to abstract away all that constitutes and distinguishes them, and to respect them not in their uniqueness but as uniform and abstract atoms, which they are not. Furthermore, since the wider society institutionalizes and enforces the dominant culture, it obviously respects the cultural rights of the majority. The principle of equality of rights requires that it should give equal respect and resources to its minorities as well. Respecting cultures does not mean that they may not be criticized any more than respect for individuals exempts them from criticism, but rather that they should be understood in their own terms, that they should not be resented or suppressed simply for being different, that our criticisms of them should be based on criteria they can comprehend and in principle share, and that their legitimate demands should be met.

READING B

Now read the piece by Charles Taylor in Reading B at the end of the chapter. As you will see, Taylor gives two reasons for according equal respect to all cultures. First, since our identity has a cultural basis and is constituted by others' recognition of it, our sense of our worth is diminished when our culture is denied respect. Second, all cultures must be presumed to have equal worth unless proved otherwise. The presumption is based on the belief that cultures that have meant so much to so many over long periods of time are almost certain to have at least some admirable features.

1   What do you think of these arguments?

2   Is Taylor right to say that our sense of worth depends on others' acknowledgement of it?

3   Do you think that the presumption of the equal worth of all cultures is justified?

4   Can you think of a culture with nothing admirable about it?

The fourth argument views cultural diversity not from the standpoint of minorities but society as a whole, and stresses not the rights of minorities but the collective value of diversity. Its proponents argue that cultural diversity increases the available range of options and extends the parameters of freedom. It provides new sources of psychological and moral energy and vitalizes the wider society. It also expands imagination and sympathy, cultivates habits of tolerance, encourages a healthy competition between different ways of life, adds colour and beauty to social life, and deepens our appreciation of the nature and possibilities of human existence. Furthermore no culture, however rich it might be, can ever embody all that is valuable in human life. Since human capacities, values and aspirations conflict, every culture realizes some of them and neglects, marginalizes or suppresses others. Different cultures thus correct and complement each other, help each become aware of its strengths and weaknesses, and encourage critical self-reflection and mutual borrowing. In short, cultural diversity is a necessary condition and component of human freedom and development, and represents a vital public good.

ACTIVITY 5

At this point you should assess the relative strengths and weaknesses of the four arguments and explore if they are mutually consistent. You might also like to ask which of them is most likely to carry weight in a liberal society, especially Britain which, unlike the USA, does not give much importance to the language of rights.

Although the four arguments are neither equally persuasive nor free of difficulties, they do provide a reasonably convincing case for welcoming cultural diversity. They are made from within the liberal perspective and appeal to such liberal values as prudence, not causing harm to others, equality, and diversity. As such, liberal society should not have much difficulty accepting them. However, critics argue that two factors stand in the way: first, inadequate liberal capacity or disposition to be self-critical and, second, legitimate liberal fears that multiculturalism would commit it to tolerating all manner of offensive practices and values. As for the first, we can say little except to reiterate the liberal point that no doctrine, including liberalism, represents the last word in human wisdom. As for the second, we need to evolve principles that help us to decide which minority practice to encourage, allow, discourage or ban. Such principles cannot be laid down in advance and require a dialogue between the parties involved. The dialogue is more likely to be fruitful and lead to a consensus if the minorities feel sufficiently secure and self-confident, and that in turn requires that the wider society should take a more hospitable view of cultural diversity.

This leads us to the second question as to how such a multicultural political community can be held together and conduct its common affairs. Obviously, every political community needs to find stable sources of unity, especially when it is multiculturally constituted. A **political community** is a territorially concentrated group of people bound together by their acceptance of a common mode of conducting their collective affairs, including a body of institutions and shared values. These institutions and values are shared by its members collectively, as a community. They are not shared by them in a way that we might share a piece of cake, but in a way that we share streets, parks, and so on. And they are common to them not in a way that having two eyes is common to all human beings, but in the way that the dining-table is common to those seated around it. The unity of a political community lies in what all its members share not individually but

political
community

political culture collectively, not privately but publicly, in their **political culture** and not in the culture of the society as a whole.

Many discussions of national unity do not appreciate this crucial distinction, and assume that a society cannot be held together unless all its members share a comprehensive or national culture, including common customs, social practices, personal ideas, social character and traits of temperament, and become fully British, French, American, or whatever. As we saw, this is the standard view of the New Right and some influential liberal writers in Britain and elsewhere.

Careful consideration, however, suggests that this view is mistaken. As citizens, we are concerned with the political life of the country and should share common values and concerns. However, there is no obvious reason why we should also be expected to agree on *all* other matters, including those that do not pertain to public and political life. Furthermore, the cultural life of a community contains a good deal of internal diversity. It is a precipitate of countless influences, not all of which pull in the same direction. Although it possesses some internal coherence and individuality, it is never homogeneous and internally consistent. Different members of the community stress different aspects of it and define it differently. The identity of a culture is therefore constantly contested, and the dominant definition of it does no more than reflect the prevailing and inherently tentative balance of power between the contesting groups. Any attempt to define a common national culture in fixed and definitive terms imposes a false unity on it and distorts it. It is also necessarily selective and partisan, privileging some values and practices, and therefore some social groups, over others.

Margaret Thatcher provided an excellent example of this. During her period of office as Prime Minister of the United Kingdom she repeatedly insisted that since socialism was 'essentially' a 'continental' phenomenon and 'at odds with the character of the British people', she was determined to 'destroy' it in order to preserve the British national culture, which she took to consist in largely Victorian values. Her view of British culture delegitimized the Labour Party as well as all those advocating some form of economic redistribution. These groups replied that the Thatcherite view ignored scepticism, the spirit of mutual help, social concern, decency, self-mocking irony, and almost all else that they held dear and believed to be central to British culture. Each side was both right and wrong. Conflicts over the 'true identity' of a national culture can cause damage to the integrity of the culture itself, and lead to social and political conflict. Far from being the necessary basis of national unity, the so-called national culture often militates against it.

I would argue that the unity of a society is located in its shared political life, not in its cultural habits, customs and practices. Every political community that has lasted a while tends to develop a widely shared body of values, practices, institutions, myths, conceptions of its past and future, a mode of public discourse, and so on, all of which constitute its shared political culture or identity. The political culture can serve to unite the community around a specific collective self-understanding and a body of shared institutions and practices. It is not, however, non-negotiable and beyond revision. Its values and practices might discriminate against or bear unduly heavily on those who are new to it, or whose historical experiences are different, or who have long been marginalized and ignored. These groups might therefore rightly question their content or inner balance, and seek their redefinition. This is what women have done, and there is no reason why cultural minorities should be denied the right to do the same. If their grievances have a rational basis, they call for a public and open-minded dialogue. To deny the dialogue on the ground that the revision of the community's political values threatens its stability or identity is both to misconceive their nature and to be unfair to their critics. Although the values deserve respect, they reflect and register a historical moral consensus and require a critical look when the latter comes under challenge. The dialogue in such cases is never easy, both because the parties involved are likely to talk past each other on areas of such deep differences, and because one or both parties are likely to prove intransigent on matters of such great moral and emotional significance to them. However, it cannot be avoided. And even if the dialogue does not result in an agreement, it serves the vital purpose of giving the minorities a fair hearing, increasing mutual understanding and deepening the democratic process, thereby making future controversies more manageable.

This is what happened in Britain and France respectively during the Rushdie and the *foulard* affairs. British Muslims asked why freedom of expression should be more or less absolutized, why the writer's freedom should include the right to mock sacred beliefs, and why the prevailing balance between freedoms of speech and religion should not be reconsidered. The French Muslims questioned the *laicité* of the French state school, and wondered why the cross was allowed but not the headscarf (*foulard*) and why the educational process should be insulated against religious and cultural self-expression. In each case the wider society proved intransigent and refused to re-open the questions it regarded as settled. Over time and after much democratic protest, a dialogue ensued. Although it led to no changes in Britain and only to minor ones in France, it did generate debates both within and between the majority and minority communities, deepened their understanding of both themselves and each other, softened rigidities on both sides, and led to new crosscutting alliances.

What is true of the community's values is also true of its political symbols, images, myths, ceremonies, view of its history, and so on. They too reflect and reproduce a specific conception of its identity, and need to be suitably revised when they are shown to misrepresent, distort or ignore the presence, experiences and contributions of marginalized groups, or to be out of step with the changes in the social composition of the community. Old and marginalized as well as newly arrived communities can rightly ask that the political life should grant them suitable public recognition by incorporating their symbols, ceremonies, views, etc. into the collective expressions of

FIGURE 4.2 The *foulard*, or traditional Muslim headscarf, became a symbol of equal rights of religious and cultural expression in a multicultural society.

national life. Such recognition confers public legitimacy on their presence, recognizes them as valued members of the community, wins over their loyalty and helps strengthen the unity of the community. In short the unity of a multicultural political community lies not in a nebulous and indefinable national culture but in an inherently open, publicly defined and periodically reconstituted political culture.

6 Conclusion

This chapter has adopted a particular approach to culture, regarding it as equivalent to a way of life with certain common components related together in a specific way that distinguishes one 'cultural community' from others. Although modern societies are increasingly culturally plural, we have seen that multiculturalism is a normative doctrine that can take various forms. Each of the forms of multiculturalism has a different view of the appropriate regulatory policies that should govern the relations between the cultural communities and the society as a whole. I have argued that even the liberal societies, which pride themselves on their tolerance of cultural differences and claim to uphold individual rights, nevertheless experience a tension between their liberal principles and some forms of multiculturalism. Finally, I have argued that the necessary degree of unity of a society, as a multicultural political community, does not depend on a shared national culture, but on an open and self-critical political culture to which all citizens can willingly subscribe.

References

DEPARTMENT FOR EDUCATION (1994) *Education For All* (The Swann Report), London, HMSO.

D'SOUZA, D. (1991) *Illiberal Education: the politics of race and sex on campus*, New York, Vintage Books.

DU GAY, P. (1997) 'Organizing identity: making up people at work' in du Gay, P. (ed.).

DU GAY, P. (ed.) (1997) *Production of Culture/Cultures of Production*, London, Sage/The Open University (Book 4 in this series).

DU GAY, P., HALL, S., JANES, L., MACKAY, H. and NEGUS, K. (1997) *Doing Cultural Studies: the story of the Sony Walkman*, London, Sage/The Open University (Book 1 in this series).

GILROY, P. (1997) 'Diaspora and the detours of identity' in Woodward, K. (ed.) *Identity and Difference*, London, Sage/The Open University (Book 3 in this series).

GORDON, E. W. and ROBERTS, F. (1991) 'Reflections on the work of the NYS Social Studies Syllabus Review Committee' in *One Nation, Many Peoples: a declaration of cultural independence*, The Report of the New York State Social Studies Review and Development Committee.

GUTMANN, A. (ed.) (1994) *Multiculturalism*, Princeton, NJ, Princeton University Press.

KYMLICKA, W. (1995) *Multicultural Citizenship: a liberal theory of minority rights*, Oxford, Clarendon Press.

RAZ, J. (1994) *Ethics in the Public Domain*, New York, Oxford University Press.

SALAMAN, G. (1997) 'Culturing production' in du Gay, P. (ed.).

SOLOMOS, J. (1988) *Black Youth, Racism and the State*, Cambridge, Cambridge University Press.

TAYLOR, C. (1994) 'The politics of recognition' in Gutmann, A. (ed.).

WEBBER, J. (1994) *Reimagining Canada: language, culture, community and the Canadian constitution*, Kingston and Montreal, McGill, Queen's University Press.

READING A:
Dinesh D'Souza, 'Multiculturalism at Stanford'

What do you think of Western civilization? 'I think it would be a good idea.'

Mahatma Gandhi

We have demographics on our side. We have history on our side.

William King, President,
Black Student Union, Stanford University

'Hey, hey, ho, ho, Western culture's got to go,' the angry students chanted on the lawn at Stanford University. They wore blue jeans, Los Angeles Lakers T-shirts, Reeboks, Oxford button downs, Vuarnet sun glasses, baseball caps, Timex and Rolex watches. No tribal garb, Middle Eastern veils, or Japanese samurai swords were in sight. Observers could not recall a sari, kimono, or sarapa. None of the women had their feet bound or bandaged. Clearly the rejection of the ways of the West was a partial one. Nevertheless it was expressed with great passion and vehemence, and commanded respect for its very intensity.

What were these eager and intelligent students protesting about in early 1988? The weather was beautiful in California, the campus pristine, many of the students hailed from middle-class and privileged families. Yet precisely this comfortable environment seemed to contribute to a vague sense of disquiet. The students appeared to share a powerful conviction that Western culture is implacably hostile to the claims of blacks, other minorities, women, and homosexuals. When they thought about the West, what entered the protesters' minds were slavery, colonialism, the domestication of women, and the persecution of 'deviant lifestyles.'

The Stanford administration was faced with a bewildering dispute over the content of the undergraduate curriculum being conducted in a manner scarcely different from a political march or a workers' strike. The real targets of the protest – Aristotle, Aquinas, Locke, and other 'white males' – had all been dead for hundreds of years. The

students resented the fact that the ideas of these men still dominated Stanford's 'core curriculum.' They shouted slogans and carried placards demanding that the Stanford faculty and administration make major changes in the course offerings.

Viewing the Stanford controversy as indicative of a trend, the print and broadcast media descended on the campus, converting the protest into a national spectacle. One immediate advantage was the kindling of serious discussion, in the pages of newspapers such as the *Washington Post* and the *Wall Street Journal,* over what aspects of the Western heritage should be transmitted to young people through education. At the same time, however, the public spotlight brought the powerful pressure of the media to bear on the question of what books a private university should assign to students. Suddenly the curriculum seemed not an academic issue to be resolved by the faculty, or even the university community, but a political question to be publicly adjudicated in the press.

Protest against alleged Western exclusiveness in the classroom is no longer restricted to Stanford, but is commonplace, and spreading, on the American campus. Now that American society, and American education, have opened themselves to full membership and legal equality for previously oppressed groups, the new activists argue that it is time that the *content* of both the culture and the curriculum reflect the aspirations, literature, history, and distinctive point of view of these groups. Like Berkeley in its affirmative action policies, Stanford is prepared to lead the way in applying principles of diversity to what is taught in universities.

* * *

The reasons for the animus against the Western civilization course are best seen from the perspective of an articulate spokesman from the Stanford faculty. Clayborne Carson is a professor of history and Afro-American Studies at Stanford, editor of the Martin Luther King papers, and one of the pioneers of Stanford's drive to transform the 'great books' curriculum into a new sequence of required courses on 'Cultures, Ideas and Values'

(CIV), first implemented in the fall of 1989. Previously Stanford steered all incoming students through a core curriculum – and examination of the philosophy, literature, and history of the West, focusing on such thinkers and writers as Plato, Dante, Machiavelli, Voltaire, Marx, and Freud; and on such events as the ascent of Greece, the fall of Rome, medieval Christian civilization, the Renaissance and Reformation, the French and Scottish Enlightenment, and the founding of modern states. The new CIV sequence would substitute a multiple-track system, each examining an issue or field, such as Technology and Values, through a cross-cultural survey of ideas and mores. Such an approach would include Western perspectives, but also African, Japanese, Indian, and Middle Eastern ones. Since the number of texts that can be assigned and discussed in a semester is limited, the relative importance of Western thinkers would be correspondingly reduced. Some of them, such as Homer, Virgil, and Aquinas, would have to make way for new, non-Western voices. A special effort was promised not to imply any superiority of Western ideas or Western culture – all cultures would be sustained on a plane of equality.

Professor Carson is a mild-mannered man, slightly stooped, with a lilting voice. He sat on the patio of the Stanford library, the repository of the Martin Luther King papers. Although the civil rights movement began by simply trying to end legal discrimination, Carson said that now 'there is a growing understanding that bringing different groups into society, without changing society in any way, is not only wrong but not very feasible.' In the past, 'the rules of the game were set by white males.' Now they must be negotiated between different groups, all considered legitimate partners in the new debate all advancing claims of justice as well as power.

The problem with the idea of a canon – a set of required great books – was that 'the curriculum is always changing,' Carson said. 'What was deemed important to know constantly changes, and that is a politicized decision.' Now that minority students and 1960s generation professors were more fully represented on campus, 'we are pressing a different agenda.' Senior faculty, whether liberal or conservative, were 'the strongest resistance to change on this campus,' Carson said. Thus prominent liberals such as historian Carl Degler

and Ronald Rebholz of the English department opposed the new curriculum, not on political but on academic grounds, insisting that it would compromise intellectual seriousness, which was not in anyone's interest. Rebholz, who termed himself a Roosevelt Democrat, said the Western core curriculum should be retained because 'if a socialist society is ever going to work, it will need educated citizens. You don't acquire a good education without discipline.'

Younger faculty, Carson said, tend to reject the idea of a canon. 'What's one generation's standard canonical text is the next generation's pulp,' Carson said. 'How many people read the poetry of Virgil, or the orations of Cicero?' He permitted himself a chuckle. When he assigned Alice Walker's *The Color Purple* in his Western culture class, Carson said some people raised eyebrows. 'Ten years down the road you might say it didn't stand the test of time,' he conceded. But such criticism 'assumes that the point of teaching a course like this is to introduce students only to those works that have timeless value. If you make that assumption, you are limiting what you can convey to students.'

Ridiculing the idea of a preordained set of great books, Carson said, 'There is something inherently anti-intellectual about the notion of an educational institution establishing a canon.' If scholars in a field agree that a work is important, they are likely to teach it on their own. To establish a canon is to 'convey a message about the importance of a work even before students have seen for themselves the content of a work.' Canons are by nature inclusive and exclusive: they keep some people in, and leave other people out; this, Carson said, 'is just not an important game to play.'

Yet if so, how did Carson explain his failure to insist that Stanford completely jettison the idea of a required curriculum, rather than simply replacing the Western cultural emphasis with a multicultural requirement? Was this not simply an exchange of one canon for another? Ideally a multicultural sequence would not be required, Carson said; the reason it must be for the present is that the Stanford faculty and student body are not fully representative of minorities in the culture. If they were, 'then a lot of the discussion about Western culture wouldn't have taken place, because the teaching would be quite different from what it is.'

In other words, multicultural education would occur naturally; it would not require political agitation or coercion. In the interim, the only option was to require new courses – a new canon – and saddle the university with the burden of finding faculty competent to teach the new agenda.

At Stanford, Carson said, younger faculty have established a new alliance with minority students and feminists, and powerful elements in the university administration. The battle of the 1960s, Carson said, was 'a battle to get recognized. But now that we are here, we want to know why our courses are peripheral and those of Mr. Senior Faculty are central. We are working to change that.'

From the comments of this earnest faculty activist, several themes emerge which are central to the debate over what is taught in the American academy. Reflecting a 1960s' ethos of non-exclusivity, Carson seems opposed to the very idea of a canon or a principle of selection that determines which books undergraduates should read. Such principles seem to produce what may be termed 'disparate impact' on ethnic groups; in other words, white males tend to be over-represented on the reading list. Carson would rather see a political solution to the 'problem of knowledge,' in which the curriculum is refashioned to reflect and represent a diversity of ethnic cultures and values. This, he believes, is the only just approach to education in a truly pluralistic and democratic society.

Carson is one of the leading CIV proponents at Stanford. His arguments have dominated the debate since the spring of 1987, when a newly formed Rainbow Coalition of minority groups demanded a substantial revision of the three-course Western culture requirement. The requirement, established in 1980, examined fifteen great Western thinkers from a variety of perspectives or 'tracks.' The courses were popular with undergraduates; a 1985 poll found that more than 75 percent considered them a 'positive academic experience'.

The Stanford administration, however, soon came under pressure from the campus Rainbow Coalition, which included black, Hispanic, Asian, and American Indian groups. 'Western culture does not try to understand the diversity of experiences of different people,' charged Alejandro Sweet-Cordero, a member of the Movimiento Estudiantil Chicano de Aztlan, the Hispanic student group on campus. 'If you think American culture is centred on the Constitution and the Founding Fathers, then you're going to exclude a major part of what this country is,' remarked Stanford student activist William King, calling for non-Western alternatives to provide students with 'a different picture.' King added, 'It was painful to come to Stanford and find that no member of your race was in the required curriculum.' Stacey Leyton, a student member of Students United for Democracy in Education, a pro-CIV group, remarked, 'It's a strong statement you're making when the only required readings are by whites and males. You're saying that what's been written by women and people of color isn't worthy of consideration.' Freshman Joseph Green wrote in the Stanford Daily, 'I get tired of reading the thoughts of white men who would probably spit on me if they were alive to face me today ... Stanford is sending many students into the world with no knowledge of the challenges facing people of color.' And Black Student Union activist Amanda Kemp protested that the implicit message of Western culture is 'Nigger go home.'

Younger faculty had their own reasons for disliking the Western core curriculum, as Clayborne Carson suggested. The Stanford line-up from Homer to the present, complained history professor Paul Robinson, was a 'roadblock' and 'arbitrary hazard' for 'men and women under 40' who felt 'alienated' from this canon of texts. Philosophy professor John Perry said the classics were an 'albatross' around the neck of the new generation of professors. These professors emphasized that they sought a more relevant agenda than a fixed list of old books.

Somewhat at a loss about how to respond, President Donald Kennedy did what embattled executives often do in these situations: he established a task force. Ordinarily task forces purchase a good deal of time in order to cope with the new demands – at best, enthusiasm soon dissolves, and everybody forgets about the issue; at worst, the administration gains a postponement or the problem is put off to an unspecified future date. But Stanford's day of reckoning came soon, as the task force speedily put together the outlines of a new set of courses. January 17, 1987, Martin Luther King Day, Jesse Jackson spoke at Stanford's Black Student Union march and rally, denouncing the Western culture requirement. A few months later, in the spring of 1987, minority students from the Rainbow Coalition forcibly occupied President Donald Kennedy's office for five hours, issuing ten demands including the adoption of the new curriculum.

The following fall, Stanford's 72-member Faculty Senate, which has jurisdiction over curricular matters, met to consider the proposal for the first time. These deliberations took place against the backdrop of chants by students demonstrating outside the building in which the debate occurred.

Mild resistance developed to the new curriculum. English professor William Chace (now president of Wesleyan University in Connecticut) offered a counterproposal, signed by twenty-five faculty members, advocating the retention of the Western core curriculum, but expanded to include more women and minorities. Chace's proposal was voted down. A Stanford undergraduate, Lora Headrick, argued that agitation for change came from a small militant segment of faculty and students; it did not reflect broad sentiment on campus. Headrick founded a group called 'Save the Core' to collect petition signatures in favor of the 'Western civ' course.

The core curriculum debate came to a head during the first three months of 1988, when the Stanford faculty discussed whether to finally embrace the CIV proposal. From the outset, however, it was clear that the momentum was with opponents of the existing Western culture requirement.

Comparative literature professor Herbert Lindenberger supported the proposed change. 'The image of Greece as a civilizing force in the West meant one thing to the Romans who absorbed Greek culture, but it meant still something else to the Renaissance humanists who revived the Greeks to suit their own historical needs, and it meant still something different to the 19th century German scholars who created an idealized Greece to serve as a civilizing ancestor to the newly emerging German nation.'

Historian Carl Degler agreed, but said these nuances could be accommodated within the existing Western civilization course; they were not best discovered by studying other cultures. Further, Degler said, 'Few historians believe that the culture of this country has been seriously influenced by ideas from Africa, China, Japan or indigenous North America ... We are a part of the West not because this country received Italians, Scots, Germans, Greeks, Irish, Poles and Scandinavians within its borders, but because the language, religions, institutions, laws, customs, literature and yes, the prejudices, of this country were drawn overwhelmingly from Europe.'

Sounding a sharper tone, classics professor Anthony Raubitschek said that CIV advocates could teach twentieth-century pluralism and multiculturalism if they wished, but that they should retain the earlier segments of the Western culture course, which emphasized ancient and classic texts. 'I do believe in affirmative action,' Raubitschek said, 'but I do not think it should be applied to books and educational programs.'

His colleague from the classics department, Gregson Davis, shot back with a call for 'structural, not just cosmetic, change.' Davis remarked that 'Eurocentrism' was 'a deeply pernicious distortion of history that is endemic among Western intellectuals.' He added, 'To say the Zulus created no great works is deplorably racist. Haitian voodoo helps us to grasp some famous scenes from Euripides' *Bacchae* , but it also encourages us to understand the unique experience of the Haitian people – a people whose lives have vitally intersected with our own.'

French professor Raymond Giraud offered a therapeutic rationale for CIV. A Western culture program shows 'insensitivity to the feelings of those who are led to perceive themselves as outsiders to be assimilated into the dominant culture, and who resent this, or are psychologically harmed by the implication of cultural inferiority.'

In an attempt at mediation and appeasement, English professor Martin Evans, who supported the Chace proposal, appealed to the orthodoxies of the CIV crowd. 'How can we begin to understand European colonialism without paying due attention to the growth and decline of its prototype and model, the Roman empire? How can we account for the development of sexism if we have never read the writings of Saint Augustine and Saint Paul?'

One of the highlights of the debate was a impassioned speech by undergraduate William King, president of the Black Students' Union. King complained that, under the existing Western culture requirement,

> I was never taught the fact that the Khemetic or Egyptian Book of the Dead contained many of the dialectic principles attributed to Greece, but was written 3,000 years earlier; or the fact that Socrates, Herodotus, Pythagoras and Solon studied in Egypt and acknowledged that much of their knowledge of astronomy, geometry, medicine, and building came from the African civilizations in and around Egypt; or that the Hippocratic Oath acknowledges the Greeks' father of medicine Imhotep, a black Egyptian pharaoh whom they called Aesculapius.

> I was never told that algebra came from the Moslem Arabs, or numbers from India. I was never informed when it was found that the so-called dark and wooly haired Moors in Spain preserved, expanded and reintroduced the classical knowledge that the Greeks had collected, which led to the Renaissance, and that they had indoor plumbing and air conditioning. Or that European scholars flocked to the Dar El Hikma or house of wisdom in Cairo to regain the lost knowledge of the classical period and reinvigorate the dying civilization in Europe during the Middle Ages. I read the Bible without knowing St Augustine looked black like me, that the 10 Commandments were almost direct copies from the 147 Negative Confessions of Egyptian initiates, or that many of the words of Solomon came from the black pharaoh Ame-En-Eope. I didn't learn that Toussaint L'Ouverture's defeat of Napoleon in Haiti directly influenced the French Revolution, or that the Iroquois Indians in America had a representative democracy which served as a model for the American system.

Perhaps the reason King wasn't told many of these things is that they are of dubious validity, but Stanford professors were moved by his central point: 'I'm here because I believe in the process of equal representation which my ancestors and yours created.' Here was a resurrection of the notion of democratic representation, this time applied not to admissions criteria, as at Berkeley, but to the curriculum.

On March 31, 1988, at a sparsely attended meeting, the Stanford Faculty Senate voted 39–4 to change the Western culture course to a new three-course sequence called 'Cultures, Ideas and Values.' The fifteen-book requirement was abandoned. Six common texts were chosen; professors could choose others they wanted to assign. Annually the six required texts would be reexamined, and changes made if necessary. The new requirement insisted that all courses study at least one non-European culture. Professors must give 'substantial attention' to issues of race and gender. The reading list must include works by women and minorities.

Thus the term *Western* was eliminated, to remove any taint or preference for European and American thought. The term *cultures* signaled a new pluralism – not one culture but many. *Values* suggested a certain relativism, in which various systems of thought would be considered on a roughly equal plane. Certainly any hierarchy of cultural values would be alien to the spirit, if not the letter, of the new requirement. Both physically and culturally, 'other voices' would find themselves included and indeed emphasized.

In a soothing message to the parents of Stanford undergraduates, deans Thomas Wasow and Charles Junkerman explained that the great books requirement had become a 'pedagogic handicap' because it 'was conveying the message that works by women and minorities are inferior to those by men of European descent.' 'Race, gender and class now shape both the domestic and international worlds in which we and our children must live,' remarked James Rosse, vice president and provost of Stanford. A Rainbow Coalition cliché had gone from a protest existence on the street to official policy at Stanford University.

The change at Stanford reverberated across the country, reflecting powerful and well-organized movements for curricular reform and a new agenda for what should be taught – the basic raw material of a liberal education. America, the victorious Stanford activists said, had risen above provincialism and ethnocentrism. The country was moving toward a consensus on the 'new knowledge' that would reflect the new political society.

As media coverage of the controversy suggested, Stanford is at the forefront of a national movement.

'Core curricula' at such places as Columbia University and the University of Chicago are now under fierce attack in the aftermath of the Stanford transformation. At Mount Holyoke College, students are currently required to take a course in Third World culture although there is no Western culture requirement. At the University of Wisconsin, students must enroll in ethnic studies although they need not study Western civilization or even American history. At Berkeley, the faculty recently adopted an ethnic course requirement, making it the only undergraduate course that all students must take. Dartmouth College has a non-Western but no Western prerequisite for graduation. The University of Cincinnati has a new 'American Diversity and World Cultures' requirement. Penn State mandates a course relating to 'Ethnic Diversity,' effective in fall 1991. Some colleges, such as Ohio State University, are going beyond a single requirement: they are overhauling the entire curriculum to reflect what they call 'issues of race, ethnicity and gender.'

Most colleges still retain a mixture of Western classics and newly introduced texts reflecting the new minority agenda, but the late arrivals are displacing their predecessors as the crusade for curricular diversity gains momentum. Lynne Cheney, chairman of the National Endowment for the Humanities, maintains that it is now extremely rare to find students exposed to a core curriculum in Western civilization, even at major state universities and the elite colleges of the Ivy League. Perhaps Christopher Clausen, chairman of the English department at Penn State University, reflected the emerging consensus when he remarked, 'I would bet that Alice Walker's *The Color Purple* is taught in more English departments today than all of Shakespeare's plays combined.'

Source: D'Souza, 1991, pp. 59–68.

READING B:
Charles Taylor, 'The politics of recognition'

The politics of equal respect, then, at least in this more hospitable variant, can be cleared of the charge of homogenizing difference. But there is another way of formulating the charge that is harder to rebut. In this form, however, it perhaps ought not to be rebutted, or so I want to argue.

The charge I'm thinking of here is provoked by the claim sometimes made on behalf of 'difference-blind' liberalism that it can offer a neutral ground on which people of all cultures can meet and coexist. In this view, it is necessary to make a certain number of distinctions – between what is public and what is private, for instance, or between politics and religion – and only then can one relegate the contentious differences to a sphere that does not impinge on the political.

But a controversy like that over Salman Rushdie's *Satanic Verses* shows how wrong this view is. For mainstream Islam, there is no question of separating politics and religion the way we have come to expect in Western liberal society. Liberalism is not a possible meeting ground for all cultures, but is the political expression of one range of cultures, and quite incompatible with other ranges. Moreover, as many Muslims are well aware, Western liberalism is not so much an expression of the secular, postreligious outlook that happens to be popular among liberal *intellectuals* as a more organic outgrowth of Christianity – at least as seen from the alternative vantage point of Islam. The division of church and state goes back to the earliest days of Christian civilization. The early forms of the separation were very different from ours, but the basis was laid for modern developments. The very term *secular* was originally part of the Christian vocabulary.

All this is to say that liberalism can't and shouldn't claim complete cultural neutrality. Liberalism is also a fighting creed. The hospitable variant I espouse, as well as the most rigid forms, has to draw the line. There will be variations when it comes to applying the schedule of rights, but not where incitement to assassination is concerned. But this should not be seen as a contradiction.

Substantive distinctions of this kind are inescapable in politics, and at least the nonprocedural liberalism I was describing is fully ready to accept this.

But the controversy is nevertheless disturbing. It is so for the reason I mentioned above: that all societies are becoming increasingly multicultural, while at the same time becoming more porous. Indeed, these two developments go together. Their porousness means that they are more open to multinational migration; more of their members live the life of diaspora, whose center is elsewhere. In these circumstances, there is something awkward about replying simply, 'This is how we do things here.' This reply must be made in cases like the Rushdie controversy, where 'how we do things' covers issues such as the right to life and to freedom of speech. The awkwardness arises from the fact that there are substantial numbers of people who are citizens and also belong to the culture that calls into question our philosophical boundaries. The challenge is to deal with their sense of marginalization without compromising our basic political principles.

This brings us to the issue of multiculturalism as it is often debated today, which has a lot to do with the imposition of some cultures on others, and with the assumed superiority that powers this imposition. Western liberal societies are thought to be supremely guilty in this regard, partly because of their colonial past, and partly because of their marginalization of segments of their populations that stem from other cultures. It is in this context that the reply 'this is how we do things here' can seem crude and insensitive. Even if, in the nature of things, compromise is close to impossible here – one either forbids murder or allows it – the attitude presumed by the reply is seen as one of contempt. Often, in fact, this presumption is correct. Thus we arrive again at the issue of recognition.

Recognition of equal value was not what was at stake – at least in a strong sense – in the preceding section. There it was a question of whether cultural survival will be acknowledged as a legitimate goal, whether collective ends will be allowed as legitimate considerations in judicial review, or for other purposes of major social policy. The demand there was that we let cultures defend themselves, within reasonable bounds. But the further demand we are looking at here is that we all *recognize* the equal value of different cultures; that we not only let them survive, but acknowledge their *worth*.

What sense can be made of this demand? In a way, it has been operative in an unformulated state for some time. The politics of nationalism has been powered for well over a century in part by the sense that people have had of being despised or respected by others around them. Multinational societies can break up, in large part because of a lack of (perceived) recognition of the equal worth of one group by another. This is at present, I believe, the case in Canada – though my diagnosis will certainly be challenged by some. On the international scene, the tremendous sensitivity of certain supposedly closed societies to world opinion – as shown in their reactions to findings of, say, Amnesty International, or in their attempts through UNESCO to build a new world information order – attests to the importance of external recognition.

But all this is still *an sich*, not *für sich*, to use Hegelian jargon. The actors themselves are often the first to deny that they are moved by such considerations, and plead other factors, like inequality, exploitation, and injustice, as their motives. Very few Quebec independentists, for instance, can accept that what is mainly winning them their fight is a lack of recognition on the part of English Canada.

What is new, therefore, is that the demand for recognition is now explicit. And it has been made explicit, in the way I indicated above, by the spread of the idea that we are formed by recognition. We could say that, thanks to this idea, misrecognition has now graduated to the rank of a harm that can be hardheadedly enumerated along with the ones mentioned in the previous paragraph.

One of the key authors in this transition is undoubtedly the late Frantz Fanon, whose influential *Les Damnés de la Terre* (*The Wretched of the Earth*) argued that the major weapon of the colonizers was the imposition of their image of the colonized on the subjugated people. These latter, in order to be free, must first of all purge themselves of these depreciating self-images. Fanon recommended violence as the way to this freedom, matching the original violence of the alien imposition. Not all those who have drawn from

Fanon have followed him in this, but the notion that there is a struggle for a changed self-image, which takes place both within the subjugated and against the dominator, has been very widely applied. The idea has become crucial to certain strands of feminism, and is also a very important element in the contemporary debate about multiculturalism.

The main locus of this debate is the world of education in a broad sense. One important focus is university humanities departments, where demands are made to alter, enlarge, or scrap the 'canon' of accredited authors on the grounds that the one presently favored consists almost entirely of 'dead white males.' A greater place ought to be made for women, and for people of non-European races and cultures. A second focus is the secondary schools, where an attempt is being made, for instance, to develop Afrocentric curricula for pupils in mainly black schools.

The reason for these proposed changes is not, or not mainly, that all students may be missing something important through the exclusion of a certain gender or certain races or cultures, but rather that women and students from the excluded groups are given, either directly or by omission, a demeaning picture of themselves, as though all creativity and worth inhered in males of European provenance. Enlarging and changing the curriculum therefore is essential not so much in the name of a broader culture for everyone as in order to give due recognition to the hitherto excluded. The background premise of these demands is that recognition forges identity, particularly in its Fanonist application: dominant groups tend to entrench their hegemony by inculcating an image of inferiority in the subjugated. The struggle for freedom and equality must therefore pass through a revision of these images. Multicultural curricula are meant to help in this process of revision.

Although it often is not stated clearly, the logic behind some of these demands seems to depend upon a premise that we owe equal respect to all cultures. This emerges from the nature of the reproach made to the designers of traditional curricula. The claim is that the judgments of worth on which these latter were supposedly based were in fact corrupt, were marred by narrowness or insensitivity or, even worse, a desire to downgrade the excluded. The implication seems to be that absent these distorting factors, true judgments of value of different works would place all cultures more or less on the same footing. Of course, the attack could come from a more radical, neo-Nietzschean standpoint, which questions the very status of judgments of worth as such, but short of this extreme step (whose coherence I doubt), the presumption seems to be of equal worth.

I would like to maintain that there is something valid in this presumption, but that the presumption is by no means unproblematic, and involves something like an act of faith. As a presumption, the claim is that all human cultures that have animated whole societies over some considerable stretch of time have something important to say to all human beings. I have worded it in this way to exclude partial cultural milieux within a society, as well as short phases of a major culture. There is no reason to believe that, for instance, the different art forms of a given culture should all be of equal, or even of considerable, value; and every culture can go through phases of decadence.

But when I call this claim a 'presumption,' I mean that it is a starting hypothesis with which we ought to approach the study of any other culture. The validity of the claim has to be demonstrated concretely in the actual study of the culture. Indeed, for a culture sufficiently different from our own, we may have only the foggiest idea *ex ante* of in what its valuable contribution might consist. Because, for a sufficiently different culture, the very understanding of what it is to be of worth will be strange and unfamiliar to us. To approach, say, a raga with the presumptions of value implicit in the well-tempered clavier would be forever to miss the point. What has to happen is what Gadamer has called a 'fusion of horizons'. We learn to move in a broader horizon, within which what we have formerly taken for granted as the background to valuation can be situated as one possibility alongside the different background of the formerly unfamiliar culture. The 'fusion of horizons' operates through our developing new vocabularies of comparison, by means of which we can articulate these contrasts. So that if and when we ultimately find substantive support for our initial presumption, it is on the basis of an understanding of what constitutes worth that we couldn't possibly have had at the beginning. We have reached the judgment partly through transforming our standards.

We might want to argue that we owe all cultures a presumption of this kind. I will explain later on what I think this claim might be based. From this point of view, withholding the presumption might be seen as the fruit merely of prejudice or of ill will. It might even be tantamount to a denial of equal status. Something like this might lie behind the accusation leveled by supporters of multiculturalism against defenders of the traditional canon. Supposing that their reluctance to enlarge the canon comes from a mixture of prejudice and ill will, the multiculturalists charge them with the arrogance of assuming their own superiority over formerly subject peoples.

This presumption would help explain why the demands of multiculturalism build on the already established principles of the politics of equal respect. If withholding the presumption is tantamount to a denial of equality, and if important consequences flow for people's identity from the absence of recognition, then a case can be made for insisting on the universalization of the presumption as a logical extension of the politics of dignity. Just as all must have equal civil rights, and equal voting rights, regardless of race or culture, so all should enjoy the presumption that their traditional culture has value. This extension, however logically it may seem to flow from the accepted norms of equal dignity, fits uneasily within them, [...] because it challenges the 'difference-blindness' that was central to them. Yet it does indeed seem to flow from them, albeit uneasily.

I am not sure about the validity of demanding this presumption as a right. But we can leave this issue aside, because the demand made seems to be much stronger. The claim seems to be that a proper respect for equality requires more than a presumption that further study will make us see things this way, but actual judgments of equal worth applied to the customs and creations of these different cultures. Such judgments seem to be implicit in the demand that certain works be included in the canon, and in the implication that these works have not been included earlier only because of prejudice or ill will or the desire to dominate. (Of course, the demand for inclusion is

logically separable from a claim of equal worth. The demand could be: Include these because they're ours, even though they may well be inferior. But this is not how the people making the demand talk.)

But there is something very wrong with the demand in this form. It makes sense to demand as a matter of right that we approach the study of certain cultures with a presumption of their value, as described above. But it can't make sense to demand as a matter of right that we come up with a final concluding judgment that their value is great, or equal to others'. That is, if the judgment of value is to register something independent of our own wills and desires, it cannot be dictated by a principle of ethics. On examination, either we will find something of great value in culture C, or we will not. But it makes no more sense to demand that we do so than it does to demand that we find the earth round or flat, the temperature of the air hot or cold.

I have stated this rather flatly, when as everyone knows there is a vigorous controversy over the 'objectivity' of judgments in this field, and whether there is a 'truth of the matter' here, as there seems to be in natural science, or indeed, whether even in natural science 'objectivity' is a mirage. I do not have space to address this here. I have discussed it somewhat elsewhere. I don't have much sympathy for these forms of subjectivism, which I think are shot through with confusion. But there seems to be some special confusion in invoking them in this context. The moral and political thrust of the complaint concerns unjustified judgments of inferior status allegedly made of nonhegemonic cultures. But if those judgments are ultimately a question of the human will, then the issue of justification falls away. Properly speaking, one doesn't make judgments that can be right or wrong; one expresses liking or dislike, one endorses or rejects another culture. But then the complaint must shift to address the refusal to endorse, and the validity or invalidity of judgments here has nothing to do with it.

Then, however, the act of declaring another culture's creations to be of worth and the act of declaring oneself on their side, even if their creations aren't all that impressive, become indistinguishable. The difference is only in the packaging. Yet the first is normally understood as a genuine expression of respect, the second often as insufferable patronizing. The supposed beneficiaries of the politics of recognition, the people who might actually benefit from acknowledgment, make a crucial distinction between the two acts. They know that they want respect, not condescension. Any theory that wipes out the distinction seems at least *prima facie* to be distorting crucial facets of the reality it purports to deal with.

In fact, subjectivist, half-baked neo-Nietzschean theories are quite often invoked in this debate. Deriving frequently from Foucault or Derrida, they claim that all judgments of worth are based on standards that are ultimately imposed by and further entrench structures of power. It should be clear why these theories proliferate here. A favorable judgment on demand is nonsense, unless some such theories are valid. Moreover, the giving of such a judgment on demand is an act of breathtaking condescension. No one can really mean it as a genuine act of respect. It is more in the nature of a pretend act of respect given on the insistence of its supposed beneficiary. Objectively, such an act involves contempt for the latter's intelligence. To be an object of such an act of respect demeans. The proponents of neo-Nietzschean theories hope to escape this whole nexus of hypocrisy by turning the entire issue into one of power and counterpower. Then the question is no more one of respect, but of taking sides, of solidarity. But this is hardly a satisfactory solution, because in taking sides they miss the driving force of this kind of politics, which is precisely the search for recognition and respect.

Moreover, even if one could demand it of them, the last thing one wants at this stage from Eurocentered intellectuals is positive judgments of the worth of cultures that they have not intensively studied. For real judgments of worth suppose a fused horizon of standards, as we have seen; they suppose that we have been transformed by the study of the other, so that we are not only simply judging by our original familiar standards. A favorable judgment made prematurely would be not only condescending but ethnocentric. It would praise the other for being like us.

Here is another severe problem with much of the politics of multiculturalism. The peremptory demand for favorable judgments of worth is paradoxically – perhaps one should say tragically – homogenizing. For it implies that we already have the standards to make such judgments. The standards we have, however, are those of North Atlantic civilization. And so the judgments implicitly and unconsciously will cram the others into our categories. For instance, we will think of their 'artists' as creating 'works', which we then can include in our canon. By implicitly invoking our standards to judge all civilizations and cultures, the politics of difference can end up making everyone the same.

In this form, the demand for equal recognition is unacceptable. But the story doesn't simply end there. The enemies of multiculturalism in the American academy have perceived this weakness, and have used this as an excuse to turn their backs on the problem. But this won't do. A response like that attributed to Bellow [...] to the effect that we will be glad to read the Zulu Tolstoy when he comes along, shows the depths of ethnocentricity. First, there is the implicit assumption that excellence has to take forms familiar to us: the Zulus should produce a *Tolstoy*. Second, we are assuming that their contribution is yet to be made (*when* the Zulus produce a Tolstoy...). These two assumptions obviously go hand in hand. If they have to produce our kind of excellence, then obviously their only hope lies in the future. Roger Kimball [1991, p. 13] puts it more crudely: 'The multiculturalists notwithstanding, the choice facing us today is not between a 'repressive' Western culture and a multicultural paradise, but between culture and barbarism. Civilization is not a gift, it is an achievement – a fragile achievement that needs constantly to be shored up and defended from besiegers inside and out.'

There must be something midway between the unauthentic and homogenizing demand for recognition of equal worth, on the one hand, and the self-immurement within ethnocentric standards, on the other. There are other cultures, and we have to live together more and more, both on a world scale and commingled in each individual society.

What there is is the presumption of equal worth I described above: a stance we take in embarking on the study of the other. Perhaps we don't need to ask whether it's something that others can demand from us as a right. We might simply ask whether this is the way we ought to approach others.

Well, is it? How can this presumption be grounded? One ground that has been proposed is a religious one. Herder, for instance, had a view of divine providence, according to which all this variety of culture was not a mere accident but was meant to bring about a greater harmony. I can't rule out such a view. But merely on the human level, one could argue that it is reasonable to suppose that cultures that have provided the horizon of meaning for large numbers of human beings, of diverse characters and temperaments, over a long period of time – that have, in other words, articulated their sense of the good, the holy, and admirable – are almost certain to have something that deserves our admiration and respect, even if it is accompanied by much that we have to abhor and reject. Perhaps one could put it another way: it would take a supreme arrogance to discount this possibility *a priori*.

There is perhaps after all a moral issue here. We only need a sense of our own limited part in the whole human story to accept the presumption. It is only arrogance, or some analogous moral failing, that can deprive us of this. But what the presumption requires of us is not peremptory and unauthentic judgments of equal value, but a willingness to be open to comparative cultural study of the kind that must displace our horizons in the resulting fusions. What it requires above all is an admission that we are very far away from that ultimate horizons from which the relative worth of different cultures might be evident. This would mean breaking with an illusion that still holds many 'multiculturalists' – as well as their most bitter opponents – in its grip.

Reference

KIMBALL, R. (1991) 'Tenured radical', *New Criterion*, January.

Source: Taylor, 1994, pp. 95–102.

THE CENTRALITY OF CULTURE: NOTES ON THE CULTURAL REVOLUTIONS OF OUR TIME

Stuart Hall

Contents

1 Introduction

This short final chapter provides an opportunity to look back and reflect on our intellectual journey. The issues are too varied to be brought together neatly into a single framework; however, something needs to be said by way of summary about some of the main, overarching themes of the *Culture, Media and Identities* project. The chapter therefore begins by looking again at the *centrality* of culture – the enormous expansion of everything which has to do with culture in the second half of the twentieth century and its constitutive position today in all aspects of social life. Secondly, we consider the conceptual and theoretical aspects – the expanded analytic and explanatory power which the concept 'culture' has acquired in social theory. Finally, we take these considerations back to the moment of the cultural circuit – *regulation* – which is the particular focus of this volume, and look at culture in the context of the contradictory tendencies and directions of contemporary social change into the new millennium.

Why is culture at the centre of so many discussions and debates at the present time? In one sense, culture has always been important. The human and social sciences have long recognized its significance. In the humanities, the study of the languages, literatures, art forms, philosophical ideas, moral and religious systems of belief have long constituted the fundamental subject-matter, though the idea that these all composed a distinct set of meanings – a culture – has not been as common an idea as we might have supposed. In the social sciences, and in particular in sociology, what is said to be distinctive about 'social action' – as distinct from behaviour which is purely instinctual or biologically and genetically programmed – is that it requires and is relevant to meaning. Human beings are meaning-making, interpretive beings. Social action is meaningful, both to those who perform it and to those who observe it; not 'in itself', but because of the many and variable systems of meanings which human beings deploy to define what things mean and to code, organize and regulate their conduct towards one another. These systems or codes of meaning give significance to our actions. They allow us to interpret meaningfully the actions of others. Taken together, they constitute our 'cultures'. They help to ensure that all social action is 'cultural', that all social practices express or communicate a meaning and, in that sense, are 'signifying practices'.

However, it does not follow from this that the social and human sciences have always given 'culture' either the substantive centrality or the epistemological weight it deserves. This distinction between the substantive and the epistemological aspects of culture (introduced in **du Gay, Hall et al.**, 1997) is worth bearing in mind throughout the rest of this chapter. By 'substantive', we mean culture's place in the actual empirical structure and organization of cultural activities, institutions and relationships of society at any particular historical moment. By epistemological, we refer to culture's position in relation to matters of knowledge and conceptualization, that is how 'culture' is used to transform our understanding, explanations and theoretical models of the world. In what follows, we deal with substantive aspects first.

1.1   The centrality of culture: the global dimension

In the twentieth century there has been a 'cultural revolution' in the substantive, empirical and material senses of the word. Substantively, the domain constituted by the activities, institutions and practices we call 'cultural' has expanded out of all recognition. At the same time, culture has assumed a role of unparalleled significance in the structure and organization of late-modern society, in the processes of development of the global environment and in the disposition of its economic and material resources. In particular, the means of producing, circulating and exchanging culture have been dramatically expanded through the new media technologies and the information revolution. Directly, a much greater proportion of the world's human, material and technical resources than ever before go into these sectors. At the same time, indirectly, the cultural industries have become the mediating element in every other process. The old distinction which classical Marxism used to make between the economic 'base' and the ideological 'superstructure' is difficult to sustain in circumstances where the media both form a critical part of the material infrastructure of modern societies and are the principal means by which ideas and images are circulated. Today, they sustain the global circuits of economic exchange on which the worldwide movement of information, knowledge, capital, investment, the production of commodities, the trade in raw materials and the marketing of goods and ideas depend. As Harvey observed, 'the formation of a global stock market, of global commodity (even debt) futures markets, of currency and interest rate swops, together with accelerated geographical mobility of funds, meant, for the first time, the formation of a single world market for money and credit supply' (Harvey, 1989). They have made a reality of what Marx only dimly foresaw – the emergence of a truly 'global' market. The resources which once went into the 'hardware' industries of the nineteenth-century industrial age – coal, iron and steel – are now, at the turn of the third millennium, being invested in the neural systems of the future – the 'software' and digital communication technologies of the Cyber Age.

In terms of some absolute aesthetic standards of judgement and taste, the cultural products of this revolution may not compare in value with the achievements of other historical moments – the civilizations of Egypt or of ancient China, for example, or the art of the Italian Renaissance. But compared with the relative narrowness of the social elite whose lives were positively transformed by those earlier historical examples, the significance of the cultural revolutions at the end of the twentieth century resides in their global scope and scale, their breadth of impact, their democratic and popular character. The foreshortening of time and space – time–space compression, as Harvey (1989) calls it – which these new technologies make possible, introduce changes in popular consciousness, as we live increasingly in multiple and – even more disconcertingly – in 'virtual' worlds. They truncate the speed at which images travel, the distances across which commodities can be assembled, the rate at which profits can be realized (reducing the so-called 'turn-over time of capital'), even the intervals between the opening times of the different stock markets around the world – minute time-gaps in which millions of dollars can be made or lost. These are the new 'nervous systems' which thread together societies with very different histories, different ways of life, at different stages of development and dwelling in different time-zones. It is here, especially, that revolutions in culture at the global level impact on ways of life, on how people live, on how they make sense of life, on their aspirations for the future – on 'culture' in the other, more local, sense.

These global cultural shifts are creating rapid social change – but also serious cultural dislocation, in about equal measure. As Paul du Gay notes,

> ... the new electronic media not only allow the stretching of social relations across time and space, they also deepen this global interconnectedness by annihilating the distance between people and places, throwing them into intense and immediate contact with one another in a perpetual 'present', where what is happening anywhere can be happening wherever we are ... This doesn't mean that people no longer lead a local life – that they are no longer situated contextually in time and space. What it does mean is that local life is inherently dislocated – that the local does not have an 'objective' identity outside of its relationship with the global.
>
> (du Gay, 1994)

One effect of this time–space compression is the tendency towards cultural homogenization – the tendency (which is extensively debated in **du Gay** (ed., 1997), **Mackay** (ed., 1997) and in this volume) for the world, in effect, to become one place, not just spatially and temporally, but culturally: the syndrome which one theorist has termed the 'McDonaldization' of the globe. It is indeed hard to deny that the growth of the great transnational communications giants such as CNN, Time Warner and News International tends to favour the transmission of a set of standardized cultural products using standardized western technologies to every corner of the globe, eroding local particularities and differences and producing in their place a homogenized, westernized 'world-culture'. However, those of you who have followed these debates will know that the consequences of this global cultural revolution are neither as uniform nor as easy to predict as the more extreme of the 'homogenizers' suggest. For it is also a characteristic feature that these processes are very unevenly distributed across the world – subject to what Doreen Massey (1995) has called a definite 'power geometry' – and that their consequences are profoundly contradictory. Thus, there certainly are many negative consequences – so far, without solution – in terms of the cultural exports of the technologically over-developed 'West' weakening and undermining the capacities of older nation-states and emerging societies to define their own ways of life and the pace and direction of their development (see the discussion of 'cultural imperialism' by Tomlinson in this volume). But there are also many countervailing tendencies which prevent the world from becoming a culturally uniform and homogeneous space (see Hall, 1992a; **Robins**, 1997; **Miller**, 1997). Global culture itself requires and thrives on 'difference' – even if only to try to convert it into another cultural commodity for the world market (such as ethnic cuisine). It is therefore more likely to produce 'simultaneously, *new* "global" and *new* "local" identifications' (Hall, ibid.) than some uniform and homogeneous world culture.

The result of cultural mixing, or syncretism, across old frontiers may not be the obliteration of the old by the new, but the creation of some hybrid alternatives, synthesizing elements from both but reducible to neither – as is increasingly the case in the culturally diverse, multicultural societies created by the great migrations of peoples arising from war, poverty and economic hardship in the late twentieth century (see **Gilroy**, 1997, and Parekh in this volume). A good example would be the catalogue of *Translocations*, an exhibition which took place in 1997 at the Photographers Gallery in London. This showed new visual work, some of it digitally produced, by post-colonial artists and others living and working in the UK, which was instructive in this respect, capturing some of the complexities which shadow these processes:

> *Translocations* is a collection of images, ideas and meditations which seeks to explore contemporary notions of place, positioning and movement. The idea of 'place' which *Translocations* seeks to explore is the concept of place as a series of processes, marked by fluidity, flux and movement, which impact on the ways we position ourselves within the world ... *Permanent Revolution II*, an interactive multimedia installation, is a first-time collaboration between Keith Piper and Derek Richards. By tracing the continual ebbs and flows of migrating people within what has been called 'The Black Atlantic', Piper and Richards explore the role that the convergence of migrating peoples and the resulting fusions play in the development of new cultural forms. [It] poses an alternative to essentialist representations of cultural purity and homogeneity ... Roshini Kempadoo's photo installation examines the impact that time–space compression is having on those who are subject to, rather than in control of, its unequal flows and movements ...
>
> (Photographers Gallery, 1997, p. 4)

The very pace and unevenness of global cultural change often produces its own resistances, which can of course be positive but are sometimes negative, defensive reactions, against a global culture and represent powerful

Find Contentment in PreModernity

tendencies towards 'closure' (see **Woodward**, 1997). For example, the growth of Christian fundamentalism in the US, of Islamic fundamentalism in parts of the Middle East, of Hindu fundamentalism in India, the resurgence of ethnic nationalisms in Central and Eastern Europe, the anti-immigrant, 'fortress' attitude and Euro-sceptic mood of many western European societies, and cultural nationalism in the form of reassertions of heritage and tradition (see Chapter 1 of this volume), though all *very different* in their detail and particulars, can be seen, in another sense, as conservative cultural responses, part of the retreat from the dissemination of cultural diversity by the forces of cultural globalization.

All these factors, then, qualify and complicate any simplistic, purely celebratory response to cultural globalization as the dominant form of cultural change in the foreseeable future (see, for example, the critiques by Hirst and Thompson, 1996, and by Goldblatt et al., 1997). They cannot, however, entirely negate the scale of the transformation in global relationships which the information and cultural revolution constitutes. Whether we like it or not, approve or not, the new forces and relationships which this process has set in motion are unravelling many of the patterns and traditions of the past. For good or ill, culture is now one of the most dynamic – and most unpredictable – elements of historical change in the new millennium. We should not be surprised, then, that struggles over power increasingly take a symbolic and discursive rather than simply a physical and compulsive form, and that politics itself increasingly assumes the form of a 'cultural politics' (see, for example, Jordan and Weedon, 1995).

1.2   The centrality of culture: transformations of local and everyday life

We should not be mesmerized simply by matters of scale. The 'cultural revolution' we are attempting to chart in its substantive forms is equally far-reaching and penetrative at the micro level. The everyday life of ordinary folk has been revolutionized – again, not evenly or homogeneously. Richard Rogers, the architect of several of our most outstanding modern buildings (including the Lloyds building in the City of London), reminded us that,

> Since the Industrial Revolution, work has dominated our lives. You would start your first job at 15 or 16, work a 60-hour week, and fight to have a Sunday off so you could go to church. By the time you were retired, you were worn out, with a few years of life ahead of you. The structure of your existence was largely predetermined: a little religion, a mountain of work. Leisure was the snatched moment of rest before the next shift began ... Today, the average working person does a 37-hour week ... Most of us can expect to suffer un- or under-employment at some stage as the number of industrial jobs has been halved since the war and of those of us lucky to be in work, barely more than 50 per cent are in full time posts ... Other traditional occupations have declined in

FIGURE 5.1   Still from 'Permanent Revolution 2', Keith Piper/ Derek Richards, 1997.

FIGURE 5.2   Still from 'Relocating the Remains', Keith Piper, 1997.

terms of their chronological importance for us – notably child-rearing. Bringing up large families once would keep parents, particularly mothers, hard at it for most of their adult lives. Now families have shrunk in size and couples live on their own after their own children have fled, for the next 30, 40 or 50 years.

(*The Guardian*, 25 January 1997, p. 5)

What is signalled in this brief passage are the transformations in the way ordinary people live – the transformations which have occurred in the cultures of everyday life: the decline of industrial work and the rise of service and other types of occupation, with their different lifestyles, motivations, life-cycles, rhythms, perils and rewards; the increase in non-working time and the relative 'emptiness' of much commodified so-called 'leisure'; the decline in work-for-life and 'career' type prospects, in favour of what is sometimes called 'job flexibility' but is just as often bouts of unplanned unemployment; the changes in family size, patterns of generational diversity, of parenting and parental responsibility and authority; the decline of marriage in the age of greater divorce, one-parent families and a diversification of family arrangements; the ageing and 'greying' of the population, with its attendant dilemmas of providing for a longer old age without the support of spouses, generous national insurance, state-supported health care or benefit systems; the decline of church-going of a traditional kind and of the authority of traditional moral and social standards and sanctions over the conduct of the young; the generational dislocations consequent on the divergence between adult and youth ways of life, between the decline of the puritan work ethic on the one hand and the rise of a hedonistic consumer ethic on the other. These shifts are all in some way related to class and social, as well as geographical, location: but they are not class-exclusive. The middle-aged middle-executive, cut adrift from 'career prospects' in mid-course, is increasingly a phenomenon of our times – even though experiencing these dislocations at a higher level of remuneration. Some women may have better survival skills – but usually at a lower level of pay, training, job security and prospects – than most men. Black people still have twice the unemployment rate of whites. The majority are beginning to feel like the victims, not the managers, of 'culture change'.

These are only some of the dislocations *of* the cultures of everyday life. But there are also the shifts and transformations in local and everyday life precipitated *by* culture. The pace of change in this respect is remarkably different in different locations. But fewer and fewer localities are entirely beyond the reach of these unsettling and dislocating cultural forces. Think of the proliferation of social meanings and messages which pervade our mental universes; the way in which information about – our images of – other peoples, other worlds, other ways of life, different from our own, have become widely accessible; the transformation of the visual universe of urban environments – in the post-colonial city (Kingston, Bombay, Kuala Lumpur) as much as in the western metropolis – by the mediated image; the bombardment of the most humdrum aspects of our daily routines by messages, instruction, invitations, and seductions; the extension, especially in the developed or 'media-rich' parts of the world, of human capacities and practicalities – to shop, view, spend, save, choose, socialize – at a distance, 'virtually', through the new 'soft', lifestyle cultural technologies. The phrase 'culture's centrality', here, signals the way in which culture creeps into every nook and crevice of contemporary social life, creating a proliferation of secondary environments, *mediating* everything. It is present in the disembodied voices and images which address us from the screens on our local petrol station forecourt. It is a key element in the way in which the domestic environment is harnessed, through consumption, to worldwide trends and fashions. It is brought home to us through the sports and fan magazines on the racks inside, which often market a deep attachment to 'place' and locality through the culture of contemporary football. They signal a curious nostalgia for an 'imagined community', which is at its most passionate long after the lived cultures of the relevant 'localities' have been transformed out of recognition, if not actually destroyed, by economic change and industrial decline.

It is almost impossible for the ordinary citizen to get anything like an accurate picture of the historical past without having it costumed, landscaped and 'themed' into the 'culture of heritage' (see Chapter 1 of this volume). Our participation in the so-called 'community' of the Internet is hyped on the promise that it will soon enable us to assume cyber-identities different in every respect from our own – replacing the need for anything so messy and physically constrained as actual interaction. Meanwhile, culture reaches deep into the mechanics of identity formation itself. "Change your life!" the listings magazine, *Time Out,* advised readers in January 1997: "Change your image ... your job ... your love-life ... your face ... your friends ... your religion ... your socks" (see Figure 5.3). This interior probe is matched, externally, by the proliferation of instruments of surveillance (from cameras and monitors to consumer surveys and credit checks), capable of keeping the movements and tastes of an entire (unwitting) population under inspection at all times. Amidst all the talk about 'de-regulation' (see the discussion in section 3.1 below) there has been a sophistication and intensification of the means of regulation and surveillance: what some are beginning to call 'governing by culture'. In these many different ways we come to recognize that 'culture' is no soft option. It can no longer be studied as some unimportant, secondary or dependent variable in what makes the modern world move and shake, but has to be seen as something primary and constitutive, determining its shape and character as well as its inner life.

London's weekly guide

Hanks a lot!
Tom's rose-tinted spectacle
Independents' day...
Buscemi! O Russell! Solondz!

Complete
8-day
TV
guide

Change your *image* change your *job* change your *love-life* change your face change your *friends* change your *religion* change your *socks*

Change your Life!

FIGURE 5.3

1.3   The final frontier: identity and subjectivity

The impact of the cultural revolutions on global societies and on local, everyday life may seem significant and broad-ranging enough to justify the claim that the substantive expansion of 'culture' in the late-twentieth century has been unprecedented. But the mention of its impact on 'inner life' reminds us of another frontier which needs to be addressed. This concerns the centrality of culture for the constitution of subjectivity, of identity itself and of the person as a social actor. Until recently, this was regarded as the conventional line of distinction between the disciplines of sociology and psychology, even though it was always recognized that every sociological model carried within it certain psychological assumptions about the nature of the individual subject and the formation of 'self' – and vice versa. However, in a significant way, this boundary line has been weakened and eroded by questions of 'culture'. Even the most sceptical have been obliged to acknowledge that meanings are both *subjectively* valid and at the same time *objectively* present in the world – in our actions, institutions, rituals and practices. The focus on language and meaning has had the effect of blurring, if not dissolving, the common-sense frontier between the two spheres of the social and the psychic.

Perhaps the easiest way to see what is at issue here is through an example. Suppose one were allowed only three images with which to explain to a young and intelligent person recently arrived from Mars what it means to 'be English'. Which images would we choose? Let us, for argument's sake, choose two sets, at the opposite extremes. In the first set, perhaps, changing the guards at Buckingham Palace, the Lake District and the Houses of Parliament. In the second set, Docklands, a cotton mill in Shipley and Wembley Stadium. There's no need to say in detail why each set was chosen. The first signifies (carries the meaning of) tradition, a stable and well-ordered society; the evocative landscape associated with the English love of Nature and most famous English poets – the Romantics; the proud heritage of parliamentary government, the quintessential sign of what it is about England that has survived through thick and thin – Big Ben; and so on. The second set – more modern, popular, up-to-date, thrusting, entrepreneurial: post-Thatcher Britain, face turned towards the competitive world; the triumphs of the industrial revolution on which Britain's greatness was based, Victorian values, the hard graft of work and labour which built its former prosperity; and, in popular sport, a testimony to 'ordinary folk', the backbone of the nation, and to the nation coming together, across class and regional (racial and gender?) lines in the football stadium.

These may seem very oversimplified contrasting images. But we should not imagine that they do not refer to quite complex discursive and cultural formations. In an article in *The Guardian*, Martin Jacques discussed the contrasting images of 'Middle' and 'multi-cultural' England and of the complex historical lineages behind each which, he suggested, were haunting the political discourses of both major political parties in the 1997 general election:

> There are two stories of Britain. One is about creative radicals and the other is about respectable conservatives. Both exist in the national psyche, both are authentic parts of what we are. But they command unequal recognition, one official and mainstream, the other unofficial and subterranean. The official culture warmly embraces Andrew Lloyd Webber, Cilla Black and Cliff Richard as authentically British: it treats our creative anarchists like [John] Lennon and [Vivienne] Westwood as phenomena, as freaks, taking a voyeuristic pleasure in their lives and activities rather than regarding them as one of us.
>
> From time to time, there is a rebirth of cultural energy, always starting on the periphery then working its way to the centre. Now is one such moment. In the capital, it has much to do with the emergence of London as a global city, perhaps the most global city in the world, certainly in Europe. London is now more open than ever before to a kaleidoscope of global influences from food to music, from ideas to business.
>
> And above all people: the ethnic minorities now figure in our cultural life like never before. Many of the key designers in London Fashion Week were from ethnic minorities. Immigrants are frequently a source of exceptional energy. Our cultural radicalism has much to do with being both an island and being culturally porous.
>
> One might think that this explosion of energy would command the attention of our politicians. True, John Major proudly boasted about London's new vibrancy and Tony Blair is partial to Britpop. But for Major and Blair the rallying cry [was] not cultural racialism but Middle England, the template of respectable conservatism. In 1964, Harold Wilson gave more than a nod in the direction of the Beatles ... Blair and Major preferred to walk on the other side of Britain's cultural street.
>
> (Jacques, 1997, p. 17)

It would be useless to ask, which of these two sets of images represents the 'true' Englishness – for *both* are 'true', in the sense of representing certain historical and present elements which have indeed been significant in the shaping of England, an English imaginary and an English identity. Let us leave aside for the moment the troubling complications of whether this is 'English' or 'British' – and thus of Scotland, Ireland (North and South), Wales, let alone the rest of the former British Empire – noting only that 'English' as an identity exists and takes its place in this complicated, shifting, unsettled, overlapping but not interchangeable table of terms, refusing either to separate itself firmly from or to easily incorporate or accommodate the others. These are internal fault-lines – boundaries – around which differences are marked, and which are therefore the potential sites of a contestation over meaning, a 'politics of identity' (cf. **Woodward,** 1997a). Both sets, then, are 'true' (meaning is never finally fixed: see **Hall**, ed., 1997).

But that does not mean that they are complete. Their meaning is defined, partly, in relation to each other; partly by what they leave out. Suppose, for example, you insisted on replacing one of those images with a shot of Brixton High Street – would this challenge existing assumptions about Englishness as an exclusive form of 'whiteness'? Or with one of the scene outside any primary school in England at around 3.30 in the afternoon when mothers (and some fathers) collect their children – would this pose the question of whether the feminine and domestic is as adequate and compelling a way of signifying 'the nation' as a more masculine scenario?

Each individual will feel more or less drawn to, more or less compelled by, each set of images. You may not feel perfectly or adequately 'expressed' by either – something of 'who you are' remains outside, a troubling remainder, something in excess of the meaning-system which these two sets of images attempt, between them, to capture. Left to itself, this excluded remainder or supplement could well, under the right conditions, become the focus for an alternative definition – a third set – precipitating a challenge to the cultural authority of the two sets already offered and representing the birth of a new contestation over the meaning of 'Englishness', a different focus of identification – and thus, a new 'politics of identity' (Butler, 1993). However, even if you are not fully *represented* by either of the image sets offered, you will probably feel pulled more towards one than the other, seeing yourself imaged or reflected (or as they say, 'summoned into place') more by one than the other. You have begun to invest in or *identify* with one or another meaning of 'what it is to be English' and, by taking up that subject-position, are becoming more *that* sort of English person yourself than the other.

This is one, rather common-sense and descriptive way of explaining how a *national identity* comes into being (see **Hamilton**, 1997; also Hall, 1992a, and Bhabha, ed., 1990). But it may be worth spelling out the implications of what we have said. Were you 'English', in the sense defined here, in the core of your being – in your heart and soul, in your genes, in your blood – *before* you were offered the list? Or has your English identity undergone greater definition through the process of representation and identification just described? What this suggests is that identity emerges, not so much from the inner core of our 'one, true, self' alone but in the dialogue between the meanings and definitions which are *represented to us* by the discourses of a culture, and our willingness (consciously or unconsciously) to respond to the summons of those meanings, to be hailed by them, to step into the subject positions constructed for us by one of the discourses on 'Englishness' – in short, to invest our sympathies and feelings in one or other of those images, to *identify* (see **Woodward**, ed., 1997). What we call 'our identities' are probably better conceptualized as the sedimentations over time of those different identifications or positionalities we have taken up and tried to 'live', as it were, from the inside, no doubt inflected by the particular mix of circumstances, feelings, histories and experiences which are unique and peculiar to us as individual subjects. Our identities, in short, are culturally formed.

This, at any rate, is what is meant by saying that we should think of social identities as constructed *within* representation, *through* culture, not outside of them. They are the result of a process of identification which enables us to position ourselves within or to 'subject ourselves' (inside) to the definitions which cultural discourses (outside) provide. Our so-called subjectivities, then, are, partly, discursively or dialogically produced. It is therefore easy to see why our understanding of this whole process has had to be thoroughly reconstituted by our interest in culture; and why it is increasingly difficult to maintain the traditional distinction between 'inside' and 'outside', between the social and the psychic, once culture has intervened.

2   Epistemological aspects: the 'cultural turn'

So far, we have been addressing the question of the 'centrality of culture' in substantive terms, looking in particular at four dimensions: the rise of new domains, institutions and technologies associated with the cultural industries, which have transformed the traditional spheres of the economy, industry, society and culture itself; culture as a force for global historical change; the cultural transformation of everyday life; the centrality of culture in the formation of subjective and social identities. Now it is time to turn to the second aspect of culture's centrality: its *epistemological* dimensions.

As in the world and in social life, so also in terms of knowledge, theory and understanding. In recent decades, there has been a revolution in human thought around the idea of 'culture'. Within the human and social sciences we now accord culture a much greater significance and explanatory weight than used to be the case – though changing habits of thought is also a slow and uneven process, and not without its powerful rearguard actions (such as, for example, the ritual attacks launched against media or cultural studies by the traditional disciplines which feel somehow challenged or displaced by their very existence). Despite this, a major conceptual revolution is in the making in the human and social sciences. This goes beyond learning to put cultural questions more at the centre of our calculations, alongside economic processes, social institutions and the production of goods, wealth and services – important as this shift is. It refers to an approach to contemporary social analysis which has made culture a constitutive condition of existence of social life, rather than a dependent variable, provoking a paradigm shift in the humanities and social sciences in recent years which has come to be known as the 'cultural turn'.

Essentially, the 'cultural turn' began with a revolution in attitudes towards language. Language has always been the subject of specialist interest among some literary scholars and linguists. However, the concern with language which we have in mind here, refers to something broader – a concern with language as a general term for the practices of representation, giving language a privileged position in the construction and circulation of *meaning*. This 'turn' involved:

> ... a reversal of the relationship that has traditionally been held to exist between the vocabularies we use to describe things and the things themselves. The usual, common-sense assumption is that objects exist 'objectively', as it were, 'in the world' and as such are prior to and constraining of our descriptions of them. In other words, it seems normal to assume that 'molecules' and 'genes' exist prior to and independently of scientists' models of them. Or that 'society' exists independently of sociologists' descriptions of it. What these examples serve to highlight is the way in which language is assumed to be subordinate to and in the service of the world of 'fact'. However, in recent years the relationship between language and the objects it describes has been the subject of a radical rethink. Language has been promoted to an altogether more important role. Theorists from many different fields – philosophy, literature, feminism, cultural anthropology, sociology – have declared language to bring facts into being and not simply to report on them.
>
> (du Gay, 1994)

What is involved here is the whole relationship between language and what we might call 'reality'. Don't objects exist in the world independently of our language about them? In one sense, of course, they do. To return to a familiar example discussed earlier: a stone still exists regardless of our descriptions of it (see **Hall**, 1997, p. 45). However, our identification of it as a 'stone' is only possible because of a particular way of classifying objects and making them meaningful (i.e. stone as part of a classificatory system which differentiates stone from iron, wood etc.; or, on the other hand, within a different classificatory system – a stone, as opposed to a boulder, a rock, a pebble etc.). Outside of these meaning-systems (each of which gives the thing – a 'stone' – a different meaning), objects certainly exist; but they cannot be defined as 'stones', or indeed as anything else, unless there is a language or meaning-system capable of classifying them in that way and giving them a meaning by distinguishing them from other objects:

> This idea that things only have meaning through their insertion within a particular classifying system or 'language game', as the philosopher Wittgenstein would call it, has some very profound consequences [see **Woodward**, 1997a]. Taken-for-granted assumptions about the fixed or given 'nature' and 'essence' of things are immediately open to question, in any final or absolute sense, if one accepts that the meaning of any object resides not within that object itself but is a product of how that object is socially constructed through language and representation.
>
> (du Gay, 1994)

What this has done is to prise open a gap between the *existence* and the *meaning* of an object. Meaning arises, not from things in themselves –

'reality' – but from the language games and classifying systems into which they are inserted. What we think of as natural facts are therefore *also* discursive phenomena.

It is difficult to exaggerate the consequences of this for the philosophy and practice of the social sciences. Ever since the Enlightenment it has been accepted that the role of 'science' was to offer an objective, impartial, rational and 'true' account or knowledge of the world. A scientific approach, in which facts were independent of our descriptions of them, was regarded as an ultimate arbiter of truth to which the social sciences should, as far as possible, aspire:

> The idea that, whatever is the nature of the elements of which physical objects are constructed, 'atoms' are a product of a classificatory or discursive practice – atomic theory, and that they are contextual and historically contingent, and are therefore open to different forms of classification which may emerge in the future, has undercut simple notions of accuracy, truth and objectivity, and opened the floodgates to what its critics see as a tide of relativism.
>
> (du Gay, op. cit.; see also, McLennan, 1992)

The 'cultural turn' is closely related to this new attitude towards language. For culture is nothing but the sum of the different classificatory systems and discursive formations, on which language draws in order to give meaning to things. The very term 'discourse' refers to a group of statements in any domain which provides a language for talking about a topic and a way of producing a particular kind of knowledge about that topic. The term refers both to the production of knowledge through language and representation and the way that knowledge is institutionalized, shaping social practices and setting new practices into play. To say, then, that a stone is only a stone within a particular discursive or classificatory schema is not to deny that it has a material existence but it is to say that its *meaning* is the result not of its natural essence, but of its discursive character.

The 'cultural turn' expands this insight about language to social life in general. It argues that because economic and social processes themselves *depend* on meaning and have consequences for our ways of life, for who we are – our identities – and for 'how we live now', they too must be understood as cultural, as discursive practices. To take only one example, the question of creating an 'enterprise culture' seems to have become *the* critical issue, not only for corporate economic and business success in the 1980s and '90s (see **du Gay**, ed., 1997), but also for personal and social life, for politics and for our collective moral well-being and definitions of 'the good life'. It is a topic about which management gurus address us in the language of hard-headed economic calculation on *The Money Programme* and in sober, moralistic voices on *Thought For The Day*, the daily religious slot on BBC Radio 4. What is this discourse about? Is it about economics, management, morality or personal self-improvement? Where does the 'economics' stop, in this example, and the culture begin?

Giving 'culture' a determinate and constitutive role in understanding and analysing all social relations and institutions, is different from how it has been theorized for many years in the mainstream social sciences. So much so that the 'turn to culture' is sometimes represented as a total rupture of the entire theoretical universe of the social sciences. This is probably too apocalyptic a view. There have always been traditions, even within mainstream sociology in the 1950s and 1960s, which privileged questions of meaning: for example, symbolic interactionism, deviancy studies, the concern in American social science with 'values and attitudes', the legacy of Weberean approaches, the ethnographic tradition, much influenced by anthropological techniques, and so on.

So, the 'cultural turn' is probably more accurately seen, not as total rupture, but as a reconfiguration of elements, some of which have always been present in sociological analysis, but coupled with new elements – in particular, the focus on language and culture as a substantive area, not just that which provided value-integration for the rest of the social system. Indeed, in some respects, the 'cultural turn' could be read as representing a 're-turn' to certain neglected classical and traditional sociological themes after a long period dominated by more structural, functionalist or empiricist concerns. It was, after all, one of the founding figures of modern sociology, Max Weber, who in his interpretive sociology defined the *subject* of sociological investigation – 'social action' – as 'action which is relevant to meaning' – though, for many years, this was not the most frequently referenced aspect of Weber's work. Durkheim and his *Année Sociologique* school in France, another founding formation in the early history of the human and social sciences, considered the centre-piece of sociology to be the study of relationships between 'the social' and 'the symbolic'; and much of their work concerned the study of the social meanings embodied in religion as well as in the classificatory systems of so-called 'primitive societies'. This idea was foundational for social anthropology and formed the basis of modern structuralism and semiotics (see **Hall**, ed., **1997**). Claude Lévi-Strauss, for example, in his inaugural lecture on 'The scope of anthropology', which outlined the project of structuralist cultural analysis, referred to his own work as a 'continuation of the programme first inaugurated by Durkheim and Mauss'. However, this aspect of Durkheim was considered 'too idealist' for mainstream sociology (for example, by that seminal text, *The Structure of Social Action,* by Talcott Parsons, who was at that time the leading American social theorist). Even Marx, whose predominant emphases were, of course, on the primacy of the economic and the material over the cultural and the symbolic, was one of the first classical social scientists to recognize that what was distinctive about human social action as contrasted with that of animals, was that human action and behaviour was guided and informed by cultural models. (As he observed, the worst of architects was cleverer than the best of bees because the former had to construct the *model* of a building conceptually in the mind before it could be built, whereas the industrious bees could only build in limited ways guided by instinct. Nowadays, we would call this a 'discursive' or cultural conception of social practice!)

It was in the 1960s, with the work of Lévi-Strauss and Roland Barthes in France, and of Raymond Williams and Richard Hoggart in the UK, that the 'cultural turn' began to have a major impact on intellectual and academic life, and a new interdisciplinary field of study organized around culture as the privileged concept – 'cultural studies' – began to take shape, stimulated in part by the founding of the postgraduate research Centre for Contemporary Cultural Studies at the University of Birmingham in 1964. Many strands of theorizing and analysis in the human and social sciences were selectively drawn on to provide the intellectual matrix out of which 'cultural studies' developed. Without going into detail, in order to get some sense of the different theoretical discourses on which cultural studies drew, one would have to refer, *inter alia*, to the traditions of textual analysis (visual and verbal), literary criticism, art history and genre studies, social history, as well as linguistics and theories of language, in the humanities; in the social sciences, the more interactionist and culturalist aspects of mainstream sociology, deviancy studies and anthropology; critical theory (e.g. the French semiotic and post-structuralist theorists; Foucault; the 'Frankfurt School'; feminist and psychoanalytic writers); film, media and communications studies, studies of popular culture. Also important were the many non-reductionist forms of Marxism (especially those associated with the work of Antonio Gramsci and the French structuralist school led by Althusser), and their preoccupation with questions of cultural hegemony, ideology and power (see Hall, 1992b). Since those early days there has been both an enormous expansion in the teaching of, and the demand by students for, cultural studies, not just in the UK but internationally (see Grossberg et al., eds, 1992; Chen, 1996; and Ang and Stratton, 1996). Just as significant, perhaps, has been the way in which elements of cultural studies have been incorporated into the more traditional disciplines, and the manner in which the 'cultural turn' has influenced and inflected the practices of the academic mainstream – not least of all, sociology itself.

Recent commentators have begun to recognize not only the real breaks and paradigm-shifts, but also some of the affinities and continuities, between older and newer traditions of work: for example, between Weber's classical interpretive 'sociology of meaning' and Foucault's emphasis on the role of the 'discursive'. Foucault's work in the 1970s and '80s has been critically influential for the 'cultural turn' – which is why, despite the criticisms offered of his work, the *Culture, Media and Identities* project has kept returning to the debate with Foucault. What all this suggests is that the 'cultural turn' is the product of a more complex genealogy than has been widely recognized and could be interpreted as a recovery – in a new key, so to speak – of some, long-neglected and subordinated strands, in critical thought within the human and social sciences. Its overwhelming consequence has been, not – as its critics suggest – to replace one kind of reductionism (idealism) for another (materialism), but to force us to radically rethink the centrality of 'the cultural' and the articulation between the material and the cultural or symbolic factors in social analysis. This is the intellectual point of reference from which 'cultural studies' took its point of departure.

2.1   Is everything culture? Is there nothing outside discourse?

In part, then, in its epistemological sense, the centrality of culture lies in the paradigm shifts which the 'cultural turn' has provoked within traditional disciplines, the explanatory weight which the concept of culture carries, and its constitutive rather than its dependent role in social analysis. One aspect of this is the expansion of 'culture' to a wider, more inclusive range of institutions and practices. Thus we have spoken about the 'culture' of corporate enterprises, the 'culture' of the workplace, the growth of an enterprise 'culture' in public and private corporate organizations (for example, in **du Gay**, ed., 1997), the 'culture' of masculinity (**Nixon**, 1997), the 'cultures' of motherhood and the family (**Woodward**, 1997b), a 'culture' of home decoration and of shopping (in **Miller**, 1997), a 'culture' of de-regulation (in this volume), even a 'culture' of the fit, and – even more disturbingly – a 'culture' of the thin body (**Benson**, 1997). What this suggests is that *every* social activity or institution generates and requires its own distinctive 'world' of meanings and practices – its own culture. So, increasingly, the term is being applied to institutions and practices, which are manifestly *not* part of 'the cultural sphere' in the traditional sense of the word. According to this emphasis, *all* social practices, in so far as they are relevant to meaning or require meaning for their operation, have a 'cultural' dimension.

Where does this leave the traditional distinction, long a part of accepted conventional sociological wisdom, between 'material' and 'symbolic' factors, between 'things' and 'signs'? If 'culture' is in everything and everywhere, where does it begin and end? Of course, this claim for the centrality of culture does not mean – as its critics have sometimes suggested – that there is nothing but 'culture' – that everything is 'culture' and that 'culture' is everything; or, to paraphrase the now infamous observation by the deconstructionist French philosopher, Jacques Derrida, 'There is nothing outside the text'; or, as Foucault is sometimes thought to have said, 'There is nothing but discourse'. If this were what is being argued, it would certainly – and rightly – be exposed to the critique that, in this case, we had simply replaced the *economic materialism* or *sociologism* which once threatened to dominate these questions in the social sciences with a *cultural idealism* – i.e. substituting one form of reductionist argument for another. What is being argued, in fact, is *not* that 'everything is culture' but that every social practice depends on and relates to meaning; consequently, that culture is one of the constitutive conditions of existence of that practice, that every social practice has a cultural dimension. Not that there is nothing but discourse, but that every social practice *has a discursive character.*

Thus, of course, there are *political* practices, which are concerned with the disposition and exercise of power, just as there are *economic* practices, which are concerned with the production and distribution of goods and of wealth. Each of these is subject to the conditions which organize and govern political and economic life in these societies. Now, political power has very real and palpable material effects. However, its actual operation depends on how people *define situations politically.* For example, until recently, the family, gender and sexual relations were defined as outside power: that is, spheres of life to which the term 'politics' had no bearing or meaning. A 'sexual politics' would have been impossible to conceive without some shift in the definition of what constitutes 'the political'. Likewise, it is only recently – since feminism has redefined 'the political' (for example, 'the personal is political') – that we have come to recognize that there is a 'politics of the family'. And this is a matter of *meaning* – the political *has a cultural dimension.*

Similarly, the distribution of economic wealth and resources has real and tangible *material* effects for rich and poor people in society. However, the question of whether the present distribution of wealth is 'fair' or 'unjust' is a matter of meaning – that is to say, it depends on how 'justice' and 'fairness' are defined; and our economic actions will be determined, in part, on what position we take up with respect to these definitions. Consequently we can say that economic practices take place and have effects within the discursive framework of what is understood as fair and as unjust – they depend on and are 'relevant to meaning' and are consequently 'cultural practices'. As Foucault might say, the operations of the economy depend upon the discursive formation of a society at any particular moment. Clearly, this does not mean that economic processes have been dissolved into discourse or language. It does mean that the discursive or meaning-dimension is one of the constitutive conditions for the operation of the economy. The 'economic', so to speak, could not operate or have real effects without 'culture' or outside of meaning and discourse. Culture is therefore, in these examples, constitutive of 'the political' and 'the economic', just as 'the political' and 'the economic' are, in turn, constitutive of, and set limits for, culture. They are mutually constitutive of one another – which is another way of saying that they are *articulated* with each other. Thus, to be strictly accurate, we should really re-word the expanded claim about 'culture' offered above as follows: every social practice *has cultural or discursive conditions of existence.* Social practices, in so far as they depend on meaning for their operation and effects, take place 'within discourse', are 'discursive'.

3   Regulation: governing cultures

We have been teasing out the implications of the centrality of culture in both its substantive and its epistemological aspects. Given that centrality, it should be perfectly clear now why this volume on the final moment of the circuit of culture is given over to the issues around *regulation* – how this important sphere of culture is governed. This volume has posed two key questions about this process. How is the cultural sphere regulated and controlled? Which of these issues of cultural regulation are likely to emerge as points of change, rupture and debate in the next century?

In its various chapters, this volume has considered these two questions in relation to a number of selective topics of key significance in defining contemporary cultural change. It has discussed various aspects of cultural policy – the regulation and governance of culture – with respect to broadcasting and the broadcasting institutions; censorship of the arts; the relationship of minority cultures to 'mainstream', national cultural traditions; control of the international flow of cultural goods and images; the regulation of morality and representations of sexuality; and so on. It has also asked broader questions – as in Chapter 1 – about modes of cultural regulation in general. What is the relationship *between* 'culture' and other forces which exert a controlling, shaping or determining force over culture? Is it primarily politics, the economy, the state, the market which is *the* determining factor in relation to culture? Is it the state which, through legislative policies, determines the shape of culture? Or is it economic interests or market forces whose 'hidden hand' is really determining the patterns of cultural change? Is it the legislators, the moral guardians or the 'ruling classes' who determine the switch from one mode of regulation at a certain period to another – say, from the more relaxed and customary attitude taken in pre-industrial England to time-keeping at work or to the many informal holidays which people gave themselves, to the stricter time-keeping and regulated leisure of the Industrial Age? What forces *should* exercise cultural regulation? Should it be the Church which provides the moral framework for regulating sexual behaviour, as once it did? What forces in society or in economic and political life have undermined the traditional sources of moral and cultural authority and what, if anything, has taken their place? Is it through the education system, the legal framework, the parliamentary process or by administrative procedures that the state 'governs' culture – for example, the freedom of minority religious communities to practise their faith in a predominantly, if nominally, Christian 'multicultural' society?

Here, it is worth focusing specifically on the centrality of culture to issues around social regulation, morality and the governance of social conduct in late-modern societies. Why should we be concerned with regulating the 'cultural sphere' and why have cultural questions increasingly taken centre-stage in these public policy debates? At the heart of this question lies the relationship between *culture* and *power*. The more important – 'central' – culture becomes, the more significant are the forces which shape, regulate and govern it. Whatever has the capacity to influence the general shape of the culture, to control or determine the way cultural institutions work or to regulate cultural practices, exerts a definite kind of power over cultural life. We have in mind here, for example, the power to control how many and what kinds of foreign-generated television images will be beamed by satellite into the nation's homes; or the power to decide what kind of publications can and cannot be sold to minors from the top shelves of newsagents; or broader policy issues such as whether the amount of news available to the citizen on mainstream terrestrial television channels should be a matter of publicly determined broadcasting policy by the government, left to the self-regulation of the broadcasting authorities themselves, the result of the personal tastes of people like Rupert Murdoch or of companies such as the Disney Corporation, who own and control the major media corporate enterprises of the world, or exposed to the 'free play' of market forces. In short, within this perspective, whether culture, while having its own distinct and autonomous existence, is itself influenced and regulated by other determining factors? The broad question which Chapter 1 asks of all the examples in this volume is: are culture and cultural change *determined* by the economy, the market, the state, political or social power, in some *strong* sense of the word (i.e. is the shape of culture determined by forces external to culture – economic or political), or should we think of the regulation of culture and cultural change in terms of a process of mutual determination – arising, say, from the *articulation* or linkage between culture and the economy, the state or the market, which implies a *weaker* sense of determination, each setting limits and exerting pressures on the other, but neither having the overwhelming determining force to define in detail the internal operations of the other?

3.1   De-regulation and re-regulation

One very powerful theme which comes across in answer to this question is the presence of two, apparently contradictory, trends in the direction of cultural policy – towards de-regulation and towards re-regulation. In broad terms, de-regulation has become the common-sense wisdom of the new neo-liberal era. The age of large-scale, nationally owned and managed public corporations or organizations associated with or governed by a 'public' philosophy or 'culture' appears to have passed. They are associated with a more collectivist, social-democratic, 'Keynesian', public-service historical moment, which lasted among the developed industrial countries from the Second World War to the 1970s. Since then, 'public enterprise' has generally come to be ideologically associated with bureaucratic, wasteful and inefficient principles of organization and a concerted campaign has been mounted to shift from 'public' and state, to 'private' and market as the basis of regulation. The drive towards 'letting free-market forces prevail' and the strategy of 'privatization' have provided the motor force of both national and international economic and cultural strategies.

These policies were pioneered by the Reagan and Thatcher eras in the USA and the UK, quickly followed by many similar regimes elsewhere (Italy, Spain, Canada, Australia, New Zealand and so on). They were driven forwards by the global restructuring policies of international organizations such as the World Bank and the International Monetary Fund which had the effect of forcing weak post-colonial economies towards private and market solutions through 'structural adjustment programmes', with disastrous effects in the last decade, especially in Africa. Finally, the shift was much accelerated by the wholesale 'privatization' of the economy of the Soviet Union and Eastern bloc countries which accompanied the political and economic liberalization after 1989. The effects of the process of 'globalization' – weakening the relative autonomy of nation-states to determine cultural policy within their own sovereign territories, and increasing the pressures for an 'open skies' policy towards the internationalization of cultural markets – have played an increasingly significant role here, as has a little-regarded trend towards re-monopolization by the global transnationals.

The main thrust, culturally, has been to divest the state of its responsibilities in the regulation of cultural matters and to open it increasingly to the free play of market forces. Freedom, maximizing choice, increasing diversity and cultural pluralism, taking the 'nanny state' off the backs of the people – these are some of the ways in which de-regulation has been positively glossed by its supporters. However, we should be very careful not to fall for some simple dichotomy between state = regulation and market = freedom. There are at least two reasons worth bearing in mind why this simplification should be resisted. First, markets do not operate on their own. They require to be set up and policed; they depend on other social and cultural conditions of existence (the presence of trust, customs and conventions, moral and wider public considerations, the effective application of the law, inspection and accountability, training and accreditation of specialized personnel and so on) which they themselves cannot provide. Someone has to bear the social 'costs' of those who fail in the market (markets always create both 'winners' and 'losers', with wider social, not merely market consequences). Markets would soon collapse into anarchy if they were not themselves regulated. Thus the privatization programme in Britain has been followed by the creation of a plethora of regulatory bodies – Oftel, Ofwat, Ofgas etc. – which set market forces in a wider regulatory context and are rapidly developing a regulatory 'culture' of their own (in addition to the continuing involvement of statutory regulatory institutions which safeguard the 'public interest', for example in broadcasting).

Secondly, the market itself *regulates*. It allocates resources, rewards efficiency and innovation, punishes inefficiency and lack of innovation, and above all, as we noted above, creates winners and losers. These are powerful incentives – and disincentives – inducing certain forms of conduct and discouraging others (i.e. regulating conduct). And, as we have seen, markets create and require very distinctive managerial and organizational 'cultures' of their own – a body of rules, expectations, normative procedures and internalized goals (see **Salaman**, 1997). We may or may not prefer the 'freedom' of market regulation over state regulation. On the other hand, we may prefer it when some social goals are imposed by regulation on cultural activities, even if it is at the expense of individual, market-driven, 'free choice'. The main point, which is central to this whole debate, is that this is *not* a choice between freedom and constraint, but between *different modes of regulation*, each of which represents a combination of freedoms and constraints. That is why what is sometimes called 'the repressive hypothesis' (Foucault, 1978) – the idea that state regulation always and only exerts control and constraint and that the alternative to it is *pure* freedom – is seriously misleading. There is rarely in social life, if ever, a state of 'no regulation'. The critical shifts are always between one mode of regulation and another. This also explains why this volume constantly asks, not how can a particular area of culture be de-regulated, but when, how and why does it shift *from one mode of regulation to another*.

However, it is also worth observing that, right alongside the trend towards de-regulation and privatization, there has appeared, in some spheres, a powerful movement to strengthen, 'nationalize' and revitalize the regulatory regime. This is especially so in relation to questions concerning sexuality, morality, crime and violence, standards of public conduct and behaviour, parenting, 'family values' and the like. In the economic sphere, rolling back the state and advancing the free market prevails as the preferred regulatory mechanism. Elsewhere, there has been a strong socially- and morally-conservative movement to push the state forwards in a regulative capacity, in these areas where it has been absent or has distanced itself, or from which it actively withdrew in the 1960s, the era of affluence and hedonism – as its critics see it – when 'life was tested to its limits without discipline or restraint'. Just why the pressure to moral re-regulation is so powerful in this particular sphere of life is itself worth asking, since it provides clues to the pattern of cultural change which societies such as ours are undergoing.

Is this, as some people see it, a glaring contradiction? It may well be, in the sense that, freeing cultural life and making it more subject to individual choice, in one respect, may have had consequences in weakening the bonds of social authority and moral consensus in another, and it is this latter erosion which is powering the drive towards moral re-regulation. In this sense, de-regulation in one sphere requires and is complemented by re-regulation in others. This is not as contradictory as it sounds. As we argued above, there is no total or 'pure' freedom, so it is not surprising that regulation consists of different modes being applied in different spheres of life, or that the consequences of the operation of the mode of regulation in one sphere may be caught up, addressed and 'corrected' in another. If accepted, however, this account would draw us away from a simplistic, unitary conception of regulation, ideologically unified around one set of discourses, practices, meanings and values, or one 'world- view', to a more complex, differentiated and articulated view of regulation as consisting of an internally differentiated moral system, structure or set of practices (see Bocock in Chapter 2 of this volume).

It does genuinely seem as if Thatcherism, for example, did aim *both* to de-regulate the economy in relation to the state, and to re-regulate morality in relation to the market – just as, in the same way, in Victorian times, the Victorian middle-class entrepreneurial 'hero' was expected to be *both* carving out his and his family's fortunes in the public competitive world of business *and* nurturing the domestic and paternal aspect of his life in the benevolent private sphere of the patriarchal family, hearth and home. What made this apparently contradictory combination 'work' was the *articulation* between the differentiated modes of regulation applied in the two related, complementary but different spheres. Something of the same kind may be in progress now, though the contradictions between the discourses of 'freedom and choice' and of 'discipline and restraint' do produce serious and glaring disjunctions in cultural life.

3.3   Governing *by* culture

We have been looking at some of the implications for the centrality of culture in the way in which culture is governed and regulated. But it may be worth stopping here to ask ourselves why the 'governance of culture' matters. Why is it of central importance? Why should we be concerned with how broadcasting and its institutions are regulated, with what we can or cannot see on our screens or buy off the shelves in our bookshops; with whether national cultures can protect themselves against the tide of global communications networks; and with how cultural diversity is to be negotiated or with the debates and anxieties about morality and standards of sexual conduct? In the end, this volume argues, these things matter essentially for two reasons. First, because these are some of the key areas of change and debate in contemporary society, around which anxieties cluster, where traditional modes of regulation appear to have fragmented or collapsed; danger-points where a sort of collective anxiety begins to cluster, where a collective cry goes up that 'something must be done'. As such, they give us a set of symptomatic clues as to what seem to be the flashpoints, the unsettled issues, the underlying tensions, the traumas of the collective unconscious in the cultures of late-modern societies. To understand what lies behind these areas of moral contestation and cultural anxiety is to gain some indirect access to the deep-seated and contradictory currents of cultural change running beneath the surface of society. They also provide us with some preliminary indicators of major fault-lines running through the body politic, from which we can begin to chart the direction of cultural change into the third millennium. In part, this is what has guided our selection of themes and issues in the few chapters we had at our disposal to map out the contours of cultural change.

The second reason why it matters how 'culture' is shaped, governed and regulated is because, in its turn, it is culture which governs *us* – which 'regulates' our conduct, social action, human practices and thus the way people act within institutions and in society at large. But what does this mean? How does culture 'regulate' social practices? How does culture govern? This takes us back to the question of meaning, and thus to the 'cultural' or discursive dimension of social action and of human conduct discussed above. You may recall the discussion of the activity of 'building a wall' taken from Laclau and Mouffe's (1990) work (discussed in **Hall**, 1997). There we noted that 'building a wall' could be described as a 'discursive practice'. This is not because everything about building a wall is 'discourse' in the limited sense of belonging to language, thought or knowledge. To build a wall requires material resources and certain physical actions of the body, which might accurately be described as the 'non-discursive' aspect of this wall-building activity; but it also involves – and could not be accomplished without – those actions and the use of the materials being shaped by our knowledge of how walls are built, by our 'model' of walls and wall-building, which precedes and informs all our actions and their sequencing; or without the exchange of information and coordination of movements which allowed several people to collaborate together in building the wall. In short, building a wall involves physical and material factors, but it could not take place outside a system of meaning, institutionalized cultural knowledge, normative understandings and the capacity to conceptualize and use language to represent to oneself the task on which one was engaged and to build around it a collaborative and communicative 'world' of meanings – in short, 'a culture'. It is in *this* sense that 'building a wall' – deeply physical and material as it may be – is and must *also* be a cultural activity, must take place or be 'relevant to meaning', and is therefore a 'discursive practice'.

This explains why cultural regulation is so important. If culture, in fact, regulates our social practices at every turn, then those who need or wish to influence what is done in the world or how things are done will need – to put it crudely – to somehow get hold of 'culture', to shape and regulate it in some way or to some degree. The author, Perri 6 (1997), offers what many may find a surprising quote from Margaret Thatcher as an epigraph to his essay, 'Governing by cultures': 'Economics is the method but the aim is to change the soul.' He continues:

> Solving problems is generally a matter of changing how people do things, or how they see the world. However much we say we would like government to leave us alone, when we are faced with large social problems, we expect government to make every effort to change the behaviour or beliefs of those people involved either in creating or in solving those problems. Put simply, we usually expect government to try to change people's culture ... Culture is now the centre of the agenda for government reform, because we know from the findings of a wide range

of recent research that culture is perhaps the most important determinant of a combination of long-run economic success and social cohesion. The mistake of both statist left and laissez-faire right was to ignore this fact.

(Perri 6, 1997, pp. 260, 272)

This may all sound very conspiratorial and power-driven – and undoubtedly questions of power *are* implicated, which is why we have kept saying that culture is inscribed by and always operates within the 'play of power'. But there is no need to be crudely reductionist about it. We all want to do the very best for our children. But what is education if it is not the process by which society inculcates its norms, standards and values – in short, its 'culture' – into the next generation in the hope and expectation that, in this way, it will broadly guide, channel, influence and shape the actions and beliefs of future generations in line with the values and norms of its parents and the prevailing value-system of society? What is this if not regulation – moral governance by culture? What is the attempt to build an 'enterprise culture' within an organization except an effort to influence, shape, govern and regulate – albeit indirectly, perhaps, and at a distance – the way its employees feel about and act within the organization? Why would traditional moralists give a damn about what people were watching on television, unless implicitly they believed that what people see, what representations they look at, and how the world is represented to them – in short, the 'culture of television' – will influence, shape, guide, and normatively regulate their – for example – sexual conduct? Why are questions of violence and sexuality so focused on the classroom, unless we are somehow depending on the education system to teach young people what is and is not acceptable in these highly-charged areas? Why, indeed, do we talk to our friends who are in trouble, except in the expectation that what we say will change their attitudes, and this 'change of culture' will change their behaviour, and they will begin to conduct themselves in their social practices in different ways, according to a different set of cultural norms and meanings. We are not necessarily speaking about arm-twisting coercion, undue influence, crude propaganda, false information or even questionable motives here. We are talking about the dispositions of symbolic or discursive power. All our conduct and actions are shaped, influenced and thus regulated normatively by cultural meanings. Since in this sense culture regulates social practice and conduct, then it matters profoundly *who regulates culture*. The regulation *of* culture and regulation *by* culture are thus intimately and profoundly interrelated.

3.3   Governing the conduct of cultural life

It may be worth exploring these forms of 'regulation *by* culture' in somewhat more detail, in order to obtain a more complex and differentiated sense of how it works. The first form of this kind of regulation we want to draw attention to is *normative*. Human actions are guided by norms in the sense that in the course of doing something we have to be able to envisage its end or purpose, in order to reach it. And our way of doing it is guided unconsciously by our sense of 'how these things are normally and properly done in our culture' – by our tacit understandings and taken-for-granted cultural 'know-how'. We get on a bus, automatically reach in our pockets for a round bit of metal, put it in the appropriate place, and wait for a machine to deliver us a bit of paper. We have boarded a bus and paid for our ticket. We hardly need to think what we are doing – all our actions are automatic. And yet, there is nothing 'instinctual' in the proper sense, about it. Every movement we have made is normatively regulated in the sense that, from start to finish, it has been 'guided' by a set of cultural norms and knowledges. Since we haven't given our actions much active conscious thought – our actions have been institutionalized, they have sedimented into the 'taken-for-granted' of our culture, its habitus – we may be reluctant to speak here of 'meaning'. And yet, someone watching us from afar – the ticket inspector at the back of the bus, for example – would be perfectly capable of *understanding* the meaning of every action we had made. S/he would find our actions intelligible because s/he could *interpret them meaningfully* – against a set of shared cultural norms and meanings which give our actions 'relevance for meaning' in Weber's sense. Is this piece of social conduct 'cultural'? Yes. You have only to think how meaningless it would all be to some other human being who was from a different culture which did not have the concept of 'bus', 'money', 'ticket', 'paying one's way' and so on, to appreciate how profoundly 'cultural' this simple act was.

What normative regulation does is to give human conduct and practice a shape, direction and purpose; to guide our physical actions in line with certain purposes, ends and intentions; to make our actions both intelligible to others, and predictable, regular; to create an orderly world – in which each action is inscribed by the meanings and values of a shared culture. Of course, normative regulation frequently, and always in the end, breaks down – otherwise there would be no change, and the world would simply repeat itself to infinity. On the other hand, our social worlds would inevitably fall apart if social practices were entirely random and 'meaningless', if they were not regulated by shared meanings, values and norms – rules and conventions about 'how to do things', about 'how things are done in this culture'. That is why the boundaries of cultural and normative regulation are such a powerful way of marking out 'who belongs' (i.e. who does things in our way, according to our norms and meanings) and who is 'other', different, outside the discursive and normative limits of our particular ways of doing things (see **Hall**, ed., 1997; and **Woodward**, ed., 1997).

Another way in which our conduct is 'culturally regulated' is in terms of the classificatory systems which belong to and mark out each culture, which define the limits between sameness and difference, between what is sacred and profane, what is 'acceptable' and 'unacceptable' about our behaviour, our dress, our speech, our habits, what customs and practices are considered 'normal' or 'abnormal', who is 'clean' or 'unclean' (see **Woodward**, ed.,

1997). Once a person can be defined as someone whose actions are always unacceptable, regulated by norms and values we do not share, our conduct towards that person will be modified accordingly. Classifying actions, and ascribing human conduct and practice within our systems of cultural classification, is another form of cultural regulation.

A third form of regulation by culture, which was discussed earlier in a different context, is in terms of producing or 'making up' new subjects – that is to say, regulating what sorts of 'subjects' we are. (This is extensively discussed in **Woodward**, ed., 1997, and **du Gay**, ed., 1997, particularly **du Gay**, 1997.) A corporate organization wishes to become less bureaucratic, more flexible in its work and management practices, more oriented towards the customer, with a greater sense amongst the employees that their personal fates and fortunes are tied up with the efficiency, profitability and success of the organization. In a word, the organization seeks to become more 'entrepreneurial'. Of course, it can lay down all sorts of external procedures and regulations to bring this about. It can undertake staff development and retraining. It can introduce a system of bonus rewards for the kind of behaviour it regards as appropriate (and of penalties to discourage inappropriate actions). But if, at the end of the day, it is obliged to employ the same people with the same ingrained attitudes and habits, its efforts are likely to fail. In the ideology of the 'new managerialism', its reforms must penetrate more deeply – it must change the actual behaviour and conduct of its employees. It can regulate their conduct, albeit at a distance, by 'changing the culture of the organization': ultimately, by producing a different kind of employee, or better still, by transforming the individual employee from the 'bureaucratic' kind of subject he or she was in the earlier management regime to the new 'entrepreneurial' kind of subject of the new regime. In fact, it must try to regulate the culture of the organization and influence the conduct of its employees by working directly on their *subjectivities* – by producing or constructing new kinds of entrepreneurial *subject,* by *subjecting* the individual employees to a new *regime of meanings and practices.*

The beauty of this kind of regulation, if it can be done – and it goes without saying that it is rarely accomplished without conflict and resistance – is that, rather than constraining the conduct, behaviour and attitudes of the employees by the imposition of an external regime of social control, it endeavours to get employees subjectively to *regulate themselves.* The strategy is to get the subjects to align their own personal and subjective motivations and aspirations with the motivations of the organization, to redefine their skills and capacities in line with the personal and professional job-specifications of the firm, to internalize organizational objectives as their own subjective goals. They will use what Foucault calls the 'technologies of the self' to 'make themselves up', to produce themselves – in **du Gay**'s (1997) terms – as different kinds of enterprising subjects. Regulation through the medium of 'culture change' – through a shift in the 'regime of meanings' and by the production of new subjectivities, within a new set of organizational disciplines – is another, powerful, mode of 'governing *by* culture'.

4   Conclusion

In this short final chapter, we have looked at the question of the centrality of culture from several different vantage points. First, we considered the substantive expansion of culture – its growing centrality to global processes of formation and change, its penetration into the detail of everyday life and the local and its constitutive role in the formation of identities and subjectivities. Then we turned to the epistemological centrality of culture – its constitutive position in the humanities and social sciences today and the shifts in theorization and analysis associated with the 'cultural turn'. We tried to review what is meant by the claim advanced by this conceptual 'turn' that every social practice takes place 'within culture'.

In the second half of the chapter, we brought these wide-ranging considerations back to the central theme of this book – the regulation of culture. We looked again at why questions of the regulation and governance of culture was so important, and we tried to tease out some of the contradictory tendencies in the new regulatory modes which have emerged in recent decades – the tendencies, in different spheres, towards both re-regulation and de-regulation. Finally, we turned the tables, relating questions of the governing *of* culture to governing *by* culture – using this as an opportunity to review some of the key dimensions of the operation of culture and its centrality in the modern world. Without providing a blow-by-blow resumé of the whole argument, we hope that this summary review will have helped to identify and highlight some of the key major themes which range across the *Culture, Media and Identities* project and clarify the nature of culture – both what it is and what it does.

References

ANG, I. and STRATTON, J. (1996) 'Asianing Australia', *Cultural Studies*, Vol. 10, No. 1 (London).

BENSON, S. (1997) 'The body, health and eating disorders' in Woodward, K. (ed.).

BHABHA, H. K. (ed.) (1990) *Nation and Narration*, London, Routledge.

BUTLER, J. (1993) *Bodies That Matter: on the discursive limits of 'sex'*, London, Routledge.

CHEN, K.-H. (1996) 'Not yet the post-colonial era', *Cultural Studies*, Vol. 10, No. 1 (London).

DU GAY, P. (1994) 'Some course themes', unpublished mss, Milton Keynes, The Open University.

DU GAY, P. (1997) 'Organizing identity: making up people at work' in du Gay, P. (ed.).

DU GAY, P. (ed.) (1997) *Production of Culture/Cultures of Production*, London, Sage/The Open University (Book 4 in this series).

DU GAY, P., HALL, S., JANES, L., MACKAY, H. and NEGUS, K. (1997) *Doing Cultural Studies: the story of the Sony Walkman*, London, Sage/The Open University (Book 1 in this series).

FOUCAULT, M. (1978) *The History of Sexuality*, Harmondsworth, Allen Lane/ Penguin Books.

GILROY, P. (1997) 'Diaspora and the detours of identity' in Woodward, K. (ed.).

GOLDBLATT, D., HELD, D., MCGREW, A. and PERRATON, J. (1997) *Global Flows, Global Transformations: concepts, evidence and arguments*, Cambridge, Polity.

GROSSBERG, L. et al. (eds) (1992) *Cultural Studies*, London and New York, Routledge.

HALL, S. (1992a) 'The question of cultural identity' in Hall, S., Held, D. and McGrew, A. (eds).

HALL, S. (1992b) 'Cultural studies and its theoretical legacies' in Grossberg, L. et al. (eds).

HALL, S. (1997) 'The work of representation' in Hall, S. (ed.).

HALL, S. (ed.) (1997) *Representation: cultural representations and signifying practices*, London, Sage/The Open University (Book 2 in this series).

HALL, S., HELD, D. and MCGREW, A. (eds) *Modernity and Its Futures*, Cambridge, Polity Press/The Open University.

HAMILTON, P. (1997) 'Representing the social: France and Frenchness in post-war humanist photography' in Hall, S. (ed.).

HARVEY, D. (1989) *The Condition of Postmodernity: an enquiry into the origins of cultural change,* Oxford, Blackwell.

HIRST, P. and THOMPSON, G. (1996) *Globalization in Question: the international economy and the possibilities of governance*, Cambridge, Polity.

JACQUES, M. (1997) 'The rebel alliance of British talents', *The Guardian*, 20 February.

JORDAN, G. and WEEDON, C. (1995) *Cultural Politics*, Oxford, Blackwell.

LACLAU, E. and MOUFFE, C. (1990) 'Post-Marxism without apologies' in Laclau, E., *New Reflections on the Revolution of our Time*, London, Verso.

MACKAY, H. (ed.) (1997) *Consumption and Everyday Life*, London, Sage/The Open University.

MCLENNAN, G. (1992) 'The Enlightenment project revisited' in Hall, S., Held, D. and McGrew, A. (eds).

MASSEY, D. (1995) 'Making spaces, or, geography is political too', *Soundings*, Issue 1, pp. 193–208.

MILLER, D. (1997) 'Consumption and its consequences' in Mackay, H. (ed.).

NIXON, S. (1997) 'Exhibiting masculinity' in Hall, S. (ed.)

PARSONS, T. (1968/1937) *The Structure of Social Action*, London, Collier-Macmillan.

PERRI 6 (1997) 'Governing by cultures' in Mulgan, G. (ed.) *Life after Politics*, London, Fontana/DEMOS.

PHOTOGRAPHERS GALLERY (1997) *Great 11: Translocations*, Catalogue to exhibition.

ROBINS, K. (1997) 'What in the world's going on?' in du Gay, P. (ed.).

SALAMAN, G. (1997) 'Culturing production' in du Gay (ed.).

WOODWARD, K. (1997a) 'Concepts of identity and difference' in Woodward, K. (ed.).

WOODWARD, K. (1997b) 'Motherhood: identities, meanings and myths' in Woodward, K. (ed.).

WOODWARD, K. (ed.) (1997) *Identity and Difference*, London, Sage/The Open University (Book 3 in this series).

Acknowledgements

Grateful acknowledgement is made to the following sources for permission to reproduce material in this book:

Cover

Front cover: (upper image:) John Stillwell/PA News Photo Library; *(lower image:)* © Sue Cunningham Photographic; *(satellite dish:)* The BT Corporate Picture Library; *Back cover: (telecommunications satellite:)* Science Photo Library; *(News Bunny:)* Courtesy Live TV.

Chapter 1

Text

Reading A: Henry, I. P. (1993) *The Politics of Leisure Policy*, Macmillan Press Ltd; *Reading B:* Wright, P. (1985) *On Living in an Old Country*, Verso, © Patrick Wright; *Reading C:* Extracts from *Theatres of Memory* by Raphael Samuel are reproduced by kind permission of the publishers, Verso; *Reading D:* Scannell, P. (1989) 'Public service broadcasting and modern public life', *Media, Culture and Society*, Vol. 11, No. 2, Sage Publications Ltd.

Figures

Figures 1.1, 1.2, 1.3, 1.8, 1.9: Getty Images; *Figure 1.4:* Courtesy Covent Garden Festival/Nicky Webb Associates; *Figure 1.5:* Courtesy Wigan Metropolitan Borough Council Leisure Services Dept; *Figure 1.6:* Courtesy The Cavern; *Figure 1.7:* Courtesy Mark Luscombe-Whyte; *Figure 1.10:* Courtesy Live TV; *Figure 1.11:* John Stillwell/PA News Photo Library; *Figure 1.12:* National Trust Photographic Library/Peter Baistow.

Table

Table 1.1: Henry, I. P. (1993) *The Politics of Leisure Policy*, Macmillan Press Ltd.

Chapter 2

Text

'Stick to basics', *Daily Telegraph*, 7th January 1994; 'Porn TV ban', *The Times*, 15th November 1995, © Times Newspapers Ltd, 1995; Kelly, E. (1988) 'The US ordnances, censorship or radical law reform', in Chester, G. and Dickey, J. (eds) *Feminism and Censorship*, Prism Press; Itzen, C. (1988) 'Sex and censorship: the political implications', in Chester, G. and Dickey, J. (eds) *Feminism and Censorship*, Prism Press; Extract from Johnson, P. (1995) in the *Daily Mail*, 16th June 1995; *Reading A:* Newburn, T. (1992) *Permission and Regulation: law and morals in post-war Britain*, Routledge; *Reading B:* Segal, L. (1992) 'Introduction', in Segal, L. and McIntosh, M. (eds) *Sex Exposed: sexuality and the pornography debate*, Virago Press, a division of Little Brown & Co (UK).

Figure

Figure 2.1: Getty Images; *Figure 2.2:* Courtesy Gaze.

Chapter 3

Text

Reading B: Hamelink, C. J. (1994) *The Politics of World Communication*, reprinted by permission of Sage Publications Ltd; *Reading C:* Reprinted from *The Media and Modernity: a social theory of the media* by John B. Thompson with the permission of the publishers, Stanford University Press. © 1995 by John B. Thompson. Also by permission of Polity Press; *Reading D:* Sinclair, J. (1992) 'The decentering of cultural imperialism, televisation and globalization in the Latin world', in Jacka, E. (ed.) *Continental Shift: globalization and culture*, Local Consumption Publications, Australia.

Figures/cartoon

Figure 3.1: John Tomlinson; *cartoon, p. 127:* Hector Breeze/The Guardian.

Chapter 4

Text

Reading A: Reprinted with the permission of The Free Press, a division of Simon and Schuster, from *Illiberal Education: the politics of race and sex on campus* by Dinesh D'Souza. Copyright © 1991 by Dinesh D'Souza; *Reading B:* Taylor, Charles, 'The politics of recognition', in Gutmann, Amy (ed.) *Multiculturalism*. Copyright © 1994 by PUP. Reprinted by permission of Princeton University Press.

Figures

Figure 4.1: Andrew Yeadon; *Figure 4.2:* Joan Russell/Guzelian Photography.

Chapter 5

Text

Jacques, M. (1997) 'The rebel alliance of British talents', *The Guardian*, 20th February 1997, © The Guardian 1997.

Figure

Figure 5.1: Still from 'Permanent Revolution pt2', © Keith Piper/Derek Richards 1997; *Figure 5.2:* Still from 'Relocating the Remains', © Keith Piper 1997; *Figure 5.3:* Courtesy of Time Out.

Index